Living the Author Life

Things Thriving Authors Don't Do

Sacha Black, Zach Bohannon, James R. Essien, Janet Kitto, J. Thorn, Daniel Willcocks

Thorn Publishing, LLC

Living the Author Life: Things Thriving Authors Don't Do

Copyright © 2022 by J. Thorn

All rights reserved.

No part of this book may be reproduced in any form or by any electronic or mechanical means, including information storage and retrieval systems, without written permission from the author, except for the use of brief quotations in a book review.

Originally published as "9 Things Career Authors Don't Do."

Edited by Eve Paludan

Cover by 100Covers.com

More info at theauthorlife.com

DISCLAIMER:

By reading this collection of essays, you agree not to use the information in them as medical advice to treat any medical condition in either yourself or others. Consult your own physician for any medical issues that you may be having. Furthermore, no information contained in this collection should be construed as legal advice, nor is it intended to be a substitute for legal counsel on any subject matter. No reader of these essays should act or refrain from acting on the basis of any information included in, or accessible through, this collection without seeking the appropriate legal or other professional advice on the particular facts and circumstances at issue from a lawyer licensed in the recipient's state, country, or other appropriate licensing jurisdiction.

Contents

Introduction		1
1.	Don't Make Excuses by J. Thorn	5
2.	Don't Try to Compete with Other Authors by J. Thorn	9
3.	Don't Ignore Self-Care by J. Thorn	13
4.	Don't Treat Writing Like a Hobby by J. Thorn	17
5.	Don't Wait to be Chosen by J. Thorn	24
6.	Don't Wait for the Muse by J. Thorn	29
7.	Don't Expect a Home Run at Every At-Bat by J. Thorn	33
8.	Don't Think They Know It All by J. Thorn	37
9.	Don't Hoard Their Knowledge by J. Thorn	42

	Mornings	47
10.	Don't Sleep with Their Phones by J. Thorn	57
11.	Don't Eat Sugary Cereal for Breakfast by J. Thorn	63
12.	Don't Skip a Workout by J. Thorn	69
13.	Don't Blow Off Meditation by J. Thorn	75
14.	Don't Check Email or Social Media First Thing in the Morning by Zach Bohannon	81
15.	Don't Ignore Journaling by Zach Bohannon	87
16.	Don't Sleep In by J. Thorn	93
17.	Don't Start with Administrative Work by Zach Bohannon	99
	Exercise	105
18.	Don't Skip Workouts by J. Thorn	109
19.	Don't Socialize on the Treadmill by J. Thorn	115
20.	Don't Buy Expensive Gear by Zach Bohannon	121
21.	Don't Sacrifice Function for Convenience by Zach Bohannon	127
22.	Don't Skip a Proper Warm-up and Cooldown by Zach Bohannon	133
23.	Don't Ignore Why They Exercise by Zach Bohannon	139
24.	Don't Do the Same Routine Forever by J. Thorn	145

25.	Don't Try to Convince Others that What They're Doing Is Best by J. Thorn	151
26.	Don't Risk an Injury with Risky Behavior by J. Thorn	157

Relationships 163

27.	Don't Listen to Them by Janet Kitto	167
28.	Don't Listen to Them by Janet Kitto	171
29.	Don't Reject Change by Janet Kitto	175
30.	Don't Fight Over Money by Janet Kitto	179
31.	Don't Doubt the Words by Janet Kitto	185
32.	Don't Follow the Leader by Janet Kitto	189
33.	Don't Argue with the Process by Janet Kitto	195
34.	Don't Waste Time by Janet Kitto	201
35.	Don't Write Without the 3Cs (Challenges, Changes, and Consistency) by Janet Kitto	205

Social Media 211

36.	Don't Build an Audience on Someone Else's Platform by Zach Bohannon	220
37.	Don't Depend on Social Media for Sales by Zach Bohannon	227
38.	Don't Check Social Media First Thing in the Morning by J. Thorn	233

39.	Don't Have Social Media Apps on Their Phones by Zach Bohannon	239
40.	Don't Tell Themselves Social Networking Is Writing by J. Thorn	245
41.	Don't Spend Too Much Time Online Talking About Writing by Zach Bohannon	251
42.	Don't Think They Have to Be on Every Platform by Zach Bohannon	259
43.	Don't Believe Everyone Is on Social Media by J. Thorn	265
44.	Believe That All Readers Want to Interact with Authors by J. Thorn	271

Podcasting		277
45.	Don't Quit a Podcast Before the Seventh Episode by J. Thorn	282
46.	Don't Record Podcast Episodes with a Phone by J. Thorn	289
47.	Don't Record Podcast Episodes in a Coffee Shop by J. Thorn	295
48.	Don't Ignore Listeners Who Engage with the Show by J. Thorn	301
49.	Don't Record Episodes and Then Never Listen to Them Again by J. Thorn	307

50.	Don't Ignore Podcast Analytics by J. Thorn	312
51.	Don't Start a Podcast Because It's Trendy by J. Thorn	317
52.	Don't Ignore Other Podcasts in the Same Industry or Category by J. Thorn	321
53.	Don't Expect to Make Fast or Big Money by J. Thorn	326

Marketing		331
54.	Don't Mistake "Marketing" for "Sales" by Daniel Willcocks	335
55.	Don't Break Reader Trust by Daniel Willcocks	346
56.	Don't Think of the Short Game by Daniel Willcocks	363
57.	Don't Care About Vanity Metrics by Daniel Willcocks	369
58.	Don't Rush Launches by Daniel Willcocks	375
59.	Don't Forget the Fans by Daniel Willcocks	381
60.	Don't Hide Their Wallets by Daniel Willcocks	387
61.	Don't Stagnate by Daniel Willcocks	393

Personal Finance		401
62.	Don't Take on Excessive Debt by Sacha Black	405
63.	Don't Buy Frivolously by Sacha Black	411

64.	Don't Use Personal Accounts for Business by Sacha Black	417
65.	Don't Ignore Cash Flow Planning by Sacha Black	423
66.	Don't Ignore Retirement Savings by Sacha Black	429
67.	Don't Focus Only on Books by Sacha Black	435
68.	Don't Mix Up Passive and Active Income by Sacha Black	441
69.	Don't Ignore Professionals by Sacha Black	449
70.	Don't Hate Money by Sacha Black	455

Creative Nomad ... 461

71.	Don't Be Like Everyone Else by Janet Kitto	465
72.	Don't Choose a Life You're Not Invested In by Janet Kitto	469
73.	Don't Stay at Home by Janet Kitto	473
74.	Don't Have a Uniform by Janet Kitto	477
75.	Don't Work Empty-Handed by Janet Kitto	481
76.	Don't Practice Social Distancing by Janet Kitto	487
77.	Don't Need a Desk by Janet Kitto	491
78.	Don't Rush the End by Janet Kitto	495
79.	Don't Travel without a Home Base by Janet Kitto	501

Mindset ... 505

80.	Don't Have a Fixed Mindset by Sacha Black	509
81.	Don't Say Yes to Everything by Sacha Black	515
82.	Don't Suppress Their Obsession by Sacha Black	521
83.	Don't Try to Be Like the Crowd by Sacha Black	527
84.	Don't Stick to the Rules by Sacha Black	533
85.	Don't Take on Expectations by Sacha Black	539
86.	Don't Refuse to Leap by Sacha Black	545
87.	Don't Ignore What They Think and Fail to Speak Up by Sacha Black	551
88.	Don't Think There's Only One Way to An Author Career by Sacha Black	557
Self-Actualization		563
89.	Don't Avoid Adversity at All Costs by Jimmy Essien	569
90.	Don't Ignore the Little Voice by Jimmy Essien	575
91.	Don't Take Their Role as Writers Lightly by Jimmy Essien	581
92.	Don't Allow Themselves to Be Influenced by the Wrong Things or People by Jimmy Essien	587
93.	Don't Believe That They Will Live Forever by Jimmy Essien	593

94.	Don't Practice Things That They Don't Want to Improve by Jimmy Essien	598
95.	Don't Succumb to Imposter Syndrome by Jimmy Essien	603
96.	Don't Starve the Dark Machine by Jimmy Essien	609
97.	Don't Ignore the Rest of the Pyramid by Jimmy Essien	615
About the Authors		621

authors believe they're immune to it. Struggling writers think that every book they write will be a smash hit, while thriving authors understand that success comes from a steady and consistent stream of excellent work—a back catalog built over time. While there are exceptions to the rule, J. believes that doing the best you can for every book launch, combined with realistic expectations, is the best way to ensure success.

"Don't Think They Know It All" – You should never stop learning. Be wary of anyone who claims to know it all. As a lifelong educator and student, J. expounds on the importance of continued education and a dedication to one's craft. A thriving author knows about the learning plateau and seeks out a coach or mentor to get to the next level. An investment in books, courses, or programs is always an investment in your career as an author.

"Don't Hoard Their Knowledge" – J. has been helped by many authors on his journey. He believes that we all have a responsibility to reach back and help others who are behind us on the path. Although there is an opportunity cost to helping others, it comes back to you many times over. Also, discover how having to teach a topic forces you to become better at it.

This is the first step on your journey from a struggling writer to a thriving author. Turn the page and make sure you're avoiding the nine things that thriving authors don't do, along with some tips on what you *should* be doing.

Let us know if there is anything we can do to help you on your journey and send us a message and tell us about your progress. Your transformation from struggling writer to thriving author starts right now!

Chapter One

Don't Make Excuses by J. Thorn

Life comes at us at a blinding speed every single day. We're bombarded with issues to face, things to fix, people to deal with. Very rarely do things go exactly as we plan them, which means that most of the time, we're putting out fires because something went wrong.

When you're a writer or a publisher, both problems can be magnified because your creativity is connected to your business. It can become impossible to separate what you do as an artist versus what you do as a business owner.

How we respond to crisis can vary from person to person. Even within yourself, you probably deal with similar situations differently at different times, based on other variables. So, when something goes wrong, and you're trying to figure out what went wrong or how to fix it, you have two choices: You can accept the responsibility as an oversight or shortcoming on your part, or you can turn your blame outward and find something or someone else who you believe is the cause of the problem.

In the new political climate of the twenty-first century, blame is ubiquitous. Whether you are on one side of the aisle or the other, or even if you stand somewhere in between, wherever there's a failure, you will find no shortage of blame.

It's easy to sink into this mindset as an author. Our stories and our work are so precious that we can't fathom the possibility that something we did caused them to be anything less than excellent. Maybe our editor missed something? Maybe the cover designer didn't choose the right image? Maybe it's Amazon's fault because the algorithm didn't favor us in the way we expected it to? And those readers leaving negative reviews wouldn't recognize a great story if it smacked them in the face. You can assign blame for everything quite easily.

Thriving authors, however, accept responsibility for things that go well and for things that don't. Even when I was most upset about something that happened to me or my business, when I gained some distance and reflected on the situation, I was almost always at fault. I wasn't trying to intentionally sabotage my own work, but sometimes that is precisely what we do, and it's nobody's fault but our own.

It's hard to accept blame, to take responsibility for something you did. Nobody wants to admit causing self-inflicted pain. It makes us feel foolish, stupid, and unworthy of the profession we've chosen. But if you're going to become a thriving author and be known as a true professional, you will accept responsibility for shortcomings, even if they weren't entirely your fault.

Why? Why would you possibly accept blame unconditionally when things go wrong? Because that is the true path of learning. Scientific studies have proven that we learn far more from our failures than from our successes. If we can step back and analyze the situation and be honest with ourselves about how we performed, we're much more likely not to make that same mistake again. Conversely, if we automatically take credit for everything, even if the effort was not attributed to us, we gain a false sense of security and knowledge.

It hurts to admit fault and face your mistakes. I'm not saying that it is easy for any human. But if you cannot acknowledge what you don't know or what went wrong, you can't learn.

There are many colloquialisms about excuses that I would not share in mixed company, but it's safe to say that we all hate hearing them, and yet, so many of us insist on using them. Accepting responsibility for your actions is the quintessential definition of what it means to be an adult, and doing so professionally can encapsulate what it means to be a thriving author.

Being a thriving author is not about how many dollars you made per month or how many figures you earn per year. It's not defined by how many five-star reviews you've accumulated or how many readers you have on your email list. A growth mindset defines a thriving author, and an insatiable desire to grow and to learn. Therefore, excuses are irrelevant. A thriving author never makes excuses.

Chapter Two

Don't Try to Compete with Other Authors by J. Thorn

My good friend Joanna Penn likes to call it comparisonitis. I don't know if she was the first person to coin the term, but I will attribute it to her anyway.

We've all been there, myself included. I've looked at the Amazon bestseller lists or author rankings and thought, "I'm a better writer than *that* person." I have no way of knowing if that's true, but that's what I tell myself because I want to feel better about the fact that someone else who is doing almost the same thing as I am is much more successful at it than me.

There's more to this than pure envy. With generations of healthy capitalist ideas baked into our DNA, independent authors especially are prone to see their colleagues more as competitors than as peers. We theorize that every book a reader purchases within our genre that is not one of our books is patronizing a competitor of ours.

It's natural to want more, to believe that your hard work should pay off. You shouldn't feel worse about yourself if you have envious thoughts about other authors. But we all know that comparisonitis isn't going to move the needle for you. It isn't going to help you sell books, or gain you readers, or earn you more royalties.

When you look around on the retail marketplaces, or Instagram, or Twitter, or the Internet bulletin boards, you can decide how to frame your perspective. You can view those other authors as competitors or collaborators. You get to choose a negative relationship with those authors or a positive one.

The truth is, those other authors are not your competitors. In this day and age, you are competing with Netflix, Hulu, Amazon Prime, video games, smartphones, subscription services, careers, relationships, finances, and so on. We are in a time when people have little bandwidth for attention. There is a deficit of available time and a surplus of things to fill it. If books were the only distraction, then maybe other authors might be considered your competition, but reading must fight for space among all of the other digital distractions available to people, and it appears as though the number of people who read is shrinking.

Every year, studies are published that demonstrate how little people read. The average American reads roughly one book per year. That means many Americans never read a book.

Does this mean you should quit writing, stop publishing, and start coding video games? I guess if you enjoy video games, then this would be an option for you, but if you are a novelist, then you will probably want to continue writing novels. But you don't have to do it alone.

I've been a fan of collaboration for a long time. I've collaborated creatively and financially with many authors in all parts of the world. I've co-written novels and co-bundled digital box sets as a marketing strategy. I collaborate daily with multiple people on multiple podcasts. I run writer's retreats and events, which, by their very definition, are collaborative endeavors.

Without question, these relationships with other authors and people in the publishing community have been responsible for allowing me to become a thriving author. I cannot sustain my lifestyle or support my family by holing up in a cabin in the woods and writing fiction by myself all day long. Some authors can, but they are the outliers, the exception to the rule.

What is it about collaboration that can transform a writer like me from a hobbyist to a professional?

It all comes back to learning. The more you collaborate, the more you learn, and the better you become at whatever it is you are doing. As a musician for most of my life, I've seen this firsthand because being in a band is organically collaborative. People come in with different ideas, and even though one person may have written a song, it must be performed by the band, and therefore, collaboration happens.

Although the same intensity of collaboration is not required as an author, you can still benefit from it. Instead of viewing those bestsellers above you as competitors, see them as collaborators. Find one of their books that you enjoy and send that book to your email list. Do it without expectation, because the more people we can get reading, the better off we will all be.

Thriving authors know that the path to success, the way to declare a victory, is to create more readers. And rarely will readers read only a single author. Most people who enjoy the act of reading will read many authors within a single genre, and they will read across genres. Creating lifelong readers is a collaborative effort by authors who are competing against the other digital distractions threatening to take eyeballs off the page.

Not only will collaborative efforts within the publishing industry help to create more readers, but those efforts will help you to build lifelong relationships. I have friends and business partners who I met online when I first began my author journey. They have become like brothers and sisters to me, family members I can count on during dark times. I can go to them and ask for advice or help because we've collaborated instead of competed. I do the same for them, and together, we help each other along.

Thriving authors don't leave negative reviews on other people's books. They don't take hateful and spiteful actions against other authors who might be enjoying more success than them. If you want to become everything you want to be, then help others do the same.

Chapter Three

Don't Ignore Self-Care by J. Thorn

Nobody ever wants to welcome pain into their lives, but unfortunately, it goes with the territory and is part of being human.

I've been fortunate—or unfortunate, depending on how you view it—to have to deal with excruciating pain multiple times during my author career. After being diagnosed with a chronic health condition, I found it almost impossible to get out of bed, let alone be creative, or drag myself to the page.

Those are the moments when we're most reminded to practice self-care, which is not something most thriving authors do willingly.

I cringe at some of the advice I hear about sacrifice. You may have heard some of the same things. Authors have said things about diet, as it pertains to finances. I've heard recommendations to eat only ramen noodles to save money. I can imagine taking such a radical approach to physical health to save a few dollars. That is not to say that you should never eat processed ramen noodles (although I would make that argument), but we cannot subsist on noodles alone, and we'll pay the price for it later.

In the same vein and more so in the entrepreneurial circles, I've heard advice such as, "You can sleep when you're dead." In other words, work yourself for long hours, and if you're short on time, simply cut into your sleep cycle because that is somehow not essential.

Rather than go on with more damaging examples of some of the dangerous advice I've heard through the years, it might be better to take a closer look at what you can do when pain arrives because it eventually will.

The first thing you must do is triage. Identify what is causing the pain and take steps to eliminate it. Easier said than done, and you'll often need help and the advice of a doctor to do so, but if you are in pain, you will probably be unable to do anything else. Once the pain subsides or you can manage it in a way that allows you to remain productive, the next step is how to stop it from happening again or by preventing it in the first place.

Most thriving authors I know have a system of habits in place to address the critical elements of a healthy lifestyle: Exercise, diet, sleep, and reflection. You might see different labels for these things, but they all mean the same thing, and while they're not the only four habits that a thriving author needs to establish, they are the core of everything.

Exercise, or body movement, is fundamental and not optional. Authors who spend extended periods at a desk tend to be the unhealthiest and not just in terms of body mass or weight. Inactivity can be as deadly as smoking cigarettes. It doesn't matter whether you walk, run, swim, lift weights, or do yoga; you need some exercise regimen within your life, preferably daily. Recommendations vary, but at a minimum, I strive for 30 minutes of exercise a day, five days a week.

Our standard American diet, or SAD for short, is genuinely that. We're bloated on complex carbohydrates, processed food, and insidious amounts of sugar that have created an epidemic. We are more overweight and obese than we have ever been, and the projected health costs are staggering.

New fad diets appear all the time, and disciples of these habits will argue that theirs is the best. There is no right way to eat, and the label "diet" implies a temporary change in eating habits to obtain a goal such as weight loss. Instead, consider the way you eat every day for the rest of your life. Put simply, eat whole foods, and avoid processed ones. Eliminate sugar and alcohol. That's it. If you do just that, you can improve how you feel almost instantly and add quality years to your life.

Sleep is no joke. The effects of sleep deprivation are worse than drunk driving when it takes place out on the road. Your ability to function, let alone concentrate, is severely compromised when you are sleep-deprived. There is no magic number of hours of sleep that is perfect for everyone, although 7 to 9 hours seem to be ideal for most of the population.

Black out the room as best you can. Put down all electronic devices at least two hours before trying to fall asleep, and once you wake up in the morning, try to get natural light on your face as soon as possible. Again, there are dozens of books and studies on how to optimize sleep, but having a routine and keeping electronic devices out of the bedroom will go a long way toward improving yours.

Instead of calling the fourth component meditation, I'm calling it reflection. For some, meditation has a religious connotation, even though it shouldn't. But meditation isn't the only form of reflection. Journaling, quiet walks, and prayers are also ways to reflect. It doesn't matter which one of these work for you. What matters is that you have dedicated time daily to think about what it is you're doing and how you're doing it.

If your days are jam-packed from one end to the other with nonstop items or events, your brain does not get the necessary downtime to process what is happening. Most of the scientific research around learning suggests that students need time to reflect on what they've learned to implement those new skills and thriving authors are no different.

What's the point of all this? If you go through the challenging and rigorous process of changing your lifestyle through exercise, diet, sleep, and reflection, what can you expect out of it? The short answer is everything.

Since I've changed my lifestyle, I'm much less prone to bouts of anxiety or depression. I feel good and energetic on most days, and when I do encounter pain—which I still do—my body is optimized to deal with it in the healthiest way possible.

Amateurs consider themselves victims, but thriving authors take control of their lives and their destiny. Although the changes will be severe at first, the long-term benefits will not only make you a better writer but a healthy person for as many days as you have left.

Chapter Four

Don't Treat Writing Like a Hobby by J. Thorn

Imagine you're walking through town, and you see a sign on what was a previously vacant storefront. It reads, "New bakery coming soon. As soon as I receive all of my baking equipment and supplies for free or through donations, I'll be able to make pastries and sell them to you."

That would be an odd sign and not one you're likely to see. And yet, this is what many independent authors expect when they start publishing their work on retail platforms.

Just like the baker who must invest money in equipment, supplies, labor, and rent, so must you invest in your author business. If you do not invest in your writing, then you are a hobbyist, not a thriving author, which is fine as long as you understand the distinction between the two.

It's easy to understand how this mindset originates. You've probably started writing in the evenings or on the weekend, or whenever you had free time. You most likely didn't graduate from college and immediately decide you're going to make a living as a novelist. Instead, you've been reading and writing for your whole life, learning about the craft and slowly writing a little bit every day. And again, this is how most of us have started. The problem comes when you cross the threshold between amateur and pro, and that distinction is made the first time you ask someone else to pay you money for your story.

Your aunt Helen may have graduated with a BA in English from State College in 1979. She probably reads a lot and doesn't make mistakes when she writes out her birthday card to you every year. But that does not make Aunt Helen a professional editor.

The problem usually surfaces when we decide we want to upload our book to a retail sales platform, and therefore, it needs to be edited, and it needs a cover design. It's tempting to believe you can edit your work, or use a program like spellcheck to clean it up, or enlist a friend in place of a professional editor.

Software tools make it easy to dabble in graphic manipulation so that you can create what you think is a fantastic book cover. But beware, these are the telltale signs that you are not a thriving author.

You have a choice in this circumstance. You can do things for yourself on the cheap, or you can hire a professional to do the job. As long as you're not asking other people to pay their hard-earned money for your book, then it's not as imperative to hire professionals to work on your book. But if you expect that book to be sold in the physical or virtual marketplace, it is irresponsible and unethical to put out a knowingly inferior product because you don't have the funds to do so correctly.

Thriving authors realize that investing in books is part of the business in the same way that someone opening a bakery wouldn't expect to do it with zero capital. We understand that the moment we enter a commercial marketplace, we are bound by a moral imperative to give people the quality they expect. It's not easy, especially when you're just starting. I tell authors that if you don't have the money to pay for a professional edit or cover design, then save up until you do. If you are writing in your spare time and you're not paying bills from your writing, then what is the hurry? Save your money, so when the time comes, you can invest in your business properly.

Some will argue that it's not necessary to pay for professional services. That with the ease of use of most of the platforms today, authors can use beta readers or read reviews and then make improvements based on that feedback. This is irresponsible, especially because the people who are leaving reviews have most likely already paid for your book and did not get the experience you promised. Before you decide to upload your book to a retail marketplace, you have the responsibility of making sure it is a quality product.

How much you should pay for a professional edit or cover design depends on where you are on your author journey. When I first began writing and publishing books to Amazon, I didn't have a lot of money saved up, and so my editing and cover budget reflected that. But like everything about the profession, the more you learn, the better you get. And as I began to sell books because I had a quality product, I was able to reinvest that money back into my business and hire better editors and cover designers. But you start where you can and do the best you can do as long as you're not knowingly cutting corners, believing that it's good enough when it isn't.

Amateurs don't like to hear this. They want to make the argument that paying professional freelancers to help you publish your book is a form of gatekeeping and that it's unfair. However, what's unfair is putting out a product of inferior quality and then, asking someone to pay for it. Furthermore, even if you are entirely self-serving, a reader who has a poor experience with your unedited book or homemade book cover is highly unlikely to give you another chance, which means you've lost a reader for life.

Thriving authors understand that the moment you put a price tag on your book, you are in business, and therefore, you must function as one. You must responsibly invest in the assets you create and strive to do the best work you can, putting out the best product possible. And when it comes to competing with the millions of books sold on the retail platforms, you won't stand a chance if you've cobbled together your cover from free stock photos or paid Aunt Helen in gift cards to edit your book.

If you were a thriving author, and you are if you are reading this book, then treat your writing as you would any other business. Invest in it, and if you do it well, those investments will pay off in the long run.

Don't Wait to be Chosen by J. Thorn

It happens to all of us. Whether you're a hobbyist or a thriving author, the day will come when you will see that message in your inbox. A publisher you've never heard of is impressed with your book, and they are inviting you to enter a contest for just a small submission fee of $100.

You jump up from your chair and throw your hands into the air, excited about the possibilities. You imagine how winning this contest could completely change your career. The big publishers in New York will come looking for you, and agents will be throwing money at your feet.

You know where this is going, and even though you're smiling, you're probably cringing a little on the inside because you've either entered one of these contests or you have seriously considered it.

Most of the time, these invites are generated by a bot that scrapes Amazon and collects author names and contact information into a spreadsheet where an unscrupulous opportunist can use the data to promote their writing contest. It doesn't mean that every contest is a scam, but you need to understand that every contest is completely subjective. Winning a contest or an award for writing is a form of external validation with many factors involved, and not necessarily the ones you think.

Art is not the same as sports. In athletics, two people or teams compete against each other according to a strict set of rules which are designed to determine a specific outcome: a winner. Whether that's through the use of points or some other system, the nature of sports is such that a winner and loser is usually uncontested.

Art does not work this way. Art connects with people on an emotional level, and what is beautiful art to you might not be beautiful to me, and therefore, to declare a "winner" among a group of unrelated pieces of art does not seem to make much sense, even though we do it all the time.

Contests aren't the only way that writers seek external validation. Another method is querying agents in hopes of securing a traditional publishing deal. I, for one, am not above this. I have openly declared that I'm seeking this external validation. I want to know if my writing is good enough to please the gatekeepers of a system that has been in place for many decades. But I understand why I have that desire, what it takes, and what I have to be willing to give up in order to achieve it.

If you take the same perspective with contests and the traditional publishing path, there's nothing wrong with that. But if your only source of validation comes from external sources, you will never be in control of your success or happiness because it will always be dependent on someone else's opinion.

Thriving authors tend to be internally motivated. We are the people who have a compulsion to write. Most of the world sees writing as a form of punishment, especially during elementary school days, but not us. If we don't write on any given day, we can feel off or dejected. The thing that most people hate to do is something we look forward to.

Because of that, most of our motivation is internal. Thriving authors write for catharsis. We create in a way to search for meaning in our world. We hope to educate or inform others as we move through life, and doing so with the written medium is our specialty.

When your motivation comes from the inside, you care much less about things such as awards, contests, external validation from the traditional industry, Amazon bestseller ranks, and ratings. We do what we do because we are driven to do it, not because of the outcomes attached to it.

It's natural for newer writers to want to be acknowledged, to be told that they have "the gift." But the reality is, nobody can bestow that upon us. We must choose ourselves and then take action toward becoming that person. While some people have more of a natural talent in the art of storytelling, everyone can become a better writer through deliberate practice and thoughtful reflection.

In a strange twist of irony, as you become a better writer motivated internally, you begin to get attention from those around you. If you sit down to the page and do your best every day, over time, industry professionals and readers will take notice. Instead of receiving invitations to join a contest with a small fee, you'll get requests for bulk book sales or speaking engagements. A thriving author can shift the paradigm so that the internal validation will eventually produce external results and not the other way around.

Despite what you might read on the Internet, there has never been a better time to be a writer. While it's true that there have never been more books available to the world than there are right now, the writers who care about craft and quality will always surface to the top. If you are internally motivated and you don't care as much about the recognition or rewards, you're more likely to come to the screen every day and do your best.

Over time, thriving authors recognize that internal motivation, although difficult, is the only path forward because relying on external motivation is not sustainable. You cannot count on someone else to pick you, to pick your book, to put you on a pedestal. If you show up every day and do the work, you are more likely to get the world's attention than you are submitting to that contest, along with the $100 submission fee.

Chapter Five

Don't Wait to be Chosen by J. Thorn

It happens to all of us. Whether you're a hobbyist or a thriving author, the day will come when you will see that message in your inbox. A publisher you've never heard of is impressed with your book, and they are inviting you to enter a contest for just a small submission fee of $100.

You jump up from your chair and throw your hands into the air, excited about the possibilities. You imagine how winning this contest could completely change your career. The big publishers in New York will come looking for you, and agents will be throwing money at your feet.

You know where this is going, and even though you're smiling, you're probably cringing a little on the inside because you've either entered one of these contests or you have seriously considered it.

Most of the time, these invites are generated by a bot that scrapes Amazon and collects author names and contact information into a spreadsheet where an unscrupulous opportunist can use the data to promote their writing contest. It doesn't mean that every contest is a scam, but you need to understand that every contest is completely subjective. Winning a contest or an award for writing is a form of external validation with many factors involved, and not necessarily the ones you think.

Art is not the same as sports. In athletics, two people or teams compete against each other according to a strict set of rules which are designed to determine a specific outcome: a winner. Whether that's through the use of points or some other system, the nature of sports is such that a winner and loser is usually uncontested.

Art does not work this way. Art connects with people on an emotional level, and what is beautiful art to you might not be beautiful to me, and therefore, to declare a "winner" among a group of unrelated pieces of art does not seem to make much sense, even though we do it all the time.

Contests aren't the only way that writers seek external validation. Another method is querying agents in hopes of securing a traditional publishing deal. I, for one, am not above this. I have openly declared that I'm seeking this external validation. I want to know if my writing is good enough to please the gatekeepers of a system that has been in place for many decades. But I understand why I have that desire, what it takes, and what I have to be willing to give up in order to achieve it.

If you take the same perspective with contests and the traditional publishing path, there's nothing wrong with that. But if your only source of validation comes from external sources, you will never be in control of your success or happiness because it will always be dependent on someone else's opinion.

Thriving authors tend to be internally motivated. We are the people who have a compulsion to write. Most of the world sees writing as a form of punishment, especially during elementary school days, but not us. If we don't write on any given day, we can feel off or dejected. The thing that most people hate to do is something we look forward to.

Because of that, most of our motivation is internal. Thriving authors write for catharsis. We create in a way to search for meaning in our world. We hope to educate or inform others as we move through life, and doing so with the written medium is our specialty.

When your motivation comes from the inside, you care much less about things such as awards, contests, external validation from the traditional industry, Amazon bestseller ranks, and ratings. We do what we do because we are driven to do it, not because of the outcomes attached to it.

It's natural for newer writers to want to be acknowledged, to be told that they have "the gift." But the reality is, nobody can bestow that upon us. We must choose ourselves and then take action toward becoming that person. While some people have more of a natural talent in the art of storytelling, everyone can become a better writer through deliberate practice and thoughtful reflection.

In a strange twist of irony, as you become a better writer motivated internally, you begin to get attention from those around you. If you sit down to the page and do your best every day, over time, industry professionals and readers will take notice. Instead of receiving invitations to join a contest with a small fee, you'll get requests for bulk book sales or speaking engagements. A thriving author can shift the paradigm so that the internal validation will eventually produce external results and not the other way around.

Despite what you might read on the Internet, there has never been a better time to be a writer. While it's true that there have never been more books available to the world than there are right now, the writers who care about craft and quality will always surface to the top. If you are internally motivated and you don't care as much about the recognition or rewards, you're more likely to come to the screen every day and do your best.

Over time, thriving authors recognize that internal motivation, although difficult, is the only path forward because relying on external motivation is not sustainable. You cannot count on someone else to pick you, to pick your book, to put you on a pedestal. If you show up every day and do the work, you are more likely to get the world's attention than you are submitting to that contest, along with the $100 submission fee.

Chapter Six

Don't Wait for the Muse by J. Thorn

You've made your coffee and sat down at your desk. You turned off your phone, taken the dog out, and fired up the computer. But now, you're sitting and staring at the white screen with a black blinking cursor. You have writer's block. Or so, that is what you tell yourself.

This problem doesn't happen as often to other professionals. When I was in college, I worked on construction sites for my father. I can't remember a time when I showed up and saw the plumber sitting in his car, scratching his head, claiming he wasn't sure he could hook up the toilets today because he had plumber's block.

Whenever I use this example, writers who like to make excuses will often claim that plumbing isn't a creative endeavor, and therefore, it's not a fair comparison. I respond by creating the same fictional scenario with a brain surgeon. Although I've never been in an operating room for brain surgery, I suspect there aren't many instances of a doctor showing up and refusing to operate because they're just not feeling it that day, that they have brain surgeon's block.

This is not to minimize or make light of the fact that there are times when we don't feel like writing. If you are anything like me, you have this feeling every time you sit down at the keyboard. I hate writing, but I love having written. It isn't until I start the process that I get past my initial resistance. If I gave up at that same moment every day, I would never get any writing done.

Another angle to the issue of writer's block has to do with waiting for the Muse. Many writers—often those with the least experience—believe that writing is done in a fit of passion and creative energy. An author is struck with an idea, and their fingers race across the keyboard as the Muse dictates the story through them. This is pure fantasy.

Thriving authors don't wait for the Muse. We don't sit down and wait for inspiration to strike before we do the work. Thriving authors understand that doing the work is what creates the inspiration, and it's what motivates you to keep writing.

But the struggle is real, and so, how can you make sure you come to the page every day motivated and ready to write?

Well, you can continue to believe in the Muse and simply sit there until she arrives. Or you can take charge of your work and your creative output by creating habits and systems that will virtually guarantee that you'll never have writer's block.

Our plumber has all of his tools in his van. He arranges them in a way that makes them easy to access. He keeps his tools clean and functioning properly, so he's not slowed down by a broken one. Our plumber uses an alarm clock to make sure he gets to the job site on time, and he gets there using GPS, so that he's not late or lost. Once he's on the site, the plumber looks over the work order provided by the foreman, so he knows exactly what he needs to do that day. At that point, the plumber grabs the necessary tool and begins work. It doesn't mean he's always thrilled to be there or that he wouldn't rather be somewhere else than having his head stuck behind a toilet. But rest assured, our plumber isn't standing in the unfinished bathroom waiting for the water Muse to strike him with inspiration. He's built a system and a set of habits that puts him in the right place, at the right time, with the right tools. And thriving authors can do the same thing.

At the end of the day, I clean off my physical desktop and my virtual desktop. I put away any tools I may have used that day. I close my browser, and I shut down my computer. Before I do that, I glance to see what it is I will be writing the next morning so that my subconscious can mull over it while I sleep.

When I get up in the morning, and after I've attended to my morning routine, I sit down at my desk, and I reverse the process. I take out my tools, I start my computer, and I open the page to begin writing. This is my system, and these are my habits. Although this is only a single example of how I leverage the power of tiny, consistent routines, you can see how this effect multiplies over time.

I never wonder what I should be working on or what I am supposed to be typing. Whether it's fiction or nonfiction, I create 2 to 3 bullet points every evening to use as a catalyst to get me started on writing in the morning, and if I think about those bullet points right before I go to bed, my brain is already working on them. It's rare that I sit down the next morning and stare at the blank page with no idea of where to begin.

If you know anything about plumbers, you'll know that is not the type of job you can leave unfinished. Once a plumber has disconnected a sewage pipe or turned off the water, he must complete the task before turning it back on so that he doesn't create a mess.

In other words, the hardest part for a plumber is getting started, and the same can be valid for authors. If you create a system that launches you into the work without much thought, you're more likely to defeat resistance, and once you start, you have a better chance of finishing the session.

Thriving authors can't rely on the Muse because she's unpredictable and unreliable. If we could pay our mortgage only when the Muse inspired us, then this wouldn't matter. But even so, creating a writing environment is the best way to ensure the words will get done. It doesn't mean you'll be excited to sit down at the blank page every day, but it does mean you're developing a long-term habit.

Amateurs wait for inspiration to do the work, but thriving authors work to generate the inspiration.

Chapter Seven

Don't Expect a Home Run at Every At-Bat by J. Thorn

You've done everything right. You're excited about the new book launch and prepare to rake in the royalties. After reading all of the most recent posts on the proper way to do a book launch, as well as listening to all of the industry podcasts, you feel as though you have everything lined up perfectly.

Many of the authors on social media make it look simple. Do X, Y, and Z to get the results you want. In some ways, it seems unlikely that you could hit anything except a home run with your book launch.

Book launch coaches and people who will guide you through the process can show you what you should be doing to maximize discoverability and eventually, sales. Some of these coaches are good at what they do and very well-meaning, but they often gloss over the fact that even if you do everything properly, there is no guarantee that you will have a successful book launch.

Therefore, there are two paths you can take when it comes to setting your expectations about releasing a new book. You can do everything you are supposed to do and therefore, feel entitled to success. Follow the recipe, check off the boxes, and success will follow. The other option is to be realistic in your expectations and understand that doing everything you're supposed to do is not a guarantee of the results you wish to see.

Enter the Pareto Principle. The Pareto Principle is the idea often known as the 80/20 rule. Eighty percent of your results will come from only 20% of your efforts. Conversely, this means that the majority of what we do doesn't move the needle for us.

The Pareto Principle, as it relates to a book launch or an author's catalog, can be a difficult pill to swallow for the amateur, but thriving authors understand this universal concept. Generally speaking, if you release ten books, 8 or 9 of them will not be successful. To put a more positive spin on this, the sales from 1 or 2 books will be eclipsed by those of the other 8 or 9. Most of the books you publish will not hit a home run. That's the bad news. The good news is that you can still score a lot of runs by hitting singles.

If you're not familiar with baseball, allow me to explain. Many of the authors I know in the community who rely on fiction as their primary source of revenue do so on a back catalog of dozens of books. If you have 30 or 40, or 50 books in your catalog, then you only need to sell a few of those every day to make a living. This is the entire concept that 20BooksTo50K® was founded upon. But we're not talking 20 home runs. If you write 20 books, the majority of your royalties will be coming from just a few of those titles, and

DON'T EXPECT A HOME RUN AT EVERY AT-BAT BY J. THORN

a slow drip of sales on the rest, combined with more robust sales on a handful, can still be enough to make a living.

So, how do you work this into a launch strategy? Should you just assume failure and not try? Absolutely not. As a thriving author, you are going to give your book the best chance of success every time you publish one. You will treat each title the same way, maximizing your efforts to get it in front of as many readers as possible, especially ones who enjoy the type of books you are writing. But at the same time, you'll have realistic expectations about how that book will do. If you don't, it can cost you a lot of money.

For example, if you don't have realistic expectations about how many books you will sell in the first month, you're more likely to overspend on paid advertising, trying to win your money back like a desperate gambler at a casino blackjack table.

A thriving author is someone who wants to write for their entire life. An amateur simply wants to write one book. If you only want to write one book, then the odds of that one book being a home run are stacked against you. It's not impossible, but it's unlikely.

Always do your best for every book launch because it's impossible to tell which of those 1 or 2 books out of 10 will conform to the Pareto Principle. I have had books that I thought would be a surefire success and have not sold very many copies and others for which I had low expectations and was then surprised by the sales numbers. Nobody knows, because if they did, there would be no such thing as a Hollywood box-office flop. No production company would spend millions of dollars on a film if they didn't think it was going to be a smashing success.

Therefore, do the best you can but keep your expectations realistic. Understand that even though it may seem as though many authors quit their full-time jobs after publishing their first book, it's highly unlikely that it will happen for you.

Beware of survivorship bias in reading the stories of those authors who succeeded as a one-book wonder because those who didn't are not writing about it or sharing their accounts on the Internet.

As a thriving author, when you hit that home run (and you will eventually if you persist long enough), you'll appreciate it that much more. And once you've been able to identify the book in your catalog that is likely to earn 80% of your revenue, you'll be able to adjust your advertising budget and other expenditures accordingly.

Don't Think They Know It All by J. Thorn

Luckily it doesn't happen very often, but I'm always shocked when I encounter an author who does not read. Even more importantly, an author who doesn't read books on craft.

There's no shortage of opportunities for learning in our current climate. Whether it's an online course, a membership site, a mastermind group, or a new book, there's never been more information on how to become a master of the craft—a thriving author.

Some writers who I respect do not have a growth mindset. They believe that the skill set they have is good enough and because they have a fan base and can sell books, why should they spend more money or time getting better at what they do? This is representative of a fixed mindset, a belief that one can only get so much better at an individual skill, and therefore, it would be a waste of time to try and improve upon it.

In a way, I can understand this rationale because of the learning plateau. When you learn a new skill, you immediately believe you're better than you think you are at said skill. Once you get over that initial presumption of mastery, the growth curve is steep, which means you will see the most measurable improvement early on in the learning process. The more you learn about something, the rate of growth slows until it hits what might be termed a learning plateau.

The learning plateau is the place beyond intermediate-level learning and in the shadow of mastery, assuming mastery is a lifelong pursuit that we never achieve. On this plateau, it's easy to convince yourself that you've learned all there is to learn about that skill or that any improvement above the plateau will be so minimal that it wouldn't matter.

Once you've reached the plateau, you have a decision to make. You can accept your perceived reality in that you're not going to get much better at whatever it is you're doing, or you can embrace a growth mindset and realize that no matter how good you are at something, you can always be better. Thriving authors never live on the learning plateau, and they embrace the growth mindset.

Why wouldn't you want to push past the learning plateau? Why wouldn't you always want to become a better writer? While intellectually I don't think any author would argue that they are a master and don't need to improve, there's a practical matter involved that skews our perspective—money.

In almost every circumstance, deliberate practice is an investment. Yes, you will learn how to become a better writer by writing—writing a lot. But if you don't have a teacher or professional guidance, someone who can provide deliberate feedback, you might be making the same mistakes repeatedly and therefore, getting stuck on the learning plateau even though you think you're improving.

A writing coach or mentor can point out the nuanced areas of growth in your craft and help you master those, taking your writing to the next level. But whether that advice comes through one-on-one coaching, an online course, a membership site, or a book, it almost always costs money as it should. It takes time and energy to help a student, and teachers deserve to be compensated for that.

Therefore, a thriving author doesn't need to justify the expense of additional learning. Money invested in coaching, or books, or courses, is an investment in the business. Even though a thriving author is beyond the initial learning curve when it comes to the rudimentary skills of writing, there is always room for improvement, and incrementally over time, this can become glaringly obvious.

I considered myself past the learning curve and a decent writer before I earned my Story Grid certification. But when I learned about the craft and the art of story after investing in that certification, it has paid off in immeasurable ways. The books I write today are far better than the ones I wrote ten years ago, even if the casual reader can't tell the difference. Over time, the gap between who you are what you've become grows and is directly proportional to the number of books you sell or the number of royalty checks hitting your bank account.

Whenever I come across a book that has anything to do with the craft of writing or the business of being an author, I don't hesitate. I buy the book and read it. This is an investment in my future, and over time, the cumulative effect is more important than I can measure.

I'm somewhat more deliberate when it comes to online courses or writing events, but I will still make reasonably quick decisions when it comes to these because I know the short-term cost is going to be worth the long-term gain. For example, I took one of Seth Godin's Akimbo workshops on marketing, and I know that my approach to reaching readers has been fundamentally improved and will continue to get better, based on the principles that now govern my strategy.

Thriving authors don't want to write the same book over and over again. If you're doing it for the money, beware, because this might be the situation where you find yourself. And no matter how much you might like the story, the world, or the genre at the beginning of the process, feeling obligated to continue writing in that series might start to feel more like a job than a passion.

Continually learning and improving, investing money in online courses or writing coaches, is a virtual guarantee that you won't write the same book twice. Things you learn will forever change your approach, and each iteration of your skillset will make your future books even better.

Within reason, allocate a percentage of your operating budget toward education and self-improvement, which will be a smart investment in you and your future.

Don't Hoard Their Knowledge by J. Thorn

It doesn't matter how long you've been at this; someone is going to approach you and ask you for advice on what you're doing. You might not be a thriving author yet, but that doesn't matter because whether you're an amateur or not, there will always be someone who is ahead of you on the journey and someone who is behind you.

Years ago, my friend Jim convinced me to start a podcast for horror writers. I'd only been at it for a few years at that time and certainly didn't feel as though I was an authority in the industry. I remember asking him what I could possibly offer a listener, and he told me that anyone who hadn't yet published would be interested in what I had to say and that changed my opinion on the idea. I realized that I didn't have to be a world-class expert to be able to teach and help other people, I just needed to be able to explain what I'd done to someone who hadn't done it yet.

But like everything, there's always a cost involved. Entrepreneurs like to call this the opportunity cost, which means, what are you giving up in opportunity to do whatever it is you're spending time on now? Whether it's in your business or your personal life, every minute or dollar invested in one thing is a minute or dollar not invested in something else. Therefore, it's a legitimate question: Should I spend my time helping other people or not?

Helping other people can be a frustrating and time-intensive process. Even if you are an introvert and you channel all of your help through email, there is still a cost in time involved. When people are asking you for advice, you have to spend time thinking about what you're going to say as well as communicating that back to them.

In some circumstances, I've spent time providing free and honest advice to people who either ignored my advice or never tried it and continued coming back with more questions. As a teacher, this is a frustrating situation to be in, but unfortunately, it is all too common. Most people will not take action on the advice they receive, even if they believe it will help them. It is only human nature, and all you have to do is look at the statistics from online courses for evidence. The vast majority of people who purchase or register for an online course never get past the first lesson, and almost none finish the course.

Therefore, on the surface, it might seem as though helping other people is a futile gesture, and that you'd be better off spending your time working on your craft or business, but I can tell you that it isn't.

After spending years as a classroom teacher and earning multiple degrees in history and education, I understand that learning is not a one-off occurrence. If people learned simply by being told what to do once, we would all have a much easier time raising our children. As a parent or even a pet owner realizes, merely saying something to your child or dog once doesn't mean they've learned and internalized the behavior. You'll most likely have to remind them frequently. Learning is not a linear process. It's not as simple as adding steps toward mastery. Some days, it may feel as though you're not making any progress with your student or child, and then all of a sudden, they reach a new level of mastery.

And while we can all agree that it's altruistic and generous to be able to help other people who are behind you on the journey, there's also a personal gain to be had, and it's not trivial.

In my experience, I've discovered that any time I'm forced to teach something, I'm also forced to learn it. Having to show or explain a skill or process to someone else enables me to more closely examine what I do and how I do it so that I can best communicate that to someone who hasn't.

The most talented or gifted in our industry don't necessarily make the best teachers. Michael Jordan was arguably the best basketball player ever played the game, but he was not a good coach. The same analogy holds for gifted editors or writers. Knowing the craft or the ways around the business is a different skill set than teaching it to someone else.

Thriving authors don't get to where they are by being selfish. Most of my friends and colleagues, the people who I had looked up to when I was inexperienced, have a long history of giving back. Whether they share their expertise via free blogs, podcasts, or low-cost books, these authors give back to the community that supports them, and their generosity bolsters their reputation as good people.

Even responding to email can fundamentally change someone's perspective or approach and have a ripple effect throughout their entire career. Some authors have an email handler or simply ignore their inbox altogether. I don't. For the past ten years, nobody else has managed my inbox, and I personally respond to every message (except for spam) that is sent to me. I'm not being self-congratulatory or patting myself on the back with praise, but I need to commit to give back and help those behind me as my mentors did for me at some point in the past.

Yes, there is an absolutely real opportunity cost at play here. If you are writing books for authors, developing online courses, or even answering emails from fellow authors, that is time you're not spending on your books or craft. However, I believe the kind gesture will come back to you threefold, and so what might appear to be a short-term loss will become a long-term gain.

There isn't one right way to help other authors on their journey. Find the method or medium that best suits you as a person and then give your help without condition in the same way that others have done for you.

Mornings

You're having one of two reactions right now—dreading what you're about to read because it's the ugly truth or celebrating it because you're a "morning person."

Mornings don't have to be cold, dark, and ugly. Well, in some parts of the world, at certain times of the year, they are, but you know what I mean.

To transform from a struggling writer to a thriving author, you must optimize those first few hours of your day, regardless of what time your day begins. The majority of us are in our most productive and creative frame of mind soon after we wake from a good night's sleep.

In this section, J. Thorn and Zach Bohannon identify nine things that thriving authors don't do when it comes to mornings. So grab a clean protein, a green juice, and a hot cup of coffee as we steer you clear of many potential a.m. obstacles.

Here's a quick summary of the valuable lessons you can expect to learn in this section:

"Don't Pull an All-Nighter" – J. explains why pulling an all-nighter is terrible for your health and your work. When it comes to pulling all-nighters—it's the equivalent of being under the influence of alcohol or drugs. So whether you skip dinner or black out your room, the key to waking with maximized brainpower is getting 7 to 8 hours of quality sleep.

"Don't Sleep with Their Phones" – J. believes that the way we use our phones now is not what Steve Jobs envisioned when he designed the first iPhone. Using your phone before you go to bed causes all kinds of problems with your sleep patterns. Scrolling through the newsfeeds while you're lying in bed after you've just awakened is giving the world permission to hijack your day.

"Don't Eat Sugary Cereal for Breakfast" – J. clarifies what your mother always told you, that breakfast really is the most important meal of the day. Although bagels, French toast, and pancakes have been traditional breakfast foods for Western culture, especially Americans, those are not necessarily healthier choices than sugary cereal. So if you want to fuel your brain, sugar is something you should avoid at all costs.

"Don't Skip a Workout" – J. believes that working out is essential to living the life as a thriving author, and yet, the older we get, the more difficult working out becomes. Getting up in the morning and getting your blood moving will not only wake you up, but it will also bring your brain to life and give you the energy you need to get through the day. He has realized that working out before breakfast (so that you don't feel sick at the gym and so that your body is burning calories from places where it has stored excess calories), is optimal and therefore, morning workouts might be the best approach.

"Don't Blow Off Meditation" – J. understands how easy it is to skip meditation in the morning. However, morning meditation can help your brain become more equipped to deal with all of the challenges you face during the day and throughout your life. In addition, meditating at night can be challenging as you might be so calm that you fall asleep.

"Don't Check Email or Social Media First Thing in the Morning" – Zach explains why you need to be protective of your mental headspace, especially early in the morning. Even something as seemingly productive as listening to podcasts can hurt your daily productivity. To protect your creative energy, you'll need to limit the number of barriers and distractions you put between you and the work that matters.

"Don't Ignore Journaling" – Zach has had a love-hate relationship with journaling over the years, and it has gone in and out of his morning routine. Whether you journal daily or occasionally, journaling offers time for deep reflection and allows you to appreciate your experiences and connect with your emotions on a personal level. Journaling helps you to appreciate things in your life or to cope with certain emotions you might be feeling and to do so at that moment.

"Don't Sleep In" – J. is a champion for early bedtimes and knows that going to bed earlier can fix many sleep issues. The solution to not sleeping in and sacrificing your writing time is to go to bed earlier. If you don't sleep in and make it a point to get up earlier than you must, a whole host of other options become available to you.

"Don't Start with Administrative Work" – Zach understands that you can't ignore the business side of writing as a thriving author. He would strongly suggest scheduling the time for administrative work later in the morning, in the afternoon, or at night, and to focus your creative energy and willpower on writing first thing in the morning. Make writing your first task of the day.

Don't Pull an All-Nighter by J. Thorn

Late-night study jams chock-full of Doritos and Mountain Dew. If you're like me, you might have survived college this way. Even though our professors warned us that cramming for an exam or writing a paper at the last minute didn't work, we tried it anyway.

Most skills are best built by doing focused and repetitive practice over long periods. For example, I used to tell my guitar students that practicing 20 minutes a day is much more valuable than jamming for several hours on a Sunday afternoon. Your body needs to develop muscle memory repeatedly, and it's optimal if you don't overload your system with infrequent spikes of activity.

And consider that neurologically speaking, most of us aren't our best when it comes to working late at night—or through the night. We have to deal with decision fatigue throughout the day—one study estimates that the average human makes 32,000 decisions in a single day. It's no wonder that so many writers identify the early morning as their prime time to draft.

But then, there are deadlines. As Douglas Adams famously said, "I love deadlines. I like the whooshing sound they make as they fly by." What can you do if you have a major deadline?

By then, it's too late. If you feel as though you must work through the night to make a deadline, then you're already in a jam. But hopefully, you can put yourself in a better place for the next deadline, whether it's external or self-imposed.

Start by mapping out your project, doing the math, and sticking to it. If you need to complete a 50,000-word draft in 30 days, you're looking at approximately 1,200 words a day—NaNoWriMo anyone? If you miss a day or two, you can make it up on another day without sacrificing hours of sleep to meet the deadline.

Why is it so important to not procrastinate? Unless you're a freshman at State U., why don't thriving authors pull all-nighters to hit a deadline?

First of all, the quality of the work will undoubtedly suffer. You already know the words you put down at 3 a.m. after five hours of typing are going to be garbage. At that point, you're going for quantity over quality.

But there's an even more serious aspect at play when it comes to pulling all-nighters—it's the equivalent of being under the influence of alcohol or drugs. Tests have been done that show conclusively that people who are sleep-deprived make the same mistakes and are prone to the same frequency of accidents as drunks on New Year's Eve.

Most normal humans require at least 7-8 hours of uninterrupted sleep per night. And just so you know, staying up for long stretches and then "sleeping in" days later doesn't reset the equilibrium. When your body is sleep-deprived, damage is being done to your biological system. Some people need only 6 hours of sleep and some need 9. You have to know your body well enough to make the call. Ideally, you should go to bed when you're tired and get out of bed when you wake up.

So if you're not ready to, or can't abandon the alarm clock, there are several things you can do to optimize your sleep and get your body the rest it needs.

If possible, getting blackout drapes or blinds for your bedroom will block all ambient light, which can wreak havoc on your sleep cycle. You want to get your room as dark as possible. If new blinds or drapes aren't in your budget or aren't feasible, consider a sleep mask instead. Find one that's comfortable and easy to use so that you'll use it every night.

Another way to ensure you'll get 7 or 8 hours of solid sleep is to turn off your devices at least 2 hours before you go to bed. Phones, laptops, televisions, and screens of all kinds emit blue light, which, on a biological level, tell your body that it's time to get up. Using these devices right before bed will make it harder to fall asleep.

Cold has been proven to contribute to quality sleep. Open a window, turn on a fan, or consider purchasing a cold blanket, which will keep your body temperature down. Although uncomfortable at first, your body will regulate, and eventually, you'll be warm enough to sleep.

The digestion of food requires a ton of energy by your body, and if you eat too late in the day, that digestion will happen as you lay down, which can cause problems from sleep apnea to heartburn. If you typically go to bed by 9 p.m., then consider finishing your evening meal by 6 p.m., or better yet, leverage the power of an intermittent fast by eating your last meal of the day by 2 p.m. If you don't snack at night, you'll "break fast" with your first meal in the morning, which has proven mitochondrial benefits in addition to making it easier for you to sleep.

If you need something to calm your nerves after a long day, make yourself a cup of hot herbal tea. The warm liquid will relax you, satiate a bit to minimize hunger pangs, and help you fall asleep, depending on what type of herbal tea you drink. I prefer chamomile, lavender, or natural mint as a soothing way to end a long day.

Whether you skip dinner or black out your room, the key to waking with maximized brainpower is getting 7 to 8 hours of quality sleep. Despite the myths and the legends, there is nothing heroic or productive about pulling an all-nighter, which is why it's something thriving authors don't do. You can't "catch up" on sleep easily, and even if you could, procrastination is not a healthy habit.

Go to bed early and be rested. Your body—and your work—will thank you.

DON'T SLEEP WITH THEIR PHONES BY J. THORN

The smartphone. Along with the advances of the Internet, it's the incredible device that has transformed our lives and changed our culture forever. It has allowed us to communicate instantly with people all over the world and opened up markets for us that never existed before, allowing us to publish our books globally, and creating a level of convenience that has been unrivaled in human history.

So why are we the most anxious and depressed we've ever been?

I don't necessarily have an issue with the technology. I am not a Luddite, and I never have been. In fact, I was creating websites with Notepad in the early 90s. But smartphones have changed the way we live in radical ways that are probably causing long-term damage.

If you watch the now legendary 2007 keynote given by Steve Jobs where he introduced to the world the very first iPhone, you will see that what we use phones for now was not what he had intended. Jobs was proud to deliver a phone that also allowed you to carry your music around with you, which is completely different from the way the devices have been co-opted with the rise of social media.

I still have a phone. It's almost impossible to get through the day without having one. However, there are some things you can do that will change the relationship of your phone for the better, and give you back control of your life.

Because a smartphone functions as a computer in your pocket, it's tempting to use it for everything out of sheer convenience. You can communicate with your aunt, pay a bill, and change the channel on your TV, all with your smartphone. Because of this level of convenience, many people never turn them off. At night, we place our smartphones on a nightstand, or maybe even next to our pillow, and use the alarm on the phone to wake us up.

This can be problematic for many reasons, and believe it or not, you have a choice. You do not have to leave your phone on all night, and you certainly don't have to use it as an alarm clock.

For just a few dollars at any big-box store, you can purchase a dedicated alarm clock that will wake you up just as well as your phone alarm.

Using your phone before you go to bed causes all kinds of problems with your sleep patterns. That's been documented by scientists and therapists all over the world. But we're not focusing on what happens with your phone at night, but rather, on what happens with your phone first thing in the morning.

If you're like most people, you use your alarm on your phone to wake yourself. When you reach for the phone, you then turn off the alarm and will probably be tempted to scroll through your notifications. It's very likely that you will check messages, including email, work and personal. That split-second decision you've just made has altered the trajectory of your entire day. If you're scrolling news sites instead of checking messages, or in addition to checking messages, you have also polluted your mind with the problems of the world before you've even been able to get out of bed.

You could take a radical approach and remove all of the apps from your phone, or suppress all notifications, and therefore, use the alarm app on your phone to wake up. But those are still just a click away, and if you aren't strong enough to resist those temptations, you will find yourself sliding back into old habits.

The simplest approach and the best choice is to turn off your phone or put it in another room.

You can rely on a standard alarm clock to wake you up, and then once you are up, you'll be able to go about your other more meaningful morning routines such as journaling, meditation, or exercise. There will be time later for you to check messages and notifications. Scrolling through the newsfeeds while you're lying in bed after you've just awakened is giving the world permission to hijack your day.

In fact, you might want to postpone checking any messages or newsfeeds until after you've done your most creative work. If you're distracted by a message or a news story, it might be more difficult for you to get your daily words written. And if you are a thriving author, there are few things more important than your daily words.

I'm a firm believer in stacking. Stacking everything. For example, while I'm on the treadmill at the gym, I allow myself to watch television or listen to podcasts. I do this because I know that after 30 minutes, my time will be up, and I won't look up after three hours of listening to podcasts and realize I've burned that much time. Plus, I'm already doing an activity that I know is healthy and beneficial and because I hate working out, watching television while I'm on the exercise bike helps me to reach that goal.

Ideally, you would like to wait until you finish your morning routine before you turn on your phone. That might not always be possible, given your family or work situation, but that should be the aspiration for everyone.

What you do in the morning is critical for what happens during the rest of the day. And if you start your day by dealing with someone else's problems in the form of email messages, or internalizing the tragedies of the world by scrolling a newsfeed, you are robbing yourself of the ability to manifest the gift that you have been given.

It's easy to blame the phone for everything or to point the finger at social media, and while I believe that a lot of our problems stem from the use of these technologies, it is not the technologies themselves that have caused the problem. We have to become better at managing the services and devices. With one simple change, by no longer using your phone's alarm to wake up daily, you're stacking the deck of success in your favor.

Don't Eat Sugary Cereal for Breakfast by J. Thorn

When you were are a little kid, you would rush down to the kitchen and grab an empty bowl before reaching for the carton of milk in the refrigerator. You'd pour yourself a bowl of Sugary Fruit Fruits or maybe some Sugar Ball chocolate cereal before rushing to the living room and watching Saturday morning cartoons.

But you're not a kid anymore. And quite honestly, it wasn't all that healthy when we did it, and just because we are "okay" now doesn't mean it was healthy. There was a time when parents put a baby seat on the floor of the back seat whenever they took a trip in the car, but nobody today would claim that that was fine because we're (most of us, but not all) still alive today.

There are many ways to approach your morning sustenance. Some people like to eat breakfast as their cornerstone meal, where they get most of their calories and nutrition early, while others prefer to fast and wait until a midday meal to eat. There's no one right way to eat or right when to eat, although there have been advances in science that have shown us that there are some things that should be nonnegotiable if you want to make sure your brain is in optimal performance to become a thriving author.

It's easy to grab for what's most convenient when it comes to breakfast. You're probably in a hurry and trying to rush out the door, maybe even taking care of the kids and getting them ready for school. But ultimately, you always have a choice when it comes to what you put into your body, especially whatever goes into your mouth first during the day.

Although bagels, French toast, and pancakes have been traditional breakfast foods for Western culture, especially Americans, those are not necessarily healthier choices than sugary cereal. As Dr. Mark Hyman likes to say on the Doctor's Farmacy podcast, bagels and donuts are the same below the neck. In other words, complex carbs, including things made with flour, are processed by your body as sugar, with the same impact as if it were processed sugar, honey, or organic sugar cane. To your body, below the neck, it's all sugar.

There's definitely something comforting about eating cereal in the morning. It's one of those traditions that we simply accept because we've probably been doing it most of our lives. For decades, Big Food has done an incredible job of marketing sugar as a breakfast food in the form of cereal. Even the so-called "healthy" cereals are loaded with added sugar.

You might think that it's an impossible choice to make. Cereal is so easy. Pour it into a bowl and add milk. Even the worst cooks among us can put together that recipe. But if you want to fuel your brain, sugar is something you should avoid at all costs.

Although many studies are just now being published, there seems to be a strong correlation between sugar and brain deterioration, including diseases like Alzheimer's and dementia, not to mention all of the physical consequences resulting from the consumption of sugar. And although you might not want to hear it, no amount of sugar is healthy. All of us can tolerate *some* sugar, especially sugars that come from natural sources like low-glycemic fruits—berries and such. But by and large, avoid sugars and sweeteners of all kinds.

What are your other options when it comes to breakfast?

If you have the luxury of time, cooking yourself breakfast with fresh ingredients is always the best approach. Eggs, whole wheat toast, fresh vegetables, and fruit. Any combination of these ingredients will provide healthy fuel for the rest of your day. Some people with calorie restrictions or dietary issues might not be able to eat one or more of those types of food. I know because I am one of them.

I prefer to eat a clean protein along with two portions of vegetables and two portions of fruit every morning. I can get this combination in several different ways.

A clean protein for me is fish or chicken that is fresh, organic, and not shot full of hormones or other byproducts. But that is not the only way to get a clean protein. I also make my own morning nut bars—a combination of dry roasted nuts, spices, and coconut oil. I bake these in a dish like brownies and then refrigerate the squares, pulling out one each morning to eat as my clean protein.

You might also be thinking that preparing fresh vegetables and fruits every morning is not feasible or going to take you a long time. But if you prepare these the night before and leave them in the fridge, it makes things a lot easier. If you like green juicing, you can even purchase your vegetables in a convenient bottle and drink them along with your clean protein.

If you make your own nut bars and get your nutrients from green juice, you can almost eat your breakfast as you're walking out the door. I don't think this is the optimal approach because

I think consuming food is also something to be mindful of, but it does solve the problem of eating food that is not healthy or sustaining you throughout the day.

Finally, if you are practicing any type of intermittent fasting, you can work this into not only your morning meal but your meal plan throughout the day and the week. For example, to fight some chronic diseases that I've experienced, I've reduced my overall calorie count slightly. I now eat twice a day, once around 9 a.m., and once around 2 p.m. This allows me to have a hearty breakfast and then only have one more meal to prepare and think about during the day. By having a five-hour window in which to eat, I get most of the benefits of intermittent fasting over the other 19 hours, and therefore, I don't need to fast for long periods to gain those benefits. You would be surprised how quickly your body and your habits adapt to different ways of eating, and different foods eaten at different times.

The bottom line is that we all know sugar is incredibly unhealthy. And even if you use sugar substitutes, you are still feeding the addictive behavior created by sugar.

So while you may have enjoyed that cereal with your Saturday morning cartoons, it might be time to become more intentional with what you put in your body first thing in the morning. But you don't necessarily have to give up the cartoons.

Don't Skip a Workout by J. Thorn

Working out. Hard, sweaty, gross. It's probably one of the last things I want to do when I get up in the morning.

When we're young, working out feels unnecessary but also enjoyable. Many of us grew up playing sports and thrived on the competition, giving our body what it needed while having fun at the same time.

But the older we get, the harder it is to be committed to an exercise regimen. It usually means scheduling a time to make sure exercise happens, and because it's a commitment that doesn't involve anyone but ourselves, it's quite easy to blow off.

Because you have to schedule or plan your exercise, the next big question becomes, "When?" Some people enjoy working out early in the morning, other people prefer the middle of the day, and yet others work out in the evening. Much like meditation, the best time to exercise is whatever time you'll do it. However, I would like to make a case that exercising in the morning will get optimal results for the most number of people. It doesn't mean working out at a different time of the day won't work for you because there are outliers in every situation. But a morning exercise routine makes a tremendous difference in your quality of life.

It might seem as though you need 12 hours to get everything done that everyone believes you should do in the morning. And if you did just your morning tasks in the morning, you wouldn't be finished until the afternoon. I recognize this, but I will say that I think exercise is one of the most important, if not the most important, element of any morning routine.

Getting up in the morning and getting your blood moving will not only wake you up, but it will also bring your brain to life and give you the energy you need to get through the day. I think it's good to move and stretch in the morning, such as stretching at your desk before you write. However, that should be a step towards a rigorous workout that you do at least five days a week, for approximately 30 minutes each day.

"Rigorous" is something you must define for yourself. However, if you are not getting your heart rate up and you're not breathing heavily, you're not exercising optimally. Again, it's a good start if you do light movements or stretching in the morning, but that is not the same as a workout. If you can laugh and chat with the person next to you on the treadmill, you are probably not walking fast enough to make a difference.

There are many different ways to work out, which could include everything from hiking through the woods to joining a gym. But most nutritionists and doctors recommend five days a week, 30 minutes a day, for all adults. Given our S.A.D. diet (standard American diet), many of us probably need more than five workouts a week.

If you have not been working out on a regular basis, you'll want to start by working out just a few days a week and build up to five. You must let your body get used to the demands of rigorous exercise before you go all-in on all five days.

Your exercise routine should be something you enjoy. The idea is to do something you will both do *and* enjoy. If you don't enjoy it, you won't continue to do it. I like to join a gym because when I'm paying for it, I feel an incentive to get my money's worth. I also like to join a gym because once I'm out the door, it's much harder for me to bail on my workout. If I had a treadmill in my house, it would be too easy to walk past it during my scheduled workout time.

While at the gym, I like to do at least 30 minutes of strenuous cardio. On every 5- and 10-minute interval, I do 60 seconds of sprinting—whether that's on the exercise bike or treadmill. Doing that for 30 minutes gets my heart rate up and it gets me sweating and breathing heavily, which are all things I want to have happen early in the morning.

So, why exercise in the morning?

I tend to work out before I eat breakfast so that I don't feel sick at the gym, and so that my body is burning calories from places where my body has stored excess calories, such as from around my waist.

As with many of the routines that we develop in the morning, they're much easier to systematize and make into habits. As we make decisions throughout the day, our willpower drops. And if you have to decide to go to the gym after work, there is a great chance that you won't. But if you put the most important elements of your day in the morning, before anything else can get in the way, you're more likely to follow through on them.

Personally, I found it difficult to work out in the afternoon because my adrenaline spikes, and I have a harder time falling asleep. After meditating and waking up my mind, a morning workout is a great way to wake up my body.

But the most important thing to think about, especially when it comes to a morning routine, is protecting it. The sacrifice you will make will probably be an earlier bedtime. You should not get up earlier without going to bed earlier because sleep is as critical as a proper diet and exercise.

So if you're trying to figure out how you will be able to fit in an entire morning routine, create the time by going to bed earlier. That might not always be possible, but if you're honest with yourself, you'll probably find that you are wasting time on social media, video games, or mindlessly watching television. Cutting those activities, going to bed earlier, and getting up earlier to fit in your morning routine can be transformative.

Working out is still hard. It's not something I enjoy doing; in fact, I hate working out. But I love having worked out.

DON'T BLOW OFF MEDITATION
BY J. THORN

Meditation can feel like a luxury, an indulgence for people who have time to sit and gaze at the horizon and listen to a quiet birdsong app while the rest of the world rushes off to work. Therefore, skipping meditation or not practicing some form of meditation is easy to do.

Without meditation, it can be difficult to manage anxiety, depression, or simply the hustle and bustle of modern daily life.

When you get up in the morning, there are several things that must get done. You probably need to get yourself to work or to your workspace, and you might be responsible for other living creatures like pets or children. You might even have to take care of a loved one who is sick or elderly. If you sleep through the alarm or hit the snooze button, and you don't have much time left in your morning, meditation is one of the easiest things to skip and is usually the first to go.

But that is a choice you should consider because it comes with heavy costs.

There's been a tremendous amount of research and case studies done over the past several years about the benefits of meditation. I'm not qualified to speak to those benefits, but I can share with you my experience because I have been meditating consistently for several years.

Meditation will not make you happy. It will not make you rich, more tolerant, more empathetic, or better looking. Meditation will not help you make more money, it will not help you become a better writer, it won't help your Facebook ads to be more effective. It will do nothing of these things—and all of them. Sort of.

Meditation can help your brain become more equipped to deal with all of the challenges you face during the day and throughout your life. The act of meditating is a workout for your mind in the same way that going to the gym is a workout for your body. If you meditate sporadically, or if you don't give it your best effort, you won't see results. And even if you do it regularly and you are putting in the effort, the effects won't be readily apparent. It will take some time before you'll notice the growth in the same way that your muscles won't get bigger after three workouts.

There is no one right way to meditate. Some people prefer guided meditation, which is listening to a teacher tell you what you should be doing during meditation. Several great apps provide guided meditation. Others prefer silent meditation, which is exactly the way it sounds—silent.

Some people like to sit cross-legged on a meditation cushion with their hands resting on their knees and their eyes open. Some people prefer to sit upright in a chair staring at the wall with their eyes open. Some people prefer to meditate while they walk out in nature. Some people can meditate while driving or lying down in bed, although I would not recommend closing your eyes if you're meditating while driving.

So which is the right way to meditate? Which method should you use? The answer is whatever method you will continue to do. That means you will need to experiment with several different ways of meditating.

I've tried just about all of the methods I've just described except lying in bed or driving. For obvious reasons, I don't feel as though I can focus on meditation while driving, and when I've tried meditating in bed, I've often fallen asleep.

Here's the method I'm using today. It will probably change as my method has changed several times over the years, but I think what has been consistent is building meditation into my morning routine and doing it before anything else gets in the way.

I started with five minutes. Five minutes of meditation does not sound like a lot, but if you've never meditated, five minutes will feel like an eternity. So don't start with more than five if you've never meditated before because you will feel frustrated and irritated and will be less likely to sit down to meditate the following morning.

I used to sit on a meditation cushion in a lotus position or even cross-legged, but I found that my legs fell asleep and it wasn't good for my circulation, so now, I sit upright in a chair with my feet flat on the floor and my back as straight as I can possibly make it. I have a meditation timer on my phone, but any timer will work. I found over the years that my optimal meditation duration is about 30 minutes. It is enough to calm me and set my mood for the day, but not so much that it becomes strenuous. I have meditated for 60, 70, and even 80 minutes a day at times, but I always seem to come back to 30. I've also found it difficult to meditate at night because I'm more likely to fall asleep, so I do most of my meditating in the morning.

If you're new to meditation, you will almost instantly think you're doing it wrong. You will sit down and expect to reach enlightenment where everything in the world melts away, and you are floating in a sea of your own tranquility. But that's not what it is, and anyone who is selling you that is a charlatan.

Meditation is the simple repetitive act of refocusing your mind on nothing. At first, it will be easy. You will clear your mind, and you will listen to the birds chirping outside of your window, or the hum of a fan, or maybe the rumbling of a passing truck. But almost immediately your mind will start racing, thinking about who's in that truck, or why the birds are outside of your window, or who you have to pick up on the way to work today. Your job is simply to recognize that thought and then release it. This will happen over and over again, every single day. Some days it will be easy for you to quiet your racing mind, and on other days, you will feel as though you've lost the race against your own brain. The goal of meditation is not to clear your mind. The goal of meditation is the act of clearing your mind every single time something pops into it. It is the process, not the product that matters when it comes to meditation.

Does meditation make you a better writer? I believe it does. I believe it makes you a better writer and a better human because it forces you to focus. We are in an age of constant distraction, whether that be from digital devices or people. The ability to focus your mind on a single task is something that will make you better, no matter what that task might be.

Commit to meditation for at least six months, doing it every single day. A lot of studies say you'll notice a difference in your focus in as few as three or four weeks, but I'm not sure that's enough time to see significant change. But over six months, if you are meditating, you will see change. Start at five minutes, and as you become more comfortable meditating, add a few minutes on until you work up to 30 minutes. It doesn't matter how many days, or weeks, or months it takes you to get to your optimal meditation time. You'll know when it happens, and you also know what your optimal meditation sitting time is.

People have been meditating for thousands of years, and the benefits are overwhelmingly positive. If you build meditation into your morning routine, I promise you'll see those benefits as well.

DON'T CHECK EMAIL OR SOCIAL MEDIA FIRST THING IN THE MORNING BY ZACH BOHANNON

Smartphones have brought a lot of convenience to our lives, mostly for the better. One of those amenities is how we can communicate with people, and even people we don't know, at any time we want. Unfortunately, this is also one of the significant disadvantages of technology.

Our phones are always with us, keeping us connected and readily available. They're there in our pockets or sitting on the dining room table next to our dinner plate. We keep our devices within arm's reach to both help fill those times of boredom and also to make us available to other people.

Because most people also sleep with their phones on their nightstands (which we also discussed and warned against), it's easy to spend time on your phone before you go to sleep when you really should be resting your eyes. It also leads to what we're going to talk about here, which is waking up and immediately checking your phone.

I used to do this. My alarm would go off, which, of course, was an app on my phone, and then I would pick up my phone to shut it off. With my phone in my hand, I would get my day started by seeing what I had missed while sleeping. This included checking social media and my email.

My eyes were open, but my brain was still foggy and trying to come out of a deep sleep. Yet here I was, instantly seeking an early-morning dopamine hit.

But I had no idea of the damage I was doing, not only to my creativity but also to my health.

The biggest hindrance to your creativity is not being able to focus for long, uninterrupted periods. Yet all around us, we have gadgets and apps, and advertisers and people fighting for our attention. More often than not, this happens through our smartphones.

The times where it is most difficult for me to focus is when I'm bothered by something or have something lingering and nagging in my mind. This could come in the form of something I read from the news that irritates me, a post that someone put on social media that annoyed me, or when I had a day job, an email from my boss telling me there's a problem at work and to see him as soon as I got into the office. How are you supposed to create with that kind of thing on your mind?

Knowing how essential my focused writing time is and how outside influences can negatively impact my ability to be creative, I am rightfully protective of my mental headspace.

How many times have you read something on social media that made you angry? Or have you ever opened your email moments after rolling over in the morning, only to see a message from your boss telling you there is a problem and that she needs you to come to your office as soon as you get to work? What kind of impact do you think that will have on your writing that morning before you go to your job? And couldn't your boss have just waited until you came into work to tell you that instead of making you worry until you get into the office?

Now I understand that not everyone is in a position where they can avoid checking their email in the morning. But I would do all I could to avoid it before writing. Try talking to your boss to set up some boundaries about the hours when you aren't in the office. She might not be willing to budge, but you're not going to know unless you ask.

However, not everything negative is related to social media or a day job.

I recently learned how listening to podcasts soon after I wake up, and before I start writing, negatively impacts my productivity. I would turn on a podcast while I woke up, got my coffee, took the dog out, etc. But I learned that once I have that podcast going, it's not only hard to turn it off, but for me, it's also hard to listen to just one. Even if it's a podcast about writing, I no longer allow myself to listen before I've done my most important work for the day, because listening to a podcast about writing isn't writing. Only writing is writing.

The fewer barriers and distractions you put between you and the work that matters, the more productive you'll be, and you'll easily get into the *deep work* state that Cal Newport writes about.

I read fiction for 20-30 minutes in the morning, which gets me in the mindset to write, I meditate, and then I get in the chair and start writing.

If you feel as if you can't focus in the morning, look at what you do before you get to the desk to write. As Becca Syme says, "Question the Process."

And keep your phone away. The world can wait while you do what you love.

DON'T IGNORE JOURNALING
BY ZACH BOHANNON

I'm fascinated by the habits of highly successful people. I've spent a lot of time studying them, reading books, articles, watching documentaries, and listening to interviews. It's interesting to see the overlap of habits shared between some of the world's most successful people, as well as things that some of them do differently. Most successful people have intentional morning routines.

Rarely, if ever, will I add an activity into my day just because someone else does. Meditation was a rare occurrence where I didn't want to give up on something just because I didn't enjoy it. I had seen so many different people rave about the value in it that I wanted to make it work for me. Eventually, after some experimentation, I fell in love with it, and now it seems ridiculous to go a day without meditating. I get too much value out of it.

But journaling is different.

I have a love-hate relationship with journaling. It is the one action in my morning routine that I have flip-flopped on the most. It has gone in and out of my morning routine more times than I can count. And it seems that every time I take it out, I find a reason that I need to bring it back in.

For thousands of years, people have kept journals and diaries. Journaling offers time for deep reflection and allows us to appreciate our experiences and connect with our emotions on a personal level. I've seen some people take a hard stance on reflection. They become so entrenched on putting on the blinders and driving forward that they are unwilling to appreciate what they have achieved.

I would argue, though, that in the busy world we live in today, full of distractions and screens always in our faces, that it is more important than ever to slow down and reflect.

But as I said, even believing this, I still had trouble identifying where the benefit lay for me in journaling. Luckily, I was able to find the disconnect. I discovered the exact thing that was keeping me from enjoying journaling and finding value in it.

And ironically, it's the exact opposite approach that I take to all my other habits.

I was too consistent.

Being consistent is crucial in starting and sticking with any habit. The root of change lies in consistency. If you want to start a workout habit, schedule the days and time you're going to go to the gym and stick to them. You'll begin to train your body and mind to know when it's time to exercise. As a writer, you likely already know the benefits of consistency. Finishing a book involves many focused writing sessions that come in weeks or months. Most writers that I know have a dedicated space and scheduled time to write, and the consistency of sticking to those help finish projects.

Naturally, I applied this same mindset to journaling. It became another part of my morning routine, along with exercise, meditation, and reading. When the time came, I sat down in front of my computer, opened a new entry in my journaling app, and spilled any thoughts I had onto the page. As with any new thing we are excited about, this was easy at first. But after a couple of weeks, I started having days where I would sit down to journal but not have anything to say. But hey, it was part of my usual morning routine, so I had to do it. Because of that, journaling started feeling more like a chore than it did a valuable way to spend my time. This is typically when I would remove it from my morning routine.

With the other three activities in my morning routine (exercise, meditation, and reading), there is immense value in me doing those every day. If I skip any of those activities on a given morning, the rest of my day feels off. I know that I need to move, I need to calm my mind, and I need to expand my knowledge and my craft through reading. But what if I don't have anything to reflect on at that moment?

That was the realization I came to with journaling. I knew that I was finding value in it when I had something to journal about, but that it felt like a chore when I had nothing to say. To some of you it might sound obvious, but keep in mind how much value I put into consistency, and how often I had heard that people who get a positive emotional return from journaling do it every day.

The truth is, I don't.

I find immense value in journaling when I *need* it, which doesn't happen every morning.

So I have become less consistent with journaling, and it's been a change for the better. It is no longer a regular part of my morning routine, but I have grown to understand when I need it. If I am still feeling overwhelmed or stressed about something after

I meditate, I journal. If I had an awesome day doing something special with my daughter the day before, I journal. If my wife and I had a discussion about something and I still have open loops in my mind about it, I journal. It's not always in the morning either. Lately, I have found a lot of value in dictating my journal entries. I've found that speaking my thoughts out loud has helped me sort through them even better, and I often will do them on nature walks, which only increases the benefits.

An important thing to remember about journaling is that you don't do it because you want to remember things and read about them later. Of course, it can be fun to go back and read previous journal entries now and then. I do it, though rarely. You journal to help you appreciate things in your life or to cope with certain emotions you might be feeling and to do so at that moment. No matter *why* I start a new journal entry or how I'm feeling when I do, I always feel great when I'm done.

For that reason, I can't afford *not* to do it. But I will continue to pay attention to the signs and understand when I need to journal as oppose to making it something I *have* to do at a particular time each day.

Don't Sleep In by J. Thorn

Sleep. Is there anything more nourishing than a good night's sleep? If a little bit is good, even more will be better, right?

On the other hand, most entrepreneurs like to claim they'll sleep when they're dead. There is a strange phenomenon that occurs in the start-up world where people wear their lack of sleep like a badge of honor.

When I was a teenager, there was something anti-authoritarian and rebellious about using Mountain Dew and Doritos to cram for a test or write a term paper. Later on, when I was in college, some students were already experimenting with prescription medicines like Ritalin to stay awake during exam week.

For most of our lives, we have functioned with metered sleep. Most of us use alarm clocks or some method of forcing ourselves awake to start the day or go to work. It might seem like a luxury to wake up whenever your body wakes up, but that is probably, biologically speaking, what your body needs.

Sleep seems to be the thing that we have to do to get to the next thing we have to do. While some people drastically cut the number of hours they sleep, they find that their body might need to make it up in other places.

Culturally speaking, we all seem to get up earlier than we would like to. But what if you took a different approach?

Thriving authors get as much sleep as their bodies need, but they do not use sleep as an excuse not to do the work. Thriving authors don't lie around in bed or sleep in for hours beyond what they know they should.

This advice will apply to most people, but, if you are one of the few who have Delayed Sleep Phase Syndrome or something similar, then I acknowledge that this isn't for you.

The solution to not sleeping in and sacrificing your writing time is to go to bed earlier. There is no shame in going to bed early. Many of the world's most brilliant and successful people start their days at what an ordinary person would consider an ungodly hour, such as 4 or 5 a.m.

These people believe that their brains are sharp early in the morning, and they are less distracted at that hour of the day because very few other people are awake—and that means people inside of their own house or people online. The phone is not ringing, the kids are not tugging at your skirt, and the dog might still be asleep.

But to make the decision to get up earlier, it's important not to cut down on the net number of hours of sleep you get, and therefore, it means going to bed early.

I began writing in the dark hours before I would have to leave for the day job. I knew that someday I wanted to be a thriving author, and that trying to write in the evening, exhausted from the day's activities, would not result in my best work. So even on the weekends, I decided not to sleep in. I would get up, whether it was with the aid of my alarm or naturally, and begin writing at five in the morning. Some days I would get 30 to 60 minutes of writing time in, and other days, it might only be 15 or 20 minutes. But I knew that I was getting up early with a purpose. I was not sleeping in.

If you don't sleep in and make it a point to get up earlier than you must, a whole host of other options become available to you. You can now explore the idea of journaling, you can begin a daily meditation practice, you might be able to start an exercise regimen, or all of those.

By getting up early and not sleeping in, you get to begin to work on your material first, not your boss's or your company's. Resist the temptation to check email or social media and use those precious minutes to do your most important work.

This doesn't mean that you should never sleep in. There will be times when you will be exhausted, and you will not be able to get up in the wee hours of the morning to do your most important work. But those times should be the exceptions and not the rule. If you continue to get up early and make progress, your habit or system will create the motivation. You don't need to be motivated to get up early, you will use your success to create the motivation to get up early.

Some people will claim that they are not a morning person, and while there could be biological dispositions towards being more intellectually alert in the evening versus the morning, most of us can train our bodies into a certain set of habits.

Our ancestors did not eat three meals a day. That was something that started just a few hundred years ago. And there is historical evidence to suggest that people did not always sleep through the night. Some people would get up at two or three in the morning and have a meal, or socialize with friends, or play games, before going back to sleep for another few hours. So although it is tempting to believe that just because you have done something the same way your entire life, and therefore, you cannot change, in most cases, that is not true.

But getting up early does not have to be a shock to your system. If you are the type of person who enjoys sleeping in or feels as though you are more active in the evening, start getting up just a few minutes earlier than you normally would. Set the alarm clock and when you start getting used to your new waking time, reset the alarm for a few minutes earlier. You'll be surprised at how your body will acclimate over time, and soon, you will become one of those "morning people."

Your bed can be warm and comforting, but it can also be a force of resistance. No matter what your lifestyle or what time your responsibilities begin in the morning, or afternoon, or evening, you can always get up earlier and make your most creative work your day's priority.

DON'T START WITH ADMINISTRATIVE WORK BY ZACH BOHANNON

As someone who has made a living for several years now primarily writing books, I find the stereotypical image of what an author's day looks like amusing.

I still occasionally meet people who think the typical day of an author consists of waking up around 10 in the morning, making some coffee, sitting down at the computer around noon, and then magically filling up a blank page with words. Oh, and by the way, this is all done in a remote cabin out in the woods. I write my stories in a notepad on the back deck as deer walk by, and birds land next to me, chirping beautiful songs.

Of course, you and I know this is the furthest thing from the truth.

Being an author is so much more than sitting down in front of the computer and letting the muse guide you through the next great American novel. Being an author isn't even just about writing. It's also about running a business that comes with its own set of responsibilities. On top of writing your books, you have to market them, pay taxes on those you sell, budget time and money to write and publish them, and find people to read them.

All of these tasks add up and ultimately take time away from writing, but they are necessary. And if you don't have a plan to execute and tackle them, then you're only going to find yourself overwhelmed and overworked.

Let's get this out of the way: writing sucks.

If you're someone who has written for a long time, then you know exactly what I'm talking about. We love the idea of writing and the emotional high we feel from having written, but the actual process of writing can suck. Not all the time, obviously, but there are those days where we all feel that. Middle of the book slog, anyone?

When those times happen, it can be easy to distract ourselves with some other task.

"I don't feel like writing right now, so I'll go interact with some of my readers on Facebook instead."

"This chapter is really hard. I'm going to spend some time in my email and come back to it later."

"I've been sitting here staring at the blank page for 10 minutes. This is probably a good time to go check my royalties."

"I think I have writer's block today. Maybe I should order a cover for that one book I've been thinking about writing."

Sound familiar? Of course, they do!

Because writing is hard, and writing sucks. And in those moments when we feel that way, it's easy to convince ourselves that working on other aspects of our business is just as important.

But here's the truth.

Only writing is writing.

And when you take time away from your writing, everything else is just Resistance.

That's not to say that all these other things aren't important. They are. As I said, as an author you are running a business and therefore, have a lot of responsibilities. But none of those should ever get in the way of your writing. That's not to say you can't have occasional days where you take breaks from writing, either to work through your administrative to-do list or to just take a break and have some time for yourself.

There's this author myth that a lot of people have bought into that says you have to write every single day. Personally, I don't believe that's true. But that doesn't give you the excuse to put off your writing for other tasks when you know you should be writing.

That's why you need to have a plan, and that plan should include scheduling time dedicated to working on your administrative tasks. And I would strongly suggest scheduling that time for either late in the morning, in the afternoon, or at night, and to focus your creative energy and willpower in writing first thing in the morning.

As I said earlier, it's easy to get overwhelmed by all the things we have to do for running an author business. But what I find most often when I talk to authors who are struggling with all the things they need to get done is that they are scheduling dedicated time to work on those tasks. If you are overwhelmed by the other things you need to get done, it's going to be much harder for you to write. Those open loops in your head will make that difficult. But if you know that you have already set aside the time to work on those later in the day, week, or month, then it becomes much easier for you to focus on writing.

I've experimented a lot with my schedule. I have tried writing at all different times of the day. Beyond a shadow of a doubt I can say that my absolute best creative work is done within two hours of waking up. The activities that you do before you dive into that work should be intentional because they matter. Everything I do before I sit down to work serves my body, my mind, or my soul. And I'm intentional about doing things that do not require me to make decisions or that use any of my creative energy.

We each only have so much willpower to make decisions or get things done throughout the day. If you still have a day job, how likely are you to put out your best creative efforts, or even sit down in the chair in the first place, if you wait until after you've spent eight hours at the office? Wouldn't you feel more accomplished if you wrote a chapter before you even started your job in the morning? I can promise you that the answer is yes. You might have to wake up a little earlier, but the rewards are tenfold, and I can guarantee you that you will appreciate that you did it.

These problems don't go away even if you're a full-time writer. It's easy to tell yourself, "I've got all day to get my writing done. I can check my email or spend a little time interacting with my fans on Facebook." The issue is that these are low-level tasks with little return on investment. If you want to make a living as a writer, you have to write. I know it sounds silly, but it's the truth.

Make writing your first task of the day. Be sure that you've set aside time to do other tasks, including checking email, and don't allow yourself to look at it or move to something else while you're in your writing time block. If you need help, get an app that blocks you from going to specific websites. I use a free app for Mac called SelfControl that prevents me from visiting sites I've blacklisted during a specific time interval. I also keep my phone in the other room or inside a drawer on the other side of my office when I'm drafting words.

The hardest part about writing is getting your butt in the chair and putting one word in front of another. Knock it out first thing, and you'll feel more accomplished and refreshed with an entire day ahead of you and your most important work already behind you.

EXERCISE

As you open this section, you're probably asking yourself: What does exercise have to do with being a thriving author?

The answer? Much more than you might think.

As authors, we spend far too much time in our chairs. Even with the growing popularity of dictation, which many authors do while on walks or during household chores, the majority of your workday is still going to be spent in front of the computer.

But aside from being a sedentary activity, writing is also a highly creative one that requires lots of energy in order to focus. You might be thinking that cup after cup of coffee will be enough to keep you going, but the truth is, vigorous exercise might do more for your energy levels while writing than any cup of joe.

In this section, J. Thorn and Zach Bohannon identify nine things that successful authors don't do when it comes to exercise. So throw on your running shoes and get ready to sweat as we discuss how exercising can help you to become a more productive thriving author.

Here's a quick summary of the valuable lessons you can expect to learn in this section:

"Don't Skip Workouts" – J. talks about consistency and how it's the key to holding true to a workout routine that will keep you healthy for the long haul. While there are circumstances where you won't be able to squeeze in a workout, you need to put the barriers in place that eliminate the excuses.

"Don't Socialize on the Treadmill" – J. explains why having a friend at the gym can be counterproductive. It's great to have a workout buddy to help you get to the gym, but once you're there, it's time to work.

"Don't Buy Expensive Gear" – Zach puts to rest the myth that you need equipment to work out. You don't need any, and any you might want to use can stay at the gym instead of taking up a bunch of room in your house. But even if you do want to work out at home, you'll learn ways you can do it while spending little to no money.

"Don't Sacrifice Function for Convenience" – Zach explains why he isn't a fan of weight machines and why more people need to think about their everyday lives when exercising. Doing so can make your day-to-day living easier and more pain-free. He also talks about why holding onto the rails of the treadmill is a mistake.

"Don't Skip a Proper Warm-up and Cooldown" – Zach clarifies why you should be stretching *after* a workout as opposed to before one. It's much more beneficial for you to begin your workout with light movement instead of static stretching. Also, learn why the warm-up and cooldown are the most critical parts of your workout and that you should never skip them.

"Don't Ignore Why They Exercise" – Zach believes that too many people work out without intention. They hear about exercise trends from friends or read about them in magazines and think that those exercises will work for them and pertain to their own fitness aspirations. But you have to know why you are exercising so that you can tailor your workout to meet those specific needs.

"Don't Do the Same Routine Forever" – J. makes the argument why finding a routine and sticking to it forever can be counterproductive. Our bodies adapt, and in order to keep them from getting bored, we have to change things up once in a while.

"Don't Try to Convince Others that What They're Doing Is Best" – J. cautions against telling others that their workout is the *only* workout that matters. Like the publishing industry, the fitness world is riddled with evangelists of different tactics and strategies. But you have to find the workout that works for you and is tailored to your physical needs and aspirations.

"Don't Risk an Injury with Risky Behavior" – J. warns against trying to relive the moments from your youth when the time might have passed you by. As you get older, you probably won't be able to play sports you once enjoyed in the same way. But with the proper workout routine and some common sense, you might not have to give them up forever.

QUICK NOTE: While much of what is said in this section is based on our own personal experiences and research we have done in building our own exercise routines, it's important to note that Zach spent two years in the fitness industry before transitioning to an author career. He's worked with dozens of clients as both an ACE Certified Personal Trainer and a Life Fitness Academy Certified Holistic Nutrition Coach. He ran a successful weight-loss blog and was featured in such places as RebootWithJoe.com and *BossFit Magazine*. That said, please consult your primary care physician before beginning any workout routine.

Don't Skip Workouts by J. Thorn

It's 5 a.m. and pitch-black outside. You roll over to turn off your alarm, and your fingertips are cold. It's warm in your bed, and if you hit snooze, what would be the harm?

Ten minutes later, your alarm is going off again, and again, you reach out to turn it off. What if you just skipped your workout today? What harm would it do if you skipped one time?

This is probably a scenario you've found yourself in many times, even if it wasn't about getting up to work out. There have probably been many things in your life that you intended to do in the morning but decided not to once you woke up, maybe going into work out being one of them.

It's understandable why it would be difficult to get up and continually go to the gym or do a strenuous workout when it would be so much easier to roll over and go back to sleep. But doing that reinforces bad habits, and if you do that with a workout, you will probably do that in other aspects of your life as well.

That is not to say that I never miss a workout, but it's only under circumstances that are out of my control. For example, if I have to be at the airport to catch a flight at 6 a.m., I simply do not have the time to do my normal workout in the morning before I leave for the airport. Or, if I am traveling in a place that makes it impossible for me to work out, then I will skip it that day. But I never skip a workout simply because I want to go back to sleep, or I don't feel like doing it.

Traveling is the best excuse for skipping a workout, but under most circumstances these days, it's not a very good excuse. Whether I've stayed at hotels, in the city, or at Airbnbs, there is almost always an opportunity for me to work out. There are gyms nearby, hotels have workout rooms, and some Airbnbs even have space to do simple exercises. The bottom line is, if you don't take advantage of those opportunities to work out, you are reinforcing bad habits while traveling, and you're making it easier for yourself to back out of commitments when you're not.

However, if I wake up and I'm physically sick, then I don't go to work out, but that is different than simply not feeling like I want to work out, which happens on almost every single day.

The key to not skipping workouts is to make them such a core part of your day that it's impossible not to do them, like brushing your teeth or getting dressed. You can't make a workout a choice because if you do, you probably won't go. It is human nature to avoid the work, and therefore, you must take the option to avoid the work off the table.

There are several things I do that minimize my likelihood of skipping a workout, bringing the chance of that happening down to almost zero.

First of all, I pack my workout bag the night before and I set it by the door. I put my car keys, my wallet, and my phone on top of my bag. When I get up in the morning, I use the bathroom, and then I meditate. Then, I have to walk past my bag to do anything else, and that is the time when I go to my gym. I get up early enough so that my family's transportation needs or schedule does not affect my ability to work out. I'm usually home from my workout before anyone else in my family has gotten up.

Scientifically speaking, there might not be a great advantage to working out in the morning as opposed to the evening. But from a motivational standpoint, there's no comparison. Leaving your workout until the end of the day gives you the opportunity to skip it for so many reasons. You have spent all of your decision-making power throughout the day, and it's easiest to default to nothing or not doing the workout. It's easy to tell yourself after a long day at work that you're exhausted and you just want to go home and watch Netflix. That is why I always have and continue to do my workouts as early as possible in my day.

Another way of making sure you don't skip a workout is to provide yourself with an incentive. The gym I belong to has hydro-massage chairs in the lounge for premium members. I make myself a deal. If I complete my entire workout, I get to reward myself with 10 or 15 minutes in the massage chair. You would be surprised at how effective this is in motivating me to get to the end of the workout.

I do not believe in using unhealthy incentives to create healthy habits. For example, I would not advocate a cigarette or a cupcake as a reward for finishing a workout. But something like the massage chair or something else that would be a treat for you is a great way to incentivize the activity and make it part of your day.

These ideas will certainly help you make the workout part of your routine, but the true key is to create a good habit so that all of this is automatic. It takes some time and intention to create the habit, but once it's there, you won't even have to think about it, and you'll end up heading to the gym while not even remembering that you made the decision because you won't have to.

It's easy to make excuses for yourself, but we all know when we're not fully committed. So build a healthy habit and take that option out of the equation, and you'll never have to worry about missing a workout again.

DON'T SOCIALIZE ON THE TREADMILL BY J. THORN

I like to work out at the same time every day. I've made my morning workouts part of my routine, something I do without thinking about it.

Each morning when I get to the gym, I begin my workout with 30 minutes of cardio. Because my ankles are shot from playing basketball, I like to use the cardio machines that don't put any undue stress on my joints. Usually, this means I'm riding an exercise bike or doing one of the low-impact gliders.

Once I start on my machine, I look around and invariably see two people who have come to work out together. I'll watch as they come in, laughing and talking and really enjoying each other's company. And then this next thing happens almost every single time. They get on a machine next to each other, push the buttons, start walking and then continue the conversation they were having when they walked in.

I'm sweating profusely, breathing deeply, really trying to push myself to get the most out of my cardio workout. And the entire time, these two people are laughing and joking with each other as they stroll along the treadmill.

If you can laugh, joke, and talk while you are working out on the treadmill, it's probably not doing much good. Yes, it is good to get out of the house and to start your body moving in the morning, but that is not the same as a vigorous workout. You can stretch and do a few jumping jacks when you get out of bed, but if you do not get your heart rate up to at least 80 to 85% of your maximum, then you're doing little more than stretching a few muscles that may have tightened up while you slept.

I'll also see men and women who bring a book or magazine and set it on top of the treadmill as they walk. And again, if you can focus, read, and comprehend a book or magazine while you're working out, you are probably not working out hard enough.

In almost all circumstances, in many different types of workout regimens, it is widely believed that getting 30 minutes of cardio five days a week is what you need to maintain a healthy cardiovascular system, to keep your heart and lungs working the way they're supposed to.

And in those 30 minutes of cardio, you should be pushing yourself to get your heart rate up and your blood pumping, and you should be breathing heavily. If you are not doing all of these things, you are not getting the most benefit out of your workout. You need to push your system hard during your workout for it to have any effect.

Another plateau to watch for on the cardio machines is the difficulty setting. When I first started riding a bicycle, I would set the difficulty level at number three. And after a few months, that difficulty level of three no longer felt challenging, and my workouts became much easier. And while it is human nature to enjoy that easy workout, it is not helping much. There is a plateau that occurs, and once your body adjusts to that new norm, the arduous physical activity that you are doing is no longer beneficial exercise.

If you have been walking for 5 miles a day for five weeks, you will see dramatic benefits in your day-to-day life, your health, and your energy. But if you've been walking 5 miles a day for five years, those 5 miles at the pace you're walking them has been normalized by your body, and if you measured your heart rate before you started walking and then after, it probably wouldn't be much different.

Everyone works out in different ways and prefers different activities. It doesn't mean that we all have to work out the same way to get the health benefits. But we are all bound by the same laws of physics. We share the same biology, and therefore, there are certain things that we all need to be paying attention to. The workout plateau is certainly one of them.

But going back to the people on the treadmill, there is a great benefit in sharing accountability with another person. If you know that someone else is waiting for you to pick them up before heading to the gym, you're much less likely to blow off your morning exercise. Having a partner going to the gym with you can make the difference between working out and not working out.

However, once you get to the gym, if you are doing cardio work, that should be done on your own. A spotting partner for training with weights is a different story. But if you know you need to get your 30 minutes of cardio to get your heart rate up, you do not need anyone else to help you with that, and in fact, doing so might lessen the effectiveness of it.

Socializing on the treadmill isn't limited to friends who join you at the gym either. While you're working out, get off your phone. It pains me to see people barely putting in any effort on the elliptical as they stare down at their phone while scrolling and texting. Not only is this preventing them from getting their heart rate up, but they are wrecking their necks at the same time. Aren't you at the gym to take care of your body? Put on some music and then get your phone out of sight.

Here's a simple technique that doesn't require a fancy Fitbit or an expensive electronic treadmill. At the five- and nine-minute marks of your workout, sprint—go hard at 100% for 60 seconds. Whether you're working out for 20 minutes or 30 minutes, do 60 seconds on the fives and nines and that will ensure that you're not letting your body normalize your workout. If you walk at the exact same pace during your entire workout, your body will get used to it and you're wasting your time and gym membership fees.

I know it's fun to chat with your friends and have a good time. Save that for the coffee shop after the workout because it's not doing you any good on the treadmill.

DON'T BUY EXPENSIVE GEAR
BY ZACH BOHANNON

We've all been there. You know exactly where I'm talking about.

You're sitting on the couch at 1 a.m., cruising through the channels trying to find something to watch (let's pretend for a minute that Netflix doesn't exist, and people still actually watch the expensive cable television they pay for). You come across an infomercial with some fancy new piece of fitness equipment promising you those six-pack abs you've always desired, that bikini body you'd love to have by summer, or a guaranteed way to shed pounds. Maybe it's a new spin on the treadmill or some crunch machine that looks like a torture device from Rob Zombie's living room.

You know the kind of ads I'm talking about.

These products range anywhere from $20 to north of $2,000 (or x number of easy payments of $19.95 and whatever "free" gift they are throwing in).

I don't have the exact numbers in front of me, but I'm willing to bet that earning in the fitness equipment industry ranges in the billions of dollars. And how many people do you know who have a fancy ab roller sitting in their garage, or a treadmill they've converted to a towel rack that's taking up half of their spare bedroom? Maybe you're one of those people. I am guilty, as I have fitness equipment sitting in my garage that I don't use.

We buy these things with the best of intentions, promising ourselves that we are "finally going to get on track" and that we will put the equipment to good use.

But here's the thing.

Why do we need any equipment? And even if we do, why do we feel like we need to own it?

Something I have learned about myself the hard way is that I suck at working out at home. I try and tell myself it's more convenient, but the truth is that there are too many distractions and excuses at home. I do much better when I drive to the gym with the sole intention of working out or going to the park for a walk or jog. Once I'm there, there's nothing to distract me, and I can get my workout done. Even still, I've spent hundreds of dollars in the past on gym equipment or other home workout solutions, intending to use them, but rarely ever did.

I believe that for *most* people, a gym membership is the way to go. The country's largest fitness chain is opening up more and more locations every month, and you can join for $10 a month and gain access to tens of thousands of dollars' worth of equipment that won't take up any space in your house. And worst-case scenario, if you end up not using your membership as much as you'd like, it's much easier to cancel that than it is to sell that expensive treadmill you bought.

But let's say that you're one of the people who either can't make it to the gym regularly or don't like to go there, and you can get in a good workout at home without distraction.

You don't need much or even *any* equipment.

In fact, my favorite exercise routine doesn't require any equipment or a lot of time.

Tabata is a form of HIIT (High-Intensity Interval Training) that only takes eight minutes to complete, and you can do it all with bodyweight exercises. All you need is a little bit of space, a timer, and your own body. Here's how Tabata works.

First, pick four exercises. Again, these can all be bodyweight exercises that don't require you to have any equipment. I like to get a full-body workout, so I'll typically pick an upper-body exercise, a leg exercise, a core exercise that isn't sit-ups or crunches (they're terrible on your spine), and a cardio exercise. You can Google or search on YouTube for ideas, but an example of these four exercises would be push-ups, squats, leg lifts, and jogging in place. These four exercises will give you a full-body workout, and each can be modified accordingly (e.g., if you can't do a full push-up, do push-ups from your knees or use a wall).

Next, you'll want to have an interval timer. There are plenty of free apps for smartphones, and you can also pick up timers that clip to your waistband that will allow you to set intervals. You want to set the first interval to 20 seconds and the second to 10 seconds. And you'll want to repeat this interval 16 times.

The 20-second timer acts as your "active" timer. During that 20 seconds, you'll start with the first of your four exercises and do as many reps of that exercise as you can in 20 seconds. So, let's say that you've chosen push-ups as your first exercise. You'll perform as many push-ups as you can in 20 seconds.

The 10-second timer is your rest timer. During this time, you'll take a short break as you transition to the next exercise. So in our example above, you would stand and prepare to do as many squats as you can in 20 seconds.

By the time you complete this 8-minute workout, you'll have done four rounds of each exercise, and if you put in even a moderate amount of effort, I guarantee you that you will be sweating and catching your breath.

Besides not needing equipment, a lot of space, or much time, Tabata is an adaptable workout that you can tailor to your own needs. Don't be afraid to modify it as necessary. You can start by cutting the intervals in half and only going for 4 minutes. You can also add an extra 5-10 seconds onto the rest period. Wearing a heart-rate monitor for these exercises is encouraged, and of course, speak to your primary care physician before starting any workout routine.

Of course, this section is called "Don't Buy Expensive Gear," not "Don't Buy Any Gear," so I'd be remiss if I didn't make a suggestion or two for those of you who want to work out at home.

If you want to add some strength training to your routine, resistance bands are the way to go. They are an especially great alternative if you're going to work your upper body and have trouble doing push-ups or pull-ups. Resistance bands are safe and easy for anyone to use. You can typically find a set online for around $20, like this set that I own. Resistance bands are much cheaper than weight sets, and you can take them anywhere. They're even simple to travel with.

I'm also a big fan of the TRX Suspension Trainer. It's a bit pricey, but if I were going to recommend one piece of equipment to anyone, this would be it. It's an excellent way for anyone to get resistance training into their routine using their bodyweight.

Also, don't feel compelled to buy any expensive DVD sets. There is enough quality, free workout content on YouTube so you'd never have to do the same workout twice.

Keep it simple, and remember you don't need anything. You just need to start. All of us could benefit from just moving our bodies more, and it doesn't take a fancy treadmill to do that.

Don't Sacrifice Function for Convenience by Zach Bohannon

Walking into a gym for the first time can be intimidating. I remember the first time I walked into a gym, intending to change my life. It was in 2012, and I weighed over 300 pounds. You feel self-conscious, like everyone is looking at you and judging you (which, you quickly learn, is a bunch of crap because people at the gym spend way more time looking at their phones or themselves in the mirror).

I also felt lost, unsure of what to do. I surely didn't want anyone making fun of me because I didn't know "how" to exercise. So, naturally, I got onto the treadmill. I had used treadmills before in hotel gyms, and the controls were relatively simple.

I remember trying out some of the machines scattered across the floor. While some look like torture devices, most are fairly simple to figure out.

Machines are a great place to start, especially if you don't have a grasp on what you're doing. Obviously, going to the gym and working out with machines is better than sitting on the couch at home. But I'd encourage you to move away from the machines as you get more comfortable in having an exercise routine.

I'm a big fan of functional exercise, and I think it is beneficial to anyone who works out, whether your "why" is to lose weight, get stronger, or feel better. Functional exercises promote movements that we use in everyday life. An example of this would be a squat. I do several variations of squats in my workouts because I squat down a lot in real life, whether it's to pick up something off the ground or to play with my daughter. Another example might be a fireman's carry. This is where you hold heavy weights in each of your hands and simply walk across the gym. You'll get the grocery bags from the car to the house in no time and without breaking a sweat if you put these into your workout.

But the point is, I like to use movements that happen in real life, and there's a reason I'm a big fan of performing these exercises with weights, kettlebells, resistance bands, or even just bodyweight, as opposed to using a machine.

Let's use the overhead press machine as an example. This is the machine where you sit down and grip two handles, pushing them straight up over your head.

The biggest problem with machines is they move on a rail, meaning they only have a single plane of movement. As a beginner, this can work to your advantage because they help teach you proper form. But the problem is that in real-life situations, we don't move in a single plane. If I am picking up a box of Christmas decorations over my head to put them onto a shelf in my garage, I am not raising them straight up. I am probably going to have to lean and adjust some to get them up onto that shelf. In this instance, performing overhead presses with dumbbells or kettlebells would be more functional. It forces you to control your movements and use the proper form without a machine guiding you in a way that may or may not translate to real-life situations.

Another disadvantage of the overhead press machine is that you are sitting. By sitting, you are not exercising half of your body. Now I'm not saying there isn't a place for seated overhead presses in your workout. There are times in life when we're required to push something overhead while sitting, so this is still a functional movement. But I recommend using free weights and mixing standing overhead presses with seated ones.

Functional exercise is not limited to only weight training, either.

Let me ask you a question.

When was the last time you walked up a hill with your arms straight out in front of you?

Don't hold on!

Don't. Hold. On.

What I'm talking about here is holding onto the top of the treadmill. Every day at the gym, I see *someone* doing this. They have the incline so high that they have to hold on. But if I saw someone doing this in real life, I would think the zombie apocalypse had started.

I love incline walking on the treadmill. It's a great way to get a cardio workout without taxing your joints by jogging or running, and it's a nice alternative to the days when I don't want to ride the bike. But I have a really simple rule:

If you have to hold onto the handles in front of you or the rails on either side of you, then you've got either the incline or speed set too high. Perhaps even both.

Find a happy medium that challenges you, but not so much that you have to hold on so you don't go rolling off onto the gym floor. Because *then* people would be looking at you! Besides, you're going to burn more calories by swinging your arms than you are by holding onto that rail.

If you're starting a workout routine, please don't let this discourage you from using machines. As I said, machines are a great place to start. But I encourage you to move beyond them and start blending more functional movements into your exercise.

One machine I would stay away from altogether is the crunch machine. It's terrible on your spine, and, as writers, we sit enough as it is. If you want a good core exercise, then do planks every day. They are safe, easy on your body, and work your core better than sit-ups. At the beginning or end of your workout, do a plank to failure (as long as you can hold it) and mark the time on a spreadsheet or in a notebook. It's a great way to keep track of how much fitter you're getting!

And for the love of God, please let go of the treadmill.

Don't Skip a Proper Warm-up and Cooldown
by Zach Bohannon

Time.

It seems like none of us have enough of it, which is a funny thing. It isn't as if over the years the days have gotten shorter in terms of hours. And as the old cliché goes, you have the same 24 hours that I have. But for whatever reason in our fast-moving smartphone culture, it's become a badge of honor to say, "I just don't have the time."

Because we have convinced ourselves that we never have enough time, we take shortcuts. We do stuff half-assed.

While many people have extraordinary responsibilities, more often than not, our lack of time comes back to what we are prioritizing.

And when it comes to a workout, prioritizing a proper warm-up and cooldown routine is crucial.

Just getting to the gym or putting on your running shoes can be a journey all on its own, especially if you haven't made exercise a priority in your life. So if you are already struggling to fit exercise time into your busy schedule, it can be natural to seek ways to cut your workout down to as little time as possible. But a dynamic warm-up and post-workout stretch are not the places to save time.

Time isn't the only factor here either. Some people simply feel like warming up or cooling down isn't necessary. And for many who choose not to skip warming up and cooling down, they do the wrong kinds of exercises to prepare for or recover from a workout.

But is it worth risking injury to save 2-3 minutes on either side of your workout?

Hell, no.

So let's talk about warming up first.

The Warm-up (pre-workout)

In my time as a trainer, this is one of the things I saw clients misunderstand the most.

Often before starting a session or group exercise class, I would see many clients going through a routine of stretches before we dove into the workout. I also often see this with runners. They will stretch out their legs before going on the treadmill or starting a run. I am not going to tell you that this is "wrong," but I personally advise against static stretching before a workout.

As you'll discover later, stretching is a great exercise for your post-workout cooldown, but somewhere along the way, we were taught that we are supposed to stretch before movement. If I had to guess, it's because we often see athletes on TV stretching right before the big game starts. But what the TV doesn't show us is the dynamic warm-ups these athletes are doing before they need to stretch.

Recent studies on ncbi.nlm.nih.gov have shown, however, that stretching before a workout without a dynamic warm-up can decrease performance and mobility and increase the risk of injury. And it makes sense. Stretching a tight muscle is like pulling a rubber band as hard as you can without loosening it up first.

So if you're not going to stretch before a workout, then how should you warm up?

At a minimum, some light cardio is a safe way to go. This is how I started every session with my clients. If you're at the gym, pick your favorite cardio machine, whether it's the treadmill, elliptical, or bike, and do some light cardio for 5 minutes. The goal here isn't to spike your heart rate, but to get your muscles ready for movement.

My personal warm-up routine is simple:

- Ten head circles each way.
- Ten arm circles each way.
- Fifteen leg swings per leg.
- A 5-minute brisk walk or light cycling.

There are a lot of exercises you can work into a dynamic warm-up, including high-knees and squats. But the most important thing is that you do some kind of dynamic warm-up with movement before jumping into your workout.

The Cooldown (post-workout)

Now that you're sweating and those muscles are nice and loose, it's time to stretch! I know you've been waiting this whole time!

Stretching after a workout will help alleviate how sore you are in the coming days. Soreness naturally decreases as working out becomes a habit, but stretching will continue to assist in recovery.

Again, keep your stretching routine simple. Many gyms have machines that will help you stretch different muscles, though I prefer to stretch without the aid of machines. My routine takes about 5 minutes, and in the process, I stretch my neck, arms, shoulders, back, and all the major muscles in my legs. You can find a lot of good routines on Google or YouTube.

Remember to focus on your breathing during stretching. I like to hold each stretch for three deep breaths before moving on to the next stretch. By the end of my 5-minute cooldown, my body feels good, and my heart rate has almost gotten back to normal.

In closing this section, I want to remind you to keep it simple. Warming up and cooling down are essential ingredients that make up a balanced workout, but they don't have to be complicated. Some light movement before and basic stretching after will suffice. What's important is that you aren't skipping these and that you understand their importance in preventing injuries and allowing you to have the most optimal workout possible.

And if you don't think you have the time to warm up and stretch, remember that you don't have the time *not* to.

DON'T IGNORE WHY THEY EXERCISE BY ZACH BOHANNON

We live in a word-of-mouth culture. As authors, you surely know this. You can run all the best ads, send out the most polished newsletter, or have a seemingly perfect social media campaign to promote your new book. But nothing will sell your book more than a reader saying to a friend, "Hey, I just finished reading this book, and you *have* to check it out!"

The health and fitness world isn't immune to this — many of the most popular diet and exercise fads spread by word of mouth. A person discovers the keto diet, loses some weight, and then wants to let everyone they encounter know how it changed their life. A friend might say, "You look great. What have you been doing?" and learn about the keto diet for the first time from that person. It's inspiring, and they decide that they want to become keto because it worked for their friend.

But is that really the best approach?

No two people are the same, and often we have different goals and aspirations than others. So while paleo might work for some people, others won't be able to or want to digest that much meat, regardless of how much weight their friend lost on that diet.

Exercise routines are no different. Fads come in and out, and people love to boast about what helped them reach their own goals.

You need to ask yourself an important question: *Why* do you exercise?

On the surface, it would seem that most people exercise because they want to look better naked. Let's be real; there's a reason that magazines, supplement companies, and treadmill manufacturers push this in advertising their products. Exercise for vanity is the most common reason people decide to start exercising, whether it's to lose fifty pounds or to shake off a little belly fat (or "tone," as is commonly said) to look more flattering in that bikini you really want to wear this summer. Triggering these emotions sells more magazines and ab machines that collect dust in your closet.

But there are a slew of other reasons that people exercise, and each purpose brings with it a different type of exercise you should be performing. For example, someone who has been experiencing back pain might receive the advice that they should be regularly exercising. That person would be doing themselves a disservice by going into the gym and hopping on the treadmill or following what the people at the weight rack are doing. They would benefit more from a routine including yoga, stretches, resistance-band training, and isometric exercises.

If your goal is weight loss, then your workout should focus on exercises that get your heart rate up and shed calories, such as running, incline walking, cycling, rowing, elliptical, or my personal favorite, HIIT—High-Intensity Interval Training. Toss in some resistance training with weights or bands for a balanced workout.

On the flip side, if you are trying to bulk up, doing too much cardio can be counterproductive. You want to focus on lifting heavy weights. Just please, my fellow men, don't skip leg day.

Know *why* you're exercising.

I was working in the fitness industry when CrossFit became popular. CrossFit Boxes (Box is CrossFit lingo for Gym) popped up all over the place, and people began filling them to do their WODs (Workout of the Day). As it caught on, more and more people flocked to CrossFit. And I get it. It looks and is pretty fun. But what wasn't fun were the several injured clients I had to help rehabilitate after getting injured doing CrossFit.

Now look, this isn't a knock on CrossFit. Please save your hate mail. I applaud CrossFit for building a supportive community around exercise and understand that many Boxes are safe with well-qualified trainers. But the fact is that *most* people don't - *need* to be performing Olympic lifts or seeing how many times they can jump on and off a box in two minutes. *Most* people don't need something as intense as CrossFit. *Most* people just need to move their bodies more.

Focus on your reasons for exercising. It's easy to Google workout routines that pertain to your needs, and if you are unsure, seek the help of a professional trainer who can tailor a personalized workout for you. And of course, speak with your primary care physician before starting any exercise routine.

In closing, I want to add that it's also essential that you do exercise that you enjoy. If you are trying to lose weight but hate running, then don't run. When I lost a hundred pounds in a year, I never ran. I've never even signed up for a 5k. I got my cardio through bicycling, playing hockey, and HIIT.

On the flip side, if CrossFit is what makes you want to get up off the couch and work out, then, by all means, head to your local Box and knock out those WODs. As long as you understand *why* you're working out, and you are keeping your health and well-being in mind, then have fun and get healthier.

DON'T DO THE SAME ROUTINE FOREVER BY J. THORN

I have a friend who walks five miles a day. That is a great way to exercise, and it has certainly made him a healthier person. However, he's been doing this for 10 years.

Don't get me wrong. Walking every day is commendable, and more of us should do this regularly. The problem is that our bodies (and our minds) are constantly seeking stasis—they try to regulate everything so that each moment feels like "normal," whatever that means. The first few weeks my friend walked five miles, I'm sure he was tired and his legs hurt. He was most likely breathing heavily and might have even struggled to finish his walk.

But guess what probably started to happen? As the days turned into weeks, those five miles felt easier to my friend. His maximum heart rate while walking most likely stabilized and his muscles adjusted to the strain so that five miles began to feel "normal" for his daily activity.

The same thing happens with all types of workouts. If you've never done push-ups and you decide you're going to start doing 10 every day, you'll struggle to reach 5 a day during the first week. But over time, your body adjusts, and pretty soon you can do 10 pushups easily—not even breaking a sweat.

Does that mean that walking five miles a day for years, or doing 10 push-ups every day for months is a waste of time? Absolutely not, and again it's worth noting how commendable this is for anyone. But if you do the same routine forever, the effectiveness of the routine drops off considerably. And if taken out to the extreme, the time spent exercising is wasted because you're not getting the most out of it.

When I first started working out a few years ago, I couldn't ride the exercise bike for more than five minutes straight. I'd struggle for air, my leg muscles would burn, and I'd even get dizzy. But each week, the five minutes became easier, and soon after that, I could ride five minutes on the bike while holding a conversation with someone—my body had adjusted.

Therefore, you must change your workout routine, no matter the length or type of your workout because failing to do so will result in your body coasting, which means you're not losing calories, and you're probably not improving your conditioning.

For aerobic exercises, it's usually best to increase frequency or intensity.

Frequency would mean doing the exercise for longer periods or doing the periods more often. This is a great place to start when you're beginning a regime because you have so much room to grow. Like me on the exercise bike, I could take a few weeks to double my workout time—from 5 minutes to 10 minutes—which wouldn't have a major impact on the rest of my responsibilities that day.

Intensity is increasing how hard you're working within your given time frame. Again using my exercise bike as an example, I could pedal at 60% of my capacity for five minutes. But if after a week that felt easy to me, I could pedal the same amount of time but at 80% of my capacity, which would be a more strenuous and worthwhile workout.

As you can probably tell, combining an increase in frequency and intensity at the same time can get you into better shape, but it can also lead to overexertion and injury.

I started by increasing the frequency of my workouts until I hit the maximum amount of time I had budgeted to exercise, which was 30 minutes on the bike. I added 5 minutes to my bike-riding time each week until I was able to pedal nonstop for 30 minutes. I did not worry about my pedaling speed, only that I could go for 30 minutes without stopping. Once I was able to do that, I turned my attention to intensity.

On a workout machine, you have two intensity factors to adjust. The tension or difficulty level on the bike can make your workout more strenuous because it gets harder to pedal if you move to the next level. If the bike has a "difficulty" level of 1-10, with 10 being the most difficult, I started at 1. When 30 minutes on the bike at level 1 felt easy, I bumped it up to level 2. And so on. Besides—and if you're not on a machine—you can increase intensity through your own exertion. For example, I start my ride at a comfortable pace until I hit the "5s and 9s." During my 30-minute workout, whenever the timer hits a multiple of 5 or 9 (minute marks), I pedal at 100% for 60 seconds.

Using a combination of frequency and intensity, I'm able to gradually improve the efficiency of my workout and never reach the "maximum" level on any measurement. I probably can't pedal for 30 minutes above level 7 on the bike difficulty setting, and my 100% pedaling effort should always be increasing as I get in better shape.

The point is that if I'm constantly tweaking the frequency, intensity, or both (with caution) of my routine, I will constantly challenge my body without significantly increasing the length of my workouts. After several years of riding the exercise bike, I still ride for only 30 minutes. But I've increased the difficulty level, which means I now burn almost twice as many calories as I did when I started. And by increasing my intensity by pedaling at 100% on the 5s and 9s, I've almost doubled the "distance" I travel on the exercise bike in that same 30-minute window.

It doesn't matter how you work out. Whether you swim, walk, ride a computerized exercise bike, or do push-ups in your living room, to get the most out of any workout, you can't do the same routine forever. Increasing your frequency or intensity means you'll always be pushing your body beyond its stasis, which, in turn, means you'll be in better shape.

DON'T TRY TO CONVINCE OTHERS THAT WHAT THEY'RE DOING IS BEST BY J. THORN

These days, it's incredibly complicated trying to come up with a workout that suits your physical condition and your lifestyle. There are experts who claim you should be running 5 miles a day while others claim that you should never run. Some will suggest working out with weights, while others would say you don't need weights at all.

I struggled for years in trying to figure out what I should be doing for physical exercise. As I've gotten older, the risk of injury has moved me away from competitive sports, so I had to think of other ways of getting my exercise.

I've done everything from swimming to hiking to riding a bike. These days, for the sake of ease and convenience, most of my cardiovascular workouts are done in a gym on a machine.

But it begs the question, which is, what kind of workout *should* I be doing?

Many people will happily tell you that *their* workout is the best kind of workout. Other authors will share their experience with you and insist that you should be doing what they are doing because it's working for them. They will use statistics or articles to prove to you that what they're doing works. And it might be working for them, but that doesn't mean it is going to work for you.

The truth is, the only right workout is the one you are going to do day in and day out. It is the one that you will turn into a positive habit by building a system that rewards you for completing the workout. That's it. If you find a workout that you do, and better yet, even enjoy, that is the one you should be doing, regardless of what anyone else tells you that you should be doing.

There are several different types of exercise, and you should experiment to figure out the best fit for you. You can do aerobic or anaerobic exercise, competitive or noncompetitive exercise, and even activities that are exercise but haven't traditionally been considered as such, like yoga.

Many people think of going to the gym as lifting weights, but that is only one type of workout. Building mass and strengthening muscles is definitely important and many people create workouts around this concept, but it is not the only way to work out. For people new to exercise, weights and machines can be intimidating, so much so that they lose interest in working out.

It might be worth starting with a low-impact activity like yoga, which stretches muscles and begins to get your heart rate up. More advanced yoga techniques can be just as effective as running or riding a bicycle and worth experimenting with if you're not sure how to work out.

If yoga isn't your thing, aerobic exercise is a wonderful way to keep your body in top shape. Most exercise experts will recommend 30 minutes of strenuous activity a day, five days a week. But there are many ways in which you can get strenuous activity beyond running on the treadmill.

I prefer using the machines at my gym simply because the conditions are always the same. I don't have to worry about cold weather, or storms, or getting a flat tire on my bike. You can walk on the treadmill, ride an exercise bike, or try any other number of gliding aerobic machines that can be found in most gyms these days. And if you prefer to do your workout in your own home, you can purchase these types of machines. However, it's important to recognize that you have fewer options if you have one machine at home instead of going to a gym and using all of their machines.

Being able to move from the rowing machine to the treadmill to the exercise bike to the step machine gives me variation in my workouts so that I don't get bored with any particular type of workout. I don't have to worry about reaching a plateau because each machine challenges me in a slightly different way. I also save a ton of room in my house.

And in addition to the aerobic workout or possibly instead of one, you can use a variety of free weights or weight machines to get your exercise. Some people prefer to do reps the same way at the same time or focusing on a certain part of the body, such as the abs or legs. These types of exercises can keep your muscles toned and keep you feeling good.

Others enjoy swimming as an alternative to weights or gym exercises. Getting in the pool can be a soothing experience, and much like walking on a treadmill at the gym, you always know the conditions of the pool will be the same. You won't have to fight temperature or weather, so you'll always know what you're getting into.

As you can see, there are many options when it comes to choosing a workout. Just because a certain workout or set of exercises works for one author doesn't mean it's going to work for you. And always be cautious of anyone who insists that the way that they are doing it is the only right way.

The most important thing a thriving author can do is to take care of the body that houses the mind that we rely on, day in and day out. So it's worth remembering that the only right workout is the one you'll stick to, the one you'll do every day, no matter what.

DON'T RISK AN INJURY WITH RISKY BEHAVIOR BY J. THORN

When I was a teenager, and in my 20s, I played on two or three hockey teams at the same time. In Pittsburgh, deck hockey is a popular form of street hockey that is played throughout the city. I've played deck hockey, street hockey, in-line hockey, and ice hockey. Participating in 4 to 5 games a week meant that I was able to get enough physical exercise that I didn't need to go to a gym or work out on a machine.

Hockey is a great aerobic sport, and unlike a more recreational sport like golf, it's almost impossible to play if you are not in shape. Hockey requires short bursts of intense energy followed by periods of rest, which you might recognize as one of the most effective ways of working out today, also known as at a H.I.I.T. (High-Intensity Interval Training) routine.

As a young man, I was not concerned with injury, strained muscles, or torn ligaments. But as I got older, I realized that unless I was going to take my health seriously, I couldn't continue to play four and five games a week. As we get older, our bodies become more susceptible to breaks and strains, and therefore, playing competitive sports might not be the best option.

I've had friends who had a similar experience playing other types of sports, such as soccer. Soccer is another game that requires intensity in short bursts followed by short periods of rest. Soccer puts a strain on ankles and knees, especially joints and ligaments. The game is fun and easy to play because it doesn't require much more than a ball, and therefore, many people around the world grow up playing the sport. It is no surprise that soccer is one of the most popular sports for kids, even in the United States.

But similar to hockey, soccer gets more difficult to play the older you get. Even if you remove the skill of heading, the risk of concussion while playing soccer can be equal to or greater than playing hockey. I have friends in their 30s and 40s who have suffered concussions from playing Sunday morning pickup soccer.

If you enjoy competitive sports, that doesn't mean that you have to stop playing them once you reach a certain age. However, the older you get, the more difficult it becomes to have a consistent cardiovascular workout by playing only competitive sports.

There are many alternatives to risky competitive sports that don't come with the same risks for injury.

The simplest example is working out at a gym or having an exercise machine in your home. While these might not be the most exciting forms of exercise, they provide the most consistent experience with little to no chance of unusual circumstances. When you step on the treadmill or hop on the exercise bike, especially if you are in your house or in a gym, the conditions are always the same. You know exactly how long you're going to go and what the workout will feel like.

Some people don't like to work out on machines, and therefore, running or bicycling in the neighborhood is an option. While I find biking my neighborhood much more satisfying than riding a machine in the gym, weather and road conditions don't always make that possible. Even if you live in a mild climate, there will be times when it will be impossible for you to ride. Therefore, having an alternative in your home or any gym is a wise move.

If you are the type of person who really is motivated by competitive sports, there are still options, sports you can play that won't put you at the same level of risk as something like hockey or soccer.

Swimming is a great alternative to both competitive sports and machines in the gym. You can swim by yourself or with friends.

The conditions in the swimming pool will always be consistent, meaning you can do the workout year-round no matter where you live. Also, there is the added benefit of being in the water, which is different from our day-to-day experience and something that many people find therapeutic.

But once you are no longer in high school, swimming isn't really a competitive sport. Other competitive sports include things like basketball or softball. However, both of these come with inherent risks, and I, for one, have pretty much ruined my ankles from playing basketball as an adult.

Alternatives to competitive sports might provide an even more enriching workout experience. Whether you are interested in cross-country skiing, hiking, climbing, or long-distance walking, all of these can be beneficial workouts without the risk of serious injury.

If you insist on playing competitive sports, then you must understand the risks that come along with them. If you've never broken a bone or torn a ligament, you might not understand the consequences of such an injury. Not only will you have medical bills to pay, a long healing process, and an extensive rehabilitation plan, but it's also difficult to keep mental focus if your body is experiencing physical pain. I've had chronic health issues that have made it hard for me to focus and so, even sitting at my desk on the computer can be a challenge. As long as you understand the inherent risks in playing competitive sports as you age, then you should do so cautiously.

And if you do decide to play sports, you should still consider a consistent workout routine that helps train you for that sport. Using the example of hockey, a workout routine consisting of sprints, squats, lunges, and interval training can help keep you in shape where you won't spend a whole afternoon trying to catch your breath afterward. As a bonus, it can make your workouts more fun because it gives them more of a purpose beyond simply keeping in shape or losing weight.

With so many opportunities to exercise and explore the natural world, it might be worth considering a different type of physical workout beyond the gym, one that does not include competition and a clock.

RELATIONSHIPS

As thriving authors, the reader relationship tends to be the one we talk about most and focus on, but the relationships we have with family, friends, accountability partners, editors, mentors, and, most importantly, ourselves, support and push us to get the words written. In this section, we explore the choices that each of these relationships presents.

Here's a quick summary of the valuable lessons you can expect to learn in this section:

"Don't Listen to Them" - We turn to those we know best when we start to write and call ourselves authors, but do family members and friends really understand the business decisions that we should be making? Getting validation from those closest to us is never a good idea, especially when they aren't readers in your genre.

"Don't Count the Free Ones" - You shared your book for free as soon as you finished it. Look at all those downloads! Does that mean you're going to sell lots of copies of your next book, or should you be focusing on your craft and figuring out what the reader expects in your genre? Maybe all they liked about your free book was the fact that it was free.

"Don't Reject Change" - It's your story, so can't you fight with the editor to keep your words on the page? To make a good thing better, let your editor make changes, so that your ideas are clear. It's not about who is right, it's about making the decisions that improve the reader experience.

"Don't Fight Over Money" - It doesn't sound like you're getting the support you need, but is that your partner's fault or your own belief system? Your significant other might be the only one who can push you to do the hard work.

"Don't Doubt the Words" - We all experience imposter syndrome, or resistance, or whatever you want to call it. Taking the fear and doubt out of your creative process is the only way to keep writing.

"Don't Follow the Leader" - Sharing your goals with other writers can be tough. Maybe you don't want anyone to see your weaknesses, or maybe you're not ready for success yet. Rather than taking the same actions as everyone else, let your vulnerable moments show the real work you're doing.

"Don't Argue with the Process" - You asked for help, didn't you? Stop spinning your wheels and discover why the decisions are still yours to make. Your mentor is there to fill the learning gaps you hit along the way.

"Don't Waste Time" - If you rely on a handful of excuses to hide behind, your significant other is there to support the path you want to be on.

"Don't Write Without the 3Cs (Challenges, Changes, and Consistency)" - Thriving authors know how to face challenges, deal with changes, and write consistently. Before you quit, discover how to do the impossible.

DON'T LISTEN TO THEM BY JANET KITTO

Friends and family are there to offer us support, but sometimes, they can't. Your mom wants to see your books in her local bookstore. She thinks what you write is "cute." That's certainly not what you poured yourself into, a story that is "cute" that all her friends can read. No, you practiced swordplay and created a fantastical world that an older generation can't relate to. You let your characters suffer in horrific ways.

The internal wants and needs that you shared in that manuscript have your brother questioning where you got your ideas. Obviously, Mom is blind when it comes to anything you do. The worst-case scenario is that a family member tells you that you can have the story that they always wanted to write. That's the one that's going to be a bestseller. After you publish that, then you could try and rewrite yours.

Why did you share your work with your family? Or worse, why did you want your friends to be beta readers? They aren't able to give you the feedback that you're looking for.

The meaning that you carefully crafted into your story might be lost on the friends who would rather say the story is good than hurt your feelings.

I made this mistake. I asked a family member who reads and writes in a different genre to read my first draft of a novel. She wasn't writing at that time, but I let her read my work and asked her to tell me if something wasn't clear. I naively thought I was showing her what the writing life was like, not knowing yet that everyone's creative process is different.

I allowed her to question what was happening in the scenes. If I had kept part of the story inside of my own head instead of getting it to the page, I believed that she was doing the job an editor would do.

The problem was that she didn't understand why my characters acted the way they did and would ask me to change things that I knew readers of my genre would want to read. But at that point, I didn't have readers. I had questions. Was I telling a good story? Could I publish this and make money?

We all do it. We want validation.

Not everyone in my close circle knew, but I had been trying to write all of my life. Family saw that I was sharing a hobby with my mother. This was another thing that made me "just like her." I wasn't like her at all. I was fighting to have my own voice. And it wasn't a hobby. I had 300 pages that were supposed to convince my family of that. The manuscript had a cover, and I had created front and back matter to show that I was a professional.

I continued to draft novels and began dreaming that I could create a business out of my writing. The next step, I thought, would be to meet with other women entrepreneurs in my small town. These were the store and restaurant owners, the plumber, the dog walker, the financial planners, and real estate agents.

I talked about word count and story structure, nothing that these women could relate to, and then I tried to take their marketing advice and promote myself on social media. I had nothing to say to my ideal reader when I posted because I hadn't figured out who my ideal reader was yet. I wasted time doing that promotion, and to be honest, my time networking with that group. I could have been learning about the genre I wanted to publish in. Because I wasn't making money yet from my writing, those businesswomen didn't see me as an author. They weren't the right community to support the growth I needed.

If a stranger had randomly asked me at the grocery store or at the library how I earned a living at that time, I couldn't say the word author out loud. I was stuck in my mother's reflection, my writing seen only as a hobby, and disconnected from the idea of being a thriving author.

My first push to earn as a creative came at home, where I was given the support to create a business providing author services to authors who were earning. What a mouthful. My mindset allowed my business to be unnecessarily complicated. I spent half of my day writing, the other half on client work. That was where I was comfortable until I chose to take a more significant plunge and make my business about creating wealth from my own words.

Whatever your journey is to get published, there will come a time when you stop listening to family and friends and start networking with other thriving authors. You won't need someone close to you to tell you if you're telling a good story. Your editor will work with you before you share your book with anyone. You'll see exactly what the other thriving authors see, and that's a business where your ideas earn you the lifestyle that you now can acknowledge that you deserve.

DON'T LISTEN TO THEM BY JANET KITTO

So many downloads! Amazing! Your debut novel is now in the hands of thousands of readers, thanks to those newsletter swaps you participated in. All of the social media promotion was worth it. Your first book, along with dozens of others from authors in your genre, is free to those voracious readers!

This is what we hear all the time. Getting your book into the hands of readers is what you need to focus on.

You might be thinking, I did all this hard work to launch and now my book is being read! Or, have you come to realize that no one wants to buy your book? The downloads went to readers who collect free books. How are you going to build a business if you share your work for free?

When I decided that writing books wasn't going to be a hobby for me, that I wanted to earn a living as a thriving author, there was no one to read my work because I wasn't sharing my books for free on any platform. I had self-published four titles, made a ton of rookie mistakes as an indie, then unpublished and tried to remove all evidence of promotion for those books. I went back to square one, feeling that it was too big of a dream to actually see my books in the hands of an audience.

I didn't quit. I wrote more books for the series of eight I had planned. There didn't seem to be any other choice for me because I couldn't let go of the story. I decided I would wait until the books were good enough.

That was the mindset I'd adopted.

I would focus on rewriting each book by studying story structure, and I would learn more about marketing and promoting myself. Then, once I was sure about my identity as a thriving author, I would drop my well-crafted stories onto the retail platforms and make loads of money.

Which isn't how this works. To create an identity, one must do the thing, not hide from it. A thriving author learns how to engage an audience.

I was stuck. I feared my books would never sell.

Even with better covers and professional edits, my books were likely never to get discovered. Should I give my words away for free to build an audience? I knew the answer was no, not if I wanted to be a professional, but it was also yes because I wanted to build a mailing list.

The problem with trying to answer when I was stuck was that I had chosen to hold my writing even closer to me. I'd been pushed into writing the first novel to deal with the grief of losing my dad a decade before this period closed with the loss of my mom. I hadn't been writing for an audience to buy my books, I had been writing for me.

So I decided to change my life in a significant way.

No more wasting time and not investing in myself. I hired an editor to look at the first book I wanted to republish. I tried to understand what genre I was writing for. I knew it would be a lot of work to build a relationship with each reader, even more to stay focused on the readers' expectations in the genre I had chosen to write.

Still hanging there was this choice: Do I work on becoming a thriving author, or give away what I had for free?

I knew enough not to count the readers who only wanted free books. They wouldn't help me do what I needed to do, which was to earn a living from my writing. I worked on building assets. I also planned to get my books into the library system. Those were the readers who could have my books for free.

My reading pile grew as it filled with the masterworks and bestsellers in my genre. These books would help me to understand how to write my books. I joined a mastermind and learned to have a different relationship with what I was writing and how I was writing. Instead of feeling lost and hiding behind a number of doubts, I finally found a pathway to creating revenue streams that would power my business.

Thriving authors decide what relationship they want with their readers. They create healthy boundaries for readers to be actively engaged with their books. Thriving authors interact with their readers through their list or other spaces they control.

Knowing that you can build your business in the same way that you build your identity, you do the one thing that all writers do. You write. That's the best way to create assets and engage an audience for your books.

Don't Reject Change by Janet Kitto

The first story we tell is personal. We all have a story. Whether it gets published or not, our first story gets written because we need to tell it.

I put all the feelings I had about grief into my first manuscript. I discovered NaNoWriMo about eight months after my father passed. I wrote to have closure because I didn't go home for the burial. I wasn't going to write about my anger. I wanted to explore the feelings of loss through characters who would learn how to love again. That was the story I chose to write.

I did the next NaNoWriMo and wrote another story about loss, this time about how death affected three generations. Again, I wasn't writing about my own loss or my own family. I continually denied that the story was connected in any way to me personally, but if I had been asked to change the plot or dive deeper into the choices I'd made with the story, I wouldn't have understood how the edits could have improved the book.

What if I had hired a professional editor to be involved before I'd hit the button to publish?

I made the rookie mistake of having family members and beta readers tell me what they thought of my writing. At the time, I had several years of experience in transcribing interviews for a university. I took the spoken word, all the "umm" and "ah" and broken thoughts, and I gave those discussions structure. I wasn't transcribing verbatim. I was adding value to the page. I also worked with a copy editor to transcribe criminal, family law, and provincial court documents.

The first novels that I wrote were too closely wrapped up in what I thought about myself. Instead of making the connection from an egocentric position that the skills I learned from the university and the courts helped made my work better, I honestly believed my experience proved that I knew what I was doing. This time, I was working on my own story, giving my own words structure.

Wasn't I right to do this self-publishing thing all on my own?

Editors take the time and have the patience to mentor you and to help you understand why changes are necessary for the draft that you poured your soul into. An editor can teach you how to make your ideas clear and improve the readability of your manuscript. There are also editors who can take your words, and with heavy editing, turn your work into something that doesn't even sound like you.

Let's focus on the editors who make a good thing better. Those are the editors that thriving authors work with.

I wasted years fighting (with myself) about what genre my stories were, and what I was trying to say about themes connected to family and loss. I dismissed the messages that thriving authors shared about professional editors on their blogs, in their podcasts, and in courses that I paid to learn from.

Being right can stand in the way of doing the work. Not just the practice of writing, but the relationship that you have with your words. Should you accept the changes? Reject them all? The choice remains with the writer, but do you want to always fight to be right? They're just words.

If you choose to make the most of the time you have with your editor, to write the best book that you can for the reader, then you know the power you have in your hands. More importantly, you have now decided to give that power to your editor because it was never about whether your words were right or not.

The decision to accept the changes from your editor are always about making your ideas clear and making a good thing even better.

Reader experience comes up all the time in conversation. We are readers, too, and I want nothing more than to escape into a story that has had line edits, a proofread, and a structural edit. I don't want to think about any of that while I'm reading. You know what that's like. You're taken right out of the story and possibly even shouting out loud about how ridiculous this plot point is. I want the book I'm reading to flow, the pages to turn effortlessly.

When I write, I no longer want the story to be personal. I want the books in my series to be profitable, the content to be of value to the reader.

I embrace whatever change is necessary to get my books into the hands of the right audience. I do the hard work with however many drafts it takes to get the story written. I hire professionals instead of relying on family and friends to validate that I've done the writing well. I trust that I've done the best I can, and I'm ready to see the improvements my editor will make.

Then I tell myself, it's time to write the next one.

DON'T FIGHT OVER MONEY BY JANET KITTO

"She doesn't support what I'm doing."

"He won't listen. Great writing takes time."

"If writing was like my paying job, she'd give me a break."

"He just doesn't get it."

While you figure out what you need to be a full-time author, you might feel that you don't have the support you expected from your partner. You don't have a dedicated space in your home yet, there's definitely not enough space outside of the roles you have in your family to make writing your focus, and your spouse has said, "We can't afford to lose your wages and benefits." Also, you need to be pushed to do the hard work. That's something I can relate to.

The experience I've had with my significant other while becoming a thriving author has been similar to a long journey without any direction. My husband wanted to see me earning more and contributing financially to our household, but there was never a huge push for that until he left his job, too. We traveled for ten months between 2018 and 2019, and we fought on the road about how we were going to support the new life we had created.

I saw us both as storytellers.

He would focus on photography and sell stock footage, and I was going to focus on writing books. This was a path for us to create together. He saw our travel as a transitional phase and wanted to work again, but remotely with fewer hours at the desk. He returned to a regular paycheck and health benefits for both of us once we settled on the east coast of Canada.

My husband has never doubted that I could write books. He believes there are ways for me to earn from my writing. He's been patient.

Any doubt there was about me earning a living from writing was actually my own. I thought he asked me to support him when he left the day job, and I did think he would enjoy that. I mean, why not? He supported our family financially for decades. He wanted to have a shorter commute and shorter working days, but not necessarily be working independently. He missed the people he worked with. He felt lost without the structure of working with a team.

When we have fought about money, it's been my belief system that I've struggled with. This is why he's been frustrated. Our arguments weren't about the fact that I wasn't earning as an author yet. I thought that he expected me to be doing the things I wasn't doing.

Let me explain. I was focused on learning more than the daily practice of writing. I hadn't learned how to balance my day or how much I had to push myself to do the drafting and revision.

I'd spent years watering down what I wanted. Family always came first. Now I was trying to go around the mess I'd made. He understood that there was a depth to the life I wanted. I was the one denying myself. Worse yet, I was projecting the anger that I had about my shortcomings directly at my spouse. When was I going to finish the series I started?

I slowly made my way into writing full-time, and I thought I had adjusted my belief system to appreciate that I was going from being paid by the hour to being paid for each asset I created, and ultimately finding wealth from the use of my ideas. Still, I was hung up on earning fast.

I had weekly meetings with accountability partners. I would listen to what they could achieve in a week and then wonder what I was doing wrong. I wasn't checking in with my husband, and he questioned why I was having those meetings with other authors because they didn't make me feel better about what I was trying to do.

Rather than making the fight about money, are you sure your partner is unsupportive, or like me, do you not look at the support as helpful because you haven't figured out what kind of help you need to do the hard work?

If you want your partner to value what you're writing, say so. If you want to make sure the arrangement is working for the whole family, find ways to check in and ask. Communicate what you need, how you want to celebrate when you earn a bestseller badge or hit a milestone for earnings. Tell your partner what your targets are for the week and for the year, and make sure you know what your partner wants you to appreciate in return for their choices.

The overarching component of any relationship will be to compromise.

The hardest decision you face as a thriving author isn't necessarily about the writing. It might be about the emotional demands you are confronted with to create products and services, and later to market and promote yourself.

You don't know what you're capable of, and you don't understand the time and energy you need to create. Should your partner be the one to push you to get your butt in the chair?

Not if you don't value the time you have, or realize that your partner is already on your team, especially when things don't go the way you expect them to. Don't you want to support their efforts? Their dream?

What you achieve is also what your significant other achieves. So celebrate together.

DON'T DOUBT THE WORDS BY JANET KITTO

It's time for the magic to happen. You have the keyboard ready or your dictation device at hand. This is your scheduled block for writing. You plan to finish a scene, or an essay, or the next newsletter. You are ready.

Except, you forgot to get a drink. It's essential to stay hydrated. Okay, that's done. Time to read your notes. You've been looking forward to this. Sigh. Why don't you feel like you're winning as an author? Where is your focus?

This kind of frustration shows up when self-doubt is playing a game with you. Self-doubt hides itself; we don't realize it's there behind the procrastination.

Take a look at your process. Is there any preparatory work you need to do before you begin writing? Have you cleared your mind of as many of the distractions in your life as you can?

Self-doubt is part of everyone's creative process. If you think that your writing isn't good enough, try acknowledging that fear and then write anyway. Avoiding the writing won't stop that feeling of not being enough. The doubt will show up in other ways.

Have you got a website that you don't want anyone to look at? Email automation that isn't set up? I was sure no one would sign up for updates from me, so I delayed as long as I could to have social proof that I existed as an author.

There isn't anything wrong with you. You aren't facing a blank page because you didn't do a proper outline. Trust yourself. You're ready. Being a perfectionist and trying to control how many words will flow isn't how to work through this challenge.

The one question that gets asked as much as, "Where do you get your ideas from?" is probably, "How do you deal with imposter syndrome?" I often ask myself, "How can you call yourself a writer when you can't clearly communicate your point?"

I want to fit in, not stand out, or be open for judgment. I want to feel confident about the content I write.

I'm not the only one having this experience. We are alone, but together feeling this doubt.

Once I knew that others believed in me, I started changing how I felt about the work I did when I sat down to write. The more that I studied story structure, the harder that imposter syndrome had to work to shut me down. The more I write, and the more I publish, the more I feel that I deserve to earn as a thriving author. The relationship we all have with our self is one that authors could talk about more.

You're not a trickster doing a fast shuffle with all of the right words. Even if you are feeling it, I do not think you're duplicitous. In fact, I haven't assumed anything about what you're writing. That's the reality. But we do share similar insecurities. I see that you've made the writing look natural and I am discounting the value of what you've done to share your work with me.

My journal is full of pages where I've plotted through every little thing my inner critic wanted me to consider. I plan out new routines to fuel my competency. It never hurts to tweak the system. Right?

I read how-to articles to move the insecurities confronting me over to awareness. Exhausting work, but I have to deliver. Back to the top of the page. It's time for the magic again, now that all of those issues that were blocking me are out of my head.

Answering the call to write is simply opening a door that leads you to abundance rather than scarcity.

Regardless of who has pushed you this far, this is the point where we all realize that we aren't failing, we are writing. We are facing the lies we've told our self and putting the words out there anyway.

The consistent way you show up and write will make it easier to face imposter syndrome, but I'm sorry to tell you, just because you are here doesn't mean that those imposter feelings aren't hiding behind other doubts. It's the practice of telling yourself that what you think others know is only an assumption. The fact is, you don't know what I know. You don't know how hard it was to write all of the drafts that I needed to write to finalize these thoughts.

We are all experts at telling ourselves we got lucky, but that's not the comparison I want you to focus on. I also don't want you to exhaust yourself by over-preparing or creating a long to-do list. Just write. Great minds like ours can be trained to do the writing, no special tricks required.

DON'T FOLLOW THE LEADER BY JANET KITTO

I've had several accountability partners over the past 4-1/2 years. I met a group of authors through an online course and then began meeting weekly on Skype with four of them. We were Canadian, from about as far west as you can go and as far east as Canada stretches. That was my first and my longest relationship with accountability partners.

I met more authors through communities online, but there was no agreement that we would show up at regular intervals and talk about our projects. The focus to keep a commitment to other writers, but more importantly, to myself, would come with a hefty amount of trust.

I wanted to have a closer bond with authors who felt as vulnerable as I did in this relationship. I wanted to trust that group members would do what they said they wanted to do, and in the process, I wanted to learn how to trust myself to do the same.

Accountability partners can provide feedback that reflects their values, but they also offer motivation to keep the group going. The relationship can allow you to share what you are struggling with, but your group is also there to celebrate your successes.

Which is where the problems began for me.

I was asking my group to hold me accountable for the actions I committed to. I was meeting these lovely ladies every week to discuss my weekly and quarterly goals. I wanted to be honest about my efforts, but that meant my weaknesses would be seen.

I wasn't finishing books. I wasn't publishing. I was talking about my color-coded apps and carefully constructed plans instead. My inner dialogue was heavy with doubt and dry of inspiration.

I was ready to quit.

I listened to the group, I took notes, but in comparison, I was shrinking. My partners' efforts to increase my confidence wasn't working. I shared my story each week about what I tried to do. I excelled at self-reflection. Maybe that's why they hadn't told me to leave. In some way, I must have been entertaining them with my weekly updates while silently suffering through my failures. I didn't want anyone to see my weaknesses, and I couldn't hear the genuine observations being made about my progress from my peers. There was a huge wall in front of me.

It was the success I didn't want. Why else was I struggling so much?

I moved on. Literally. I was at a point in my life where I had created the space and the freedom to travel, to own less, and to write full time. I wanted to focus on craft and figure out how to earn a living as an author. Even though that had been my focus for three years with my accountability partners, and I had carefully dissected each quarter for growth and scheduled books to be published, we were heading in different directions. I was figuring out how to travel back to Canada to find a new home when it happened.

I said thank you and goodbye.

You can't do what everyone else is doing. Maybe you need to look at your production schedule at a higher level, and weekly check-ins are counterproductive. Perhaps you feel that holding the others accountable for their progress will replace your need to get a coach or an editor.

Don't confuse the roles that other authors have in your life with your own responsibility for your actions. Every group will be different, each writer's needs and wants are as individual as their voice.

If you haven't made those decisions yet of how your project breaks down into smaller chunks to manage successfully, being in partnership with peers will push you, or the relationship will break you.

Whatever happens, you are responsible for your own work. It's important to find your process, to experiment with what you need. You are the one listening to your inner dialogue, you know what your pain points are, so don't ask your partners to understand you by talking about your goals and intentions. Show them what kind of author you are with your actions.

Accountability partners don't have to be with you for life. It's okay to grow beyond the group you start out with. If you're not growing and changing as your business grows, look for fresh ideas and new faces.

If you can be honest and transparent about why you are there with accountability partners and don't become the one who has to be rescued every week — we all meet a Needy Nelly at some point — following your own path can actually benefit the whole group.

Regardless of the level you are at, if you are fully engaged and committed, and you value the time you have with the group, and most importantly, you find the right group, they will value your insights about the mistakes you've made and be your biggest fans.

DON'T ARGUE WITH THE PROCESS BY JANET KITTO

I'm learning to ride a motorcycle again. I took a course back in 1992, rode that summer on my Suzuki GS400S, then had a child the following summer. Over the next two decades, I was never the rider, always the passenger.

My husband has had sport bikes, a track bike, dual sports, and even a minibike that came in pieces. We hoped our daughter might be interested in rebuilding that Honda Monkey and then want to ride it. Some dreams remain just that. The box of bike parts went to other hands, and like me, my daughter was happy to go along for the ride. By this time, my husband had taken several courses and even certified as a motorcycle instructor.

Something changed in me. It was a slow build in tension, a thought that maybe I could do it again. The words came out of my mouth before I could edit myself. I wanted to challenge my belief that I wasn't a rider.

I wanted a motorcycle.

These were the words my husband had wanted to hear from me for 28 years. Because if I'm honest, I didn't want that GS400S. Even with a small dose of natural ability, I wasn't confident in riding that bike. I was happy when the bike sold. I got to keep my Class 6 designation, and I remain, to this day, licensed to ride.

The old adage that you never forget how to ride is an interesting one in relation to a motorcycle. There are a lot more moving pieces and skills to master when you ride a motorbike. When my Suzuki VanVan 200 came off the truck, I had to start again with the basics. The bike is a dual sport with wide tires and a quiet rumble, but on the bike, I still have the power to run uncontrollably into anything in front of me, to fall over, to crash, to speed, to get distracted, and make mistakes that can change the course of my life. When my husband suggested we get a helmet communication system, I said, yes, absolutely.

I have a headset and microphone attached inside my helmet. My first ride of 2020 was in a gravel parking lot. I needed to practice letting out the clutch and using the accelerator with my handgrip, and watching the road in front of me, and remembering that the front brake was controlled with my right-hand lever, and my back brake was controlled with my right-foot pedal, and not to worry about the shifter yet, but get those feet off the ground and just ride. Remember to turn. Go in a circle.

Over the headset I hear, "Breathe. Just breathe. In through your nose, out through your mouth." Wouldn't it be great to listen to those words when you are writing? To have someone supporting you? To be reminded that you're okay and to just write?

Mindset is important. Regardless of why you are working with your mentor, and this can be by listening to a mentor's podcast online every week, or taking a self-study course created by a mentor, meeting online or in person, or even talking on the phone regularly. Whatever the arrangement is, you are working with your mentor for a reason. You seek out a mentor to fill the gaps you have in your writing process.

If you choose a mentor who does everything the same way you do, what benefit will there be? How will you make a shift to a new status quo? A mentor who has a different point of view can push you to heights that would be impossible if you always worked alone and stayed within a fixed mindset.

Additionally, a mentor can provide connections to a larger network of authors at every experience level and create opportunities for you to grow. A great example of this is an author mastermind. I've found myself choosing mentors who I have a lot in common with. To have the growth I've needed, I've worked with several mentors.

Part of the reason I wasn't the rider, always the passenger on the motorcycle, was that I didn't want to take the same path as my husband. I didn't want to ride to Laguna Seca and take a lap on the track. I didn't want to lean my bike over in a turn and put my knee to the ground.

I wanted to explore beaches and scenic ocean views. That's how the motorcycle came to be parked at our property, a bike exclusively for me. My husband and I have the same make and model, but mine is storm-gray in color. I'll do my best to wear down the tires evenly from edge to edge, like his, but I've got the freedom to ride my bike wherever and whenever I want. I listen and take the advice I'm given when I ride with my husband about where to ride in the lane, and how fast, and when I'm told to pull over, I pull over.

Your mentor shouldn't be defining your goals. A mentor can help you evaluate whether you are ready to take a risk or not. What a mentor should not do for you is give you the answers without pushing you to do the work and make your own decisions. A mentor will help you to ask the right questions.

At some point, as you reflect on your process, you'll examine how you feel about taking the advice of your mentor. You might even feel you can argue that what you want to do is a better idea.

A mentor isn't there to make decisions for you. A mentor can only shape what you are open to change about your methods.

By trying new methodologies, I've improved my scenes, and I've been able to express my ideas with clarity. I've grown to work within a community of authors, and I've found new readers because my writing is solidly within a commercial genre.

Every time I go out for a ride, I have a direct connection with my husband. He knows when I'm feeling stressed, he can hear that I'm tense by listening to my breath over the communication system we share. He's there to give me directions if I'm heading into the unknown. He's there to support my choices. Frustratingly, he's also there to tell me that I left my turn signal on.

That's what a mentor does. They help us become better riders—I mean writers.

DON'T WASTE TIME BY JANET KITTO

Of all the relationships we have as a thriving author, the one we have with our significant other may be the only one that doesn't relate to the words we write. What I mean is, your partner may not understand your writing habits. That doesn't stop us from talking to our partners. This is the person who unconsciously forces you to do the hard work you've been avoiding. That's why it's easy to make excuses about the book you still haven't finished.

When I heard my husband telling his friends a lot of wrong information about my writing, I realized that he had no way of knowing what I was struggling with. He was simply talking about what he was seeing, which was me talking about my goals but not taking action toward them. I shouldn't have been angry at him, although I was.

In reflection, I turned that anger toward myself, once I was honest about what had happened. My dream of publishing a series of books had slipped away, along with years that I couldn't get back. However I explained the situation, the fact was I hadn't published anything that was an asset for my business. I'd only created excuses.

That's what hurts the most. My husband had supported me from my initial leap into becoming an author right through to this stall I was in. Months had passed while I focused on learning as much as I could about more than I needed. I even set up a business to help other authors to publish because I knew what to do, I just wasn't doing it myself. I believed that writing took "a lot of time." That was a big-enough excuse to cover all of the hours I was wasting. I knew that what my husband was telling his friends was true. There weren't any books I had finished.

I scheduled weekly accountability meetings with other authors, but afterward, I was miserable and less inspired to work after I forced myself to show up and tell everyone that I had pushed out another deadline.

That was the troubling piece for me. I couldn't show up and hide at the same time. If you think you can, then ask yourself how you feel talking about your plans but having no results to show.

You either quit, or you do the work.

There is a wooded trail I often walk along with my husband. It follows the waterfront of our small town. We see eagles and osprey above us, and seals in the strait. In the early morning, we rarely see other people. That's a great place to blow off misunderstandings in a louder voice than used at home or in polite conversation. The trees don't seem to take my anger personally, and because of the distance we are from our house, I can make a number of points, however irrational, until I have nothing else to say.

Our walk along this trail typically takes 90 minutes. Once we reach the halfway point, I review every response I've given, every bit of information he provided, and through my internal processing, I realize he's right. I know I have to tell him this. He has repeatedly answered to me that he supports my journey as an author, and he is letting me have all the time I need to do the writing. I can't be upset with him. He's right to question this: if I'm not writing and publishing books, what am I doing?

Now I can talk about the real work that has to be done as we walk back home. I'm committed to earning a living from my writing. I promise myself that I will work on my ideas around money and how I contribute to my household. The eagles return, and I look up.

The first thing I do when we get back home is head to my desk. I want to get my butt in the chair while my head is still clear. My husband knows to leave me alone. I don't even have to close the door. No barrier is there to keep me from writing, so I write.

We all hit that point eventually. We get past the angry outburst, the reflective moments when we search for answers, and then understand that we've had someone by our side the entire time. And we forgive ourselves for thinking it was a waste.

Whoever your significant other is, if they've been with you along this journey, they know what's best before you get there yourself. They know your excuses and your strengths, even if they don't know what you write or who your audience is. They know those words matter to you.

Don't Write Without the 3Cs (Challenges, Changes, and Consistency) by Janet Kitto

Three Story Method, by J. Thorn and Zach Bohannon, breaks down the structure of story and scenes into three components: Conflict, Choice, and Consequence. Understanding why you need those 3Cs—if you don't already know, get a copy at Thre eStoryMethod.com—are different than the three Cs I'm going to break down now.

Thriving authors are faced with writing challenges regularly. That is the first of the 3Cs: Challenges.

In many ways, you can consider a challenge in the same way that you consider the conflict you have in your story. Something has forced you out of your status quo. I'm not talking about the challenge a writer has who spends his or her lifetime finishing a book. I mean the challenges a thriving author faces to establish a writing practice, and to plan, produce, and promote assets.

Imposter syndrome isn't something you fix and never face again. A blank page, the medical emergency of a loved one, a power outage, a new coffee shop, there are many problems we face daily to knock out our confidence and keep us from growing. I caught myself trying to measure my progress by looking at other thriving authors' work until I realized that I can only compare the work I'm doing now to what I've done previously. Little or pandemic-sized, we have to face the challenges in front of us and make a decision.

How are we going to deal with this change?

That's the second of the 3Cs: Changes. Rewrites, edits, whatever you are working on, best-laid plans and manuscripts change. The schedule you have for your novel, or your family time, or even how long you can stream your favorite new binge needs to be open to change. A thriving author plans for the worst and adapts for the better.

It's natural to compare your business to those you see in the community, especially if you've just started as a thriving author. You look at their successes like you do with your mentors. You study what they're doing and try to figure out from their process what you can borrow for your process. Maybe most of the authors you know write in very different genres than you do, and it's hard to watch your work not be discovered as quickly as your peers wearing their bestseller badges.

The best comparison scale you can use is to remember where you were six months ago, compared to where you are now. Are you repeating bad habits? Did you share your work, i.e., did you publish? Have you stuck to a schedule? Have you been paying attention to the changes that face you, and have you adapted? I bet you have, Scarlett.

Whatever feels like the impossible at that moment happens, and you've got to let go of the thing or give up. Thriving authors don't give up. We adapt. We swear. We caffeinate. I've been known to pull out a pen and stab my inner critic with new plans and ideas. I've also taken a page from Sherlock and "eliminated the impossible" because he taught me to look at what remains. Whatever I believe at that moment, "however improbable," I separate my belief from the facts. I self-assess without shutting down.

Success is coming. There's a reward for finishing. Starting with an idea, creating a draft, adding value in the revisions, then repeating the process for the success that always comes to you in the end. Regardless of the size of the asset, whether it's an ad, a podcast, or a book, you go through this cycle of creating, editing, promoting, and releasing it into the wild. Acknowledging the work you finish helps get you started on the next one.

Another good exercise is taking the excuses that rise and flip them with vengeance. Just like John Wick. You think you've written yourself into a corner? Change that to you are writing a kick-ass action scene, and the setup is epic. Don't believe you are good enough to write that scene? You've been at it for two hours, and you're exhausted? There are only 72 steps you have to climb. Raise your hands, Rocky, and run up those stairs!

Removing barriers is part of facing the third of the 3Cs: Consistency.

By now, as a thriving author, you are consistently writing. You are showing up. You write that article, you finish that story, you podcast every week at the same time. You meet your deadlines consistently. You create new content consistently. The shift has happened.

You aren't fearful of the garbage you had to write to get to the gold. You went through idea after idea until you found what you were really trying to say. All the work you've done in your relationship with the words, in the relationships you have with those who support you and the path you've chosen, and the constant attention you've given yourself has paid off.

You're motivated and more reliable, smarter, and damn, that new status quo looks amazing on you.

SOCIAL MEDIA

We live in a world seemingly ruled by social media. Look around when you're at the supermarket, sitting in a doctor's office, or waiting for a table at your favorite restaurant. Most people have their noses in their smartphones, scrolling up and down with a finger.

It can be easy then as authors to assume that we *have* to be on social media. How else will we build an audience and talk to our readers?

Social media can absolutely enhance your business, but it can also be a deep, dark hole that prevents you from getting your most important work done: writing. And is it really as important to your author business as you think it is? From two thriving authors who have basically abandoned all social media over the last year, the answer might surprise you.

In this section, J. Thorn and Zach Bohannon identify nine things successful authors don't do when it comes to social media. So post a selfie of you reading this book and join us as we help you make the best use of your time in regard to social media and your author career.

Here's a quick summary of the valuable lessons you can expect to learn in this section:

"Don't Build an Audience on Someone Else's Platform" – Zach warns against the risks of building your audience on any social media platform. Many bands were devastated when MySpace fell out of the public eye several years ago. But even if your favorite social media platform is here to stay, you're still one algorithm change away from losing touch with your entire readership.

"Don't Depend on Social Media for Sales" – Zach questions whether trying to sell your books on social media is a good use of your time. While it can be a good place to connect with your readers, the "buy my book" posts don't really work in a world where people mostly want to watch cat videos and keep up with their friends.

"Don't Check Social Media First Thing in the Morning" – J. explains the dangers of starting off your day with notifications and scrolling. In order to do your best creative work, you need to go to the desk with a clear mind and all your willpower.

"Don't Have Social Media Apps on Their Phones" – Zach argues that taking all social media apps off your phone can increase productivity and make you a happier person. There are plenty of other ways for you to check your social media. You don't always need to have access to your newsfeed in your pocket.

"Don't Tell Themselves Social Networking Is Writing" – J. discusses the danger in treating social media use as work. It's easy to tell ourselves we are making progress in our author careers by engaging on social media. But only writing is writing, and getting your work out to the world is going to have a larger return on investment than any meme you spend time creating.

"Don't Spend Too Much Time Online Talking About Writing" – Zach questions how helpful it really is to be involved in online communities with other authors. Even if you're involved in groups which are drama-free, there can still be adverse effects to spending too much time chatting about writing and the industry.

"Don't Think They Have to Be on Every Platform" – Zach talks about why it's not helpful for you to be on every social media platform, if any at all. Only be present on the platform you enjoy. People will be able to sniff out if you genuinely don't enjoy being somewhere. And if you don't like social media at all, do you need to be on any platforms?

"Don't Believe Everyone Is on Social Media" – J. questions if as many people are on social media as we think there are. Is there is a mass exodus coming to these platforms as more people grow tired of privacy issues, toxic activity in their newsfeeds, and generally wanting to be more intentional with their time?

"Don't Believe That All Readers Want to Interact with Authors" – J. pushes back on something we've all been told as authors: that readers want to engage with authors. Most readers are going to read your book without ever sending you an email or joining your list. So how much time do you really need to spend filling readers in on what you're doing in your life?

Don't Build an Audience on Someone Else's Platform by Zach Bohannon

MySpace.

Friendster.

Xanga.

LiveJournal.

Vine.

Remember those?

Depending on your age, you probably do remember most or even all of these. But in case you aren't familiar with these names, each of them was once a popular social media platform. Some, or maybe even all (I haven't checked), are still around, but you are likely not going to hear your friends ask you about them. I mean, could you imagine one of your friends coming up to you today and asking you, "Hey, have you posted in your LiveJournal lately?" Yeah, me neither.

I spent the majority of my 20s playing drums in two different heavy metal bands. MySpace was a godsend for us. For the first time in history, musicians could create music and share with the world in seconds (well, maybe minutes with those horrendous mid-2000s Internet speeds) and gain fans anywhere. It broke down barriers and disrupted the gatekeepers of the music industry. No longer did you need a record label to tell you that you were good enough or to travel the country in a conversion van to get people to hear your music. It was a great thing. My bands built good followings on MySpace, and I know of others who had tens of thousands, even hundreds of thousands, of followers on there.

Then something strange happened.

People quit caring about MySpace. The platform took a nosedive when the next hip thing came around, which ended up being Facebook. Other social media platforms like Twitter, Instagram, Pinterest, and even YouTube, also rose to popularity, making the aforementioned platforms obsolete. Some, like MySpace, had been popular for a couple of years before fading. Others (Vine) were in and out of people's minds faster than a manufactured pop song.

So what happened to the "fans" that all those bands gained through MySpace?

I can't answer that from my own experiences, as my music career was winding down around the time all of this happened. But I can tell you what would've happened. We would have been screwed, because MySpace was the only platform we were using to reach all of these people. It was the only place we were building an online presence. We hadn't built any mailing list, so we didn't have a way to contact anyone directly. Our only option would have been to post on MySpace that we were moving our fan page to Facebook, or our website, or wherever. But that would have only worked for the people who still were spending time on MySpace and saw the message. And how many of those people would take the time to follow us over to the other platform?

As of early 2020, Facebook is the largest and most popular social media platform and has been for at least ten years. They've been lucky not to fade into obscurity like the other companies we've mentioned, but that doesn't make them invulnerable to collapse. While many people feel that Facebook will remain relevant for the foreseeable future, there is a lot of evidence showing that people are beginning to question what kind of role they want social media to play in their lives, especially Facebook. With the disturbing privacy issues that Facebook has been forced to address, along with many people merely becoming sick and tired of all the noise they consume in their newsfeeds, I can envision a mass exodus from that platform within the next few years, and I'm not alone in that sentiment. Cal Newport, who is leading the revolution of Digital Minimalism, feels the same way and sees people moving back toward more meaningful connections with people in real life.

Do you want your entire business to be on Facebook when that happens? Yeah, neither do I.

Now let's assume that I'm wrong and that Facebook is here to stay, and I'm some kooky guy totally out of touch with society. Facebook can make changes to their platform at any time that can hinder your business. They've done it several times before, and they'll do it again.

A few years ago, it was relatively easy on your Facebook fan page to get all the people who liked that page to see anything you posted. Then, one day Facebook decided to change their algorithm and only show posts to 2% or 3% of the fans who liked your page. The only way then to get those posts seen was to pay to boost those posts. As of this writing, it's still like that, and most authors I know have bailed on promoting and growing their pages.

Groups have also become popular, and I know some authors with vibrant and engaging Facebook Groups. You could do a group on Facebook, but have you ever considered that that isn't the only option? Yeah, it might seem like the most convenient because most people are already spending time on Facebook and can check in on your group. At the same time, they are looking at people's malicious political opinions and cute cat photos.

There are other places to build a group. J. and I have several engaged Slack communities, and we've also used Mighty Networks. Yes, it's another website that people have to sign up for, but if they want to engage with you and be a part of the community, they won't hesitate. And when they are there, they won't be distracted by an endless scrolling feed of unrelated content. Also, Facebook could make changes to Groups at any moment, making it more difficult for you to engage with your readers.

Why then, as an author who feeds his family by writing stories for loyal readers who will buy them, would I depend on a company making billions of dollars with a virtual social slot machine app to reach those people?

Every year some Internet marketing or book marketing guru suggests that mailing lists are dead. They say no one wants to subscribe to your mailing list and that people don't read their email. Don't listen to these people. As an author, your mailing list is still your number-one tool for engaging with your audience and for letting them know when you have new books available. People are not going to get rid of their email address anytime soon, that I can guarantee you. And there's enough data out there that supports people who still open emails and that email marketing, when done correctly, still works.

I encourage you to put all of your audience-building efforts toward getting people onto your email list. If you want to use Facebook pages or groups to engage with fans, that's fine. But I wouldn't put a lot of effort into pushing people to those places to 'like' you. It's hard enough to get a reader to buy and hopefully read one of your books; then you're fortunate to get them to take another action, such as join your mailing list, leave a review, or join a Facebook group. I encourage you to focus on only one of those actions and for that action to be building your mailing list.

Don't Build an Audience on Someone Else's Platform by Zach Bohannon

MySpace.

Friendster.

Xanga.

LiveJournal.

Vine.

Remember those?

Depending on your age, you probably do remember most or even all of these. But in case you aren't familiar with these names, each of them was once a popular social media platform. Some, or maybe even all (I haven't checked), are still around, but you are likely not going to hear your friends ask you about them. I mean, could you imagine one of your friends coming up to you today and asking you, "Hey, have you posted in your LiveJournal lately?" Yeah, me neither.

I spent the majority of my 20s playing drums in two different heavy metal bands. MySpace was a godsend for us. For the first time in history, musicians could create music and share with the world in seconds (well, maybe minutes with those horrendous mid-2000s Internet speeds) and gain fans anywhere. It broke down barriers and disrupted the gatekeepers of the music industry. No longer did you need a record label to tell you that you were good enough or to travel the country in a conversion van to get people to hear your music. It was a great thing. My bands built good followings on MySpace, and I know of others who had tens of thousands, even hundreds of thousands, of followers on there.

Then something strange happened.

People quit caring about MySpace. The platform took a nosedive when the next hip thing came around, which ended up being Facebook. Other social media platforms like Twitter, Instagram, Pinterest, and even YouTube, also rose to popularity, making the aforementioned platforms obsolete. Some, like MySpace, had been popular for a couple of years before fading. Others (Vine) were in and out of people's minds faster than a manufactured pop song.

So what happened to the "fans" that all those bands gained through MySpace?

I can't answer that from my own experiences, as my music career was winding down around the time all of this happened. But I can tell you what would've happened. We would have been screwed, because MySpace was the only platform we were using to reach all of these people. It was the only place we were building an online presence. We hadn't built any mailing list, so we didn't have a way to contact anyone directly. Our only option would have been to post on MySpace that we were moving our fan page to Facebook, or our website, or wherever. But that would have only worked for the people who still were spending time on MySpace and saw the message. And how many of those people would take the time to follow us over to the other platform?

As of early 2020, Facebook is the largest and most popular social media platform and has been for at least ten years. They've been lucky not to fade into obscurity like the other companies we've mentioned, but that doesn't make them invulnerable to collapse. While many people feel that Facebook will remain relevant for the foreseeable future, there is a lot of evidence showing that people are beginning to question what kind of role they want social media to play in their lives, especially Facebook. With the disturbing privacy issues that Facebook has been forced to address, along with many people merely becoming sick and tired of all the noise they consume in their newsfeeds, I can envision a mass exodus from that platform within the next few years, and I'm not alone in that sentiment. Cal Newport, who is leading the revolution of Digital Minimalism, feels the same way and sees people moving back toward more meaningful connections with people in real life.

Do you want your entire business to be on Facebook when that happens? Yeah, neither do I.

Now let's assume that I'm wrong and that Facebook is here to stay, and I'm some kooky guy totally out of touch with society. Facebook can make changes to their platform at any time that can hinder your business. They've done it several times before, and they'll do it again.

A few years ago, it was relatively easy on your Facebook fan page to get all the people who liked that page to see anything you posted. Then, one day Facebook decided to change their algorithm and only show posts to 2% or 3% of the fans who liked your page. The only way then to get those posts seen was to pay to boost those posts. As of this writing, it's still like that, and most authors I know have bailed on promoting and growing their pages.

Groups have also become popular, and I know some authors with vibrant and engaging Facebook Groups. You could do a group on Facebook, but have you ever considered that that isn't the only option? Yeah, it might seem like the most convenient because most people are already spending time on Facebook and can check in on your group. At the same time, they are looking at people's malicious political opinions and cute cat photos.

There are other places to build a group. J. and I have several engaged Slack communities, and we've also used Mighty Networks. Yes, it's another website that people have to sign up for, but if they want to engage with you and be a part of the community, they won't hesitate. And when they are there, they won't be distracted by an endless scrolling feed of unrelated content. Also, Facebook could make changes to Groups at any moment, making it more difficult for you to engage with your readers.

Why then, as an author who feeds his family by writing stories for loyal readers who will buy them, would I depend on a company making billions of dollars with a virtual social slot machine app to reach those people?

Every year some Internet marketing or book marketing guru suggests that mailing lists are dead. They say no one wants to subscribe to your mailing list and that people don't read their email. Don't listen to these people. As an author, your mailing list is still your number-one tool for engaging with your audience and for letting them know when you have new books available. People are not going to get rid of their email address anytime soon, that I can guarantee you. And there's enough data out there that supports people who still open emails and that email marketing, when done correctly, still works.

I encourage you to put all of your audience-building efforts toward getting people onto your email list. If you want to use Facebook pages or groups to engage with fans, that's fine. But I wouldn't put a lot of effort into pushing people to those places to 'like' you. It's hard enough to get a reader to buy and hopefully read one of your books; then you're fortunate to get them to take another action, such as join your mailing list, leave a review, or join a Facebook group. I encourage you to focus on only one of those actions and for that action to be building your mailing list.

Don't Depend on Social Media for Sales by Zach Bohannon

Imagine for a moment that you're at a party. I know you're a writer and I'm sure the idea of going to a party probably gives you anxiety. Am I stereotyping? Maybe a little bit, but either way, hang with me for a minute.

You're at a party, and you're cruising through the room, taking its temperature. Maybe you're listening in on conversations, or perhaps you're trying to eye who is the most interesting-looking person who won't bore you.

Either way, you're minding your own business when, all of a sudden, someone jumps right in front of you, holding a book in their hand.

"Hi," the person says. "Will you buy my book?"

What would your reaction to this be? Would you smile, pull out your wallet, and thank the person for greeting you in such a cold manner? Would you buy the book?

I doubt it.

Now I'm sure you know where I'm going with this, so let me get a few things out of the way first.

I am *not* saying that you can't sell books on social media. You can. I've done it, even though I knew it would account for a relatively low percentage of the source of my overall sales since launching my author career in 2015 if I were to track that.

I am also not saying that social media doesn't have a place in your author platform. For me, it is no longer something I choose to spend any time on, but I understand many authors enjoy it and use it to their advantage, especially when it comes to engaging with their readers.

But if I were to reintroduce social media into my business, it wouldn't be to sell books.

People are going on social media to check in with their friends and family, argue about politics and social issues, and to watch cat videos. They aren't going on there to look at ads. Even if they are, your friends and family aren't the people you want buying your books. You want readers of your specific genre doing that. And if you depend on your Facebook page you've made for your author brand, you could be risking not being seen at all, at least not without paying. As of this writing, only 2-3% of the people who "like" your page see your post without you paying Facebook to show it to more people. I don't know about you, but I'd much rather have those people on a mailing list that I own.

Now it's no secret that Facebook is the single best targeting platform in the world. They have more data on us as individuals than any other company in the world. Even still, I always remind myself that people aren't on Facebook for you to send them to Amazon to buy a book. If I want someone to buy a book, I'd much rather spend my money on AMS (Amazon Marketing Service) ads or with one of the many reputable book deal sites, such as BookBub, Ereadernewstoday, Fussy Librarian, etc. The people seeing your books on those platforms are visiting those sites to *buy books*, not to look for a new keto-friendly recipe.

We occasionally use Facebook ads for other things, such as list-building or to get the word out about our author events, but we do not use them to sell books. Does that mean we never will again? No. J. recently ran some ads as an experiment. But as a rule of thumb, we don't depend on social media to sell books.

We also prefer to engage with our audiences through groups off of Facebook, primarily our mailing lists.

If you're a new author, this might be tough to hear. I'm sure you're asking yourself, "Then how do I get the word about my book out there if you're telling me not to depend on social media?"

Here are some great alternatives to promoting your books on social media:

- If you have an ongoing ad budget, use it on AMS ads or BookBub ads.
- Enroll your book in the KDP Select program on Amazon. Your book will have to be exclusive to Kindle, but it lowers the barrier of entry to your book as a new author for the millions of Kindle Unlimited subscribers who can borrow your book for free as part of their monthly paid subscription.
- Plan a sale. Schedule a time to discount your book to $0.99 and submit it to the sites mentioned earlier, like BookBub, Ereadernewstoday, and Fussy Librarian. Most of these sites have genre-specific mailing lists that will get your book in front of your desired audience.
- Join a multi-author promo with other authors in your genre. BookFunnel is a great site that allows authors to run these.

- Know other authors in your genre? Do list swaps with each other where you promote a book to their mailing list, then they do the same for you.

These are just a few ways. For J. and I, all of them work much better than promoting on Facebook or Twitter or Instagram.

Social media can be a good place to interact with readers and with other authors (though we challenge those assumptions as well), but it is generally not a great place to try and sell your books.

Don't Check Social Media First Thing in the Morning
by J. Thorn

So much of what we do becomes a habit, for better or for worse. Over the years, I've had many morning routines, intentionally and unintentionally, and I've discovered that you have one, whether you like it or not.

Morning routines can be categorized in one of two ways. Either you determine your morning routine, or someone else does it for you. For most people, the second option happens by default.

When our kids were toddlers, say around the ages of 2 and 4 years old, my wife and I had convinced ourselves that the mornings were not ours. Our kids were early risers, up and hankering for a cup of juice or bowl of cereal by 6 a.m., weekdays or weekends—it didn't matter. For good reason, we surrendered because that's what good parents do. We make sacrifices for our children. But unless you have extraordinary circumstances, those periods are temporary. If I walked into either of my teenagers' rooms today with a cup of juice before noon, they'd probably throw something at me.

Special needs or situations aside, eventually, you realize that your morning routine is yours to surrender. I love my wife, and I understand why she does it, but she has handed control of her morning routine to her employer. She must be at work at a certain hour, and so the job determines what she does in the morning. She'll get up as late as possible to maximize sleep. This works for her because she is not a writer. She is not creating art. My wife has no song to work on before the day job, no novel to wrestle with before her "real" job begins.

But you and I are not like my wife. Whether you're a thriving author or a part-time hustler, you understand that if you don't create time to create, nothing will get created. And while this applies to all time slots within our day, mornings tend to be most important.

If we're not intentional with what we do during our precious morning minutes, someone else will make that decision for us.

You probably sleep with your phone nearby. You might even use the alarm app on it to wake yourself in the morning. And you probably have your notifications enabled because they are turned on by default.

The problem—you are unable to ignore those notifications. They are designed specifically for that reason, especially the ones for social media accounts. So when you roll over and turn off your alarm, you're tempted with all of those notifications. Why not scroll through a few? What's the harm in checking your Twitter feed, Instagram account, or Facebook app?

By checking notifications or scrolling your social media accounts, you have now put the priorities of the rest of the world before your own. Cat videos and stupid memes might be a big deal, but what about the outrage culture that is currently infesting social media? What is going to happen when you see something that angers you, pushes your buttons, and sets you off? You've now polluted the best, purest part of the day.

Scientifically speaking, mornings are magical. Some really smart people wearing white lab coats have figured this out, and I'm sure you can find studies about them if you do a search. Even if you don't consider yourself a morning person, the fresh energy of a new day is hard to ignore.

If your nutrition is solid, you're exercising, and getting the amount of sleep your body requires, you'll wake up with a sense of optimism. You'll think about what you want to accomplish that day, what you'll write, how you're going to write yourself out of a corner in that most recent manuscript. Your brain is alert, refreshed, and ready to go.

In the evening, your decision-making abilities have been worn down throughout the day, what those social scientists would call "decision fatigue." Not only is your mind tired, but so is your body. As a human, you're susceptible to Circadian rhythms, which can dampen plans you have for a late-night creative writing jam.

Now let's return to the moment you open your eyes to grab your phone and turn off your alarm app. And let's assume you function like most of us, and you begin scrolling your social media feeds. You've now destroyed that thin line of optimism and put your thoughts and energies toward something else.

In the best-case scenario, social media is a simple, pleasurable distraction. It sucks the time out of the space allotted and might leave you with a smile or a chuckle. But in the worst-case scenario, it might have just ruined any creative mojo you had brewing from the dreaming to awakening state. Now you might be upset, angered, outraged, or irritated. You might even begin to respond, escalating those cortisol levels in your system that are designed to protect you from threats.

A few simple solutions can help you avoid the temptations that might come from this.

First, stop using your phone as an alarm clock. In fact, power it down at night. Give it a rest. Get yourself a real alarm clock, and then you won't be tempted to put that device in your hand as soon as you open your eyes.

Second, turn off the notifications or delete the social media apps from your phone entirely. You can schedule social media time on your computer, and I guarantee you that you don't need those apps on your phone as much as you think you do.

Being in control of your mornings and making good decisions to avoid temptation can have dramatic and far-reaching effects. You'll be shocked at how much happier, optimistic, and productive you can be in the morning if you're not downloading the world's problems into your brain first.

Yes, we all have bad habits. The good news is that it's just as easy to replace them with good ones.

Don't Have Social Media Apps on Their Phones by Zach Bohannon

If you're a regular listener of the Career Author Podcast, then you know that in early 2019, I quit using social media altogether, both for my author business and personal use. Even if you've never listened to the podcast, you've probably figured it out by reading my other essays.

But I didn't get to that point by one day waking up and deciding I was done with social media and ceasing to use it. There were steps. And the first step after I'd decided that I wanted to take back control of my digital life, as opposed to having it control me, was to delete social media apps (and email) from my phone.

Now I understand that quitting social media isn't for everyone. I have seen many more benefits in my own life by stepping away from it than the small amount of value I was getting from devoting any amount of time there, but that's me. My goal isn't to convince you to leave social media. But I will ask you to question what kind of role you want it to play in your life and then ask if it is currently overstepping those boundaries. I started asking myself these questions about two years ago.

Studying my behavior, I realized I had a problem. Every time my phone beeped or buzzed at me, my instinct, no matter what else I was doing, was to pick it up. I could be in the middle of a conversation with my wife, but be compelled to glance at my phone just because *it* told me to. It's not like this is uncommon. Look around, and you'll see people do it all the time. It's become ingrained in our culture. But that wasn't good enough for me.

Why was I allowing my smartphone to control me and dictate when I look at it? Shouldn't I pick it up when I need it instead of the device fighting—and usually winning—to grab my attention?

That led me to my first change, which was to disable all notifications from my phone except for two. I keep my text message notifications on because there are only a select number of people who text me, and I keep Slack notifications on because that is how J. and I communicate about business. He and I have set up specific boundaries, and as Cal Newport calls them, deep work hours, where we know not to disturb each other unless it's urgent. And considering I use the Do Not Disturb feature on my phone most of the day (definitely when I'm working), then the text message notifications don't end up disturbing me. My wife knows to call me if there's an emergency, and her calls are set up to bypass the Do Not Disturb feature.

But turning off notifications wasn't good enough. Yes, my phone was no longer sending little dopamine hits via its speakers, but I still found myself picking up my phone more often than I needed to. It was again stealing time from me in my small moments of boredom or when I needed a distraction.

I decided I needed to go a step further and begin eliminating reasons to pick up my phone. The first apps to go were the social media ones, which included Facebook, Twitter, and Instagram. I put up a barrier where I had to go into my office and get on my computer if I wanted to visit any of these sites. No more pulling my phone out of my pocket and mindlessly wandering onto these apps in my small moments of boredom. Is it a little inconvenient? Sure, but that's the point. Just because we have access to whatever we want at our fingertips doesn't mean that we need it.

It's important to remember that these apps have been specifically and scientifically designed to consume as much of your attention as possible. And that's not a theory. Employees working for these companies have admitted as such. That's why all these apps force you to scroll, urging you to keep "pulling the slot-machine lever" until you "win."

I quickly realized how much of a problem I had after I started deleting these addictive apps. I would pull out my phone and slide over to the places on my home screen where those apps had once lived, only to find they were no longer there. The scary part is, that I didn't even realize I was doing it. I was simply trying to fill those small moments of boredom with *something*.

But you know what? It's okay to be bored every once in a while. We don't have to continually fill our eyes and ears with content. In coming to that realization, I've discovered how much I enjoy being bored and living in the moment instead of trying to find a way to escape it.

Unsure or not ready to admit that you have a problem?

The iPhone has a great feature that tells you how much time you spend on your phone, going as far as breaking it down by specific apps and showing you how many times you pick up your phone in a day as well as per hour. It's a fantastic feature, but one that scared the hell out of me when Apple first added it to iOS. I ignored it like a toothache. Maybe if I didn't think about it, it would go away. But once I decided to face my addiction, it became one of my favorite tools to break that addiction.

This feature forces you to be honest about your behavior and to face it head-on. I was surprised to see how much time I was spending on my phone and within specific apps — ashamed, even. I thought about how many more books I could have read with that time or the kind of intentional time I could have had with Kathryn or with my daughter.

My phone now gives me very few reasons to pick it up. I've removed email, social media, games, and apps that I was spending way too much time on, such as YouTube. And I have to say that I'm a much happier and calmer person because of it.

DON'T TELL THEMSELVES SOCIAL NETWORKING IS WRITING BY J. THORN

Only writing is writing. These are not my words, although I find myself saying them quite often.

When you first become a thriving author, time management takes on a different level of attention. For some, it's easy to manage time. And for others, it's a nightmare.

I spent decades working in education, which meant I was not only responsible for my time daily, but I was also responsible for dozens of students and their daily structure. I had to think about long-term plans, daily plans, and then, how those wove together. After years and years of practice, I learned how to structure massive projects so that they didn't feel overwhelming and yet still got done—often before the deadline.

So when I quit my day job, I had the skills necessary to handle the transition. I was able to transfer what I did with long-term projects to a novel. But it's never that easy.

Whether you're a full-time writer, side hustler, or hobbyist, you'll have to learn how to manage your time. It's critical to take a look at the time you have available to work and then decide what to do during that time.

If you're never making the decision, you're probably realizing that things never get done. You need a plan for everything. Not goals, but a plan or a system that will provide the space to get the work done. If you sit down at the computer with an hour to work, how do you know what you can and should be doing?

Strangely, I hate writing, but I love having written. Again, not my words, but I've said them enough that they should be. Authors are a strange crew, resisting the very thing we claim we were put on this Earth to do. I'm no different. This Resistance (capital R thanks to Steven Pressfield and *The War of Art*) is something we all must battle every time we sit down at the keyboard.

If you're an independent publisher, you need to work on tasks other than just writing. You're responsible for your branding, marketing, publishing, distribution, and more. It's not only your job to write books, but you've got to sell them as well.

If you're querying agents in the hopes of landing a traditionally published book, you also need to work on tasks other than writing. Unfortunately, you will also be responsible for branding and marketing, maybe even distribution, depending on your deal. Just because you have a publisher doesn't mean you don't have to sell your own books. And all of this assumes you've spent countless hours querying agents, finding one who was able to sell your manuscript.

In either case and with any variation in between, authors must do other things than just writing. The cabin deep in the woods, with a potbelly stove and a view of the lake at sunset—nice, but fiction. Ninety-nine percent of authors don't live in this fantasy world. They probably hate writing but love having written, just like you.

Therefore, it becomes an easy and accepted form of Resistance to put other tasks ahead of your words. Remember that you chose to be an author, at whatever level you're at. Nobody has put a gun to your head and told you to type, although some days I might find that quite useful motivation.

Administrative tasks, email lists, paid promotions, giveaways, podcast interviews—and yes, social media.

Social media is probably the most accepted and overlooked form of Resistance when it comes to convincing ourselves we're writing. We'll say things like, "All of my readers are on social media. They expect me to be there." Or, "If I don't post x number of times on y platform, readers will forget about me." Or, "I've got a new book coming out, and if I don't get on social media and tell everyone, I won't sell any."

These are all excuses, and I would argue that most of them are just plain wrong. In the same way that disbursing royalties to my co-writers is not writing, and that running paid ads is not writing, social media use is not writing.

It's not as though social media itself is inherently evil. Some might say the tech giants in Silicon Valley are exploiting our primal instincts with things like notifications and likes, but let's give them the benefit of the doubt for the sake of this piece. If we assume the best, then social media is a distraction that is keeping you from your most important work—the writing.

It's easy to rationalize the use of social media instead of drafting or revising. It's tempting to blur the lines of writing and promotion and claim that without a social media presence, there's no reason to write because nobody will know about your words.

There is an element of truth to this in that the age of organic discoverability is over—it's going to be rare for the advice, "Publish it, and they will come," to still work at this stage of the independent publishing revolution. But that doesn't justify the use of your time on social media instead of writing.

For some, getting into the right mindset takes time. I feel this. If I have only 30 minutes, it's hard for me to get my head into the story, get productive words, and then wrap up. And if you write on evenings or weekends or within the margins of your day-to-day life, this might be the situation you face all the time.

If you take this approach and fill those 30 minutes with social media time instead of writing, you'll convince yourself that you need a "special" circumstance to get the good words in—like a cabin in the woods with a potbelly stove—and we've already pulled back the curtain on that myth.

Writing is writing. Yes, there will be times (many times) when you'll need to tend to some other aspect of your business, and that's valid. But if your words are getting banked on Facebook instead of into your work-in-progress, it might continue to be a work-in-progress for years to come.

DON'T SPEND TOO MUCH TIME ONLINE TALKING ABOUT WRITING BY ZACH BOHANNON

We love talking about things we're passionate about with other like-minded people. It's part of how we're wired as human beings. We tend to gravitate toward people who like to watch the same kinds of shows we do, read similar books, play the same sorts of video games, or enjoy watching or participating in certain sports. Some circumstances bring us together with people we might not usually be friends with, such as a job or a Christmas party. Still, when left to our own devices, our interests and passions typically influence our friendships.

In saying that, I love talking about the publishing industry. Whether it's the craft of writing, marketing tips, and strategies, or just good novels, I love discussing all things book publishing.

Being a writer is a fulfilling, yet often a solitary activity. As someone who enjoys alone time, I love sitting by myself and writing stories. But even still, we all desire connection, and we also love talking about our passions with others who share similar interests. I get a lot of value out of communicating with other writers, and for that matter, other creatives in general. Today, it's natural (and most convenient) to turn to social media to seek out those connections, and Facebook has made that easy with their Groups feature.

One of the last things that kept me from leaving Facebook altogether was Groups. I believe that it's essential to network with and interact with other authors, especially other independent publishers. And Facebook Groups is a convenient way to do this. As an author, you can find a Group for just about any niche or genre you're writing in. There are smaller, more focused Groups, as well as larger ones with hundreds, and sometimes thousands of people in them. Groups can not only be a great way to stay connected with other writers but also to keep up with what's going on in the industry and to see what's working for other authors. You can also share your own experiences of what is and isn't working for you.

I've been a part of a few different Facebook Groups over the last several years. Some came and went, and others remained—and probably still are—pretty active. I stayed away from the larger Groups and instead found smaller, curated communities of authors sharing marketing strategies, craft tips, and open, smart conversations about the industry.

My favorite Group was one with only thirty authors. It was a private Group where current members would have to vote on new members to be let in. This curation kept self-promotion and drama out of the Group, as well as assured its members that the conversations would remain valuable and intelligent. While there were a few less experienced authors in the Group, most were making a full-time living, some even in the high six figures and a couple in the seven-figure range.

How could I not want to be a part of a Group like that?

But once I began to question what kind of value I was getting out of being in this Group, and others, it wasn't difficult for me to step away.

With the world of independent publishing continually changing, it's crucial to stay informed so that you don't fall behind. If you want to keep up with the changes in online booksellers and the latest marketing strategies and tactics, then it's important to be plugged in. There are lots of great websites and podcasts to get this information, but authors also love discussing these sorts of things in Groups. One of the reasons I stayed connected to social media for as long as I did was for this exact reason. Rarely did I miss a big story, whether it was an algorithm change, or a shift in royalty payments, or the news that another independent author got a big traditional publishing deal or had movie rights optioned, or that there was drama brewing within one of the many writing organizations.

Again, I had to be getting value out of that. So I stayed.

Another popular topic among authors is success. When an author sells a lot of books or gets accepted for a BookBub ad or hits a big list or finally quits their day job, they love to share those stories. This is especially true in the self-publishing circles where independent authors, solely responsible for their own marketing and hence, attracting readers, love to share their experiences.

For a long time, I told myself that these stories were inspiring to me. If one of my author friends posted that they had a 10,000-word writing day, I would 'like' the post and comment about how awesome that was. One time a friend of mine posted in the small Group I was in that he had a month where he made over $100,000 after having a new series take off. Wow. It blew me away that someone I conversed with daily had found that much success by publishing novels. I was dumbfounded. Impressed. Inspired.

Or so I thought I was.

I started to notice something that I'm sure was happening subconsciously all along, but I had never stopped to think about it. I would have these really productive writing days where I wrote a lot of words and should have been proud of that. But instead, I found myself thinking about the friend who wrote 10,000 words in a day and wondering why I didn't do that.

I was making a living and supporting my family as a full-time creative, yet I would find myself wondering why I had never had a month where I had made anywhere close to a hundred thousand dollars. I knew it was possible. Someone who I consider a friend, even though we had never met in person, yet conversed daily online, had done it. It felt so close, yet so far away.

So while I was initially inspired by these remarkable successes of my colleagues, in the long-term career path, I found myself frustrated and unable to appreciate the achievements in my own journey.

Several studies done over the last few years have found this exact thing to be one of the dangerous inverse effects of social media. On social media, we are generally seeing the snapshots and highlights of other people's lives. In seeing these highlights, it's easy for us to look at ourselves and feel like we aren't doing a good enough job or aren't worthy. When I began studying and reading about the link between social media use and anxiety and depression, I became alarmed and realized that I was experiencing it myself. After this, it became much easier for me to walk away and accept that the few benefits I might get out of social media for my author career aren't worth the adverse effects I was feeling, and the potential that that could get worse. And since leaving, I've heard enough stories from writer friends about author bullying and drama that I know I've made the right choice.

That said, I stated earlier that I believe there is value in being friends with other authors and in staying connected. So how do I do that?

- Keep in touch with author friends via email
- Slack groups, which are more controlled and less distracting than Facebook
- Local indie author meetups
- Hosting and attending conferences and retreats
- Scheduled online video conferences
- When I read a novel I like, I reach out to the author and let them know

Meeting with other authors in person is by far my preferred way of connecting. This is something you can't do daily and, depending on where you live, could be difficult no matter how you look at it. But I would encourage you to look for local meetups or start one yourself. The library is a great place to start. Also, consider attending conferences or retreats. I can't overstate how powerful in-person interactions are compared to low-level, online ones. J. and I recognized the power of this long ago, and it's why we never plan a new series or talk about a big idea for an event until we can meet and do it in person.

It's easy to convince yourself that you need to be in big online writer groups. That you need to stay connected with other authors daily or that you might miss out on some significant change in the industry by *not* being in one of these groups. But talking about writing isn't writing. Only writing is writing. Remember that, and write on.

Don't Think They Have to Be on Every Platform by Zach Bohannon

Whenever we start a new endeavor, we get excited. Whether it's deciding to write a book or start a business, these projects, usually born out of passion, bring us a certain type of euphoria that is impossible to explain to someone who isn't a creative.

You probably are that creative or you at least know another creative who has gotten overly excited about a new project and jumped the gun on some things. I have at least two covers for books I was initially thrilled to write, only to see that excitement taper off before I got to the finish line. I also have a couple of different domain names for pen names or services that I initially was excited about, but I never ended up doing anything with them. I'm sure that most of us have some story like this, with things we bought now sitting around as sunk costs.

We love to tell people about our new ventures or ideas. It's natural to want to claim a title and announce it to the world. This is easy to do in our modern era with social media.

Think back to when you declared yourself an author. What was one of the first things you did? If I had to guess, you probably bought a domain name for yourself and set up social media accounts specifically to promote yourself as an author. I know that these are two of the first things I did. I did the same thing back in my 20s when I was playing in bands. Setting up accounts and announcing to the world, "I'm in a metal band!" was half the fun!

There's nothing wrong with this. In fact, you should have an author website, if for anything, then to allow people to sign up for your mailing list. And more than likely, you'll want to have some sort of social media presence.

The question then becomes, "Which social media platform should I be on?"

When I first started, the answer was, "All of them." And from talking to other authors, that seemed to be a common sentiment.

This becomes even more important to think about as you begin to publish your books and find out how hard it is to be discovered. It's easy to believe that being on more platforms will help you reach more readers.

As of this writing, these are the most popular social media platforms:

- Facebook
- Instagram
- Twitter
- Pinterest
- Tumblr
- Goodreads
- LinkedIn (nonfiction)
- YouTube
- Snapchat

If you're tuned into the author community, you're sure to find at least one big author success story for each one of these platforms. I know because I bought into those stories and thought I was missing out by not having accounts on them.

The one I remember specifically was Pinterest. I heard a couple of different stories about authors who were "crushing it" on Pinterest, whatever that means. I didn't know a thing about Pinterest other than my wife loved looking at crafts and food recipes on there, but I decided to jump in.

While I did initially find some value in building boards for story inspiration, I never got the hang of Pinterest. I couldn't grasp how it worked and how to connect with other people through the platform. But most importantly of all, I didn't enjoy the time I spent there.

So if I didn't enjoy it, why was I wasting my time? Not only were there plenty of other things I could be spending my time on (like writing), but people can tell you're on a platform just to be there. If you don't like being there, the people who do are going to be able to sniff that out, and it could wind up hurting your brand more than it could benefit it.

My advice is to pick one or two platforms that you enjoy and focus on those. Designate time for these activities (after you've done your writing) so that you aren't using social media marketing as Resistance and allowing it to get in the way of your important work, your writing. Out of all the platforms listed above, most can be a useful extension of your author brand if you genuinely enjoy being there.

The one exception to that I would say is Goodreads. I can also speak for J. in saying that we believe Goodreads is a place for readers, not authors. Yes, we are all readers. If you're writing and not reading, you have other problems. So if you want to be on Goodreads as a reader, go ahead. But do *not* promote your work there, as hardcore users will take offense. So be warned.

And if you don't like using *any* social media platforms, don't feel like you *have* to.

I no longer use any of the mentioned platforms. On the fiction side, I use my mailing list to communicate with my readers, and they are welcome and encouraged to email me as well.

On the nonfiction side, the Career Author Podcast and that website are how I communicate with listeners, as well as our Patreon-exclusive Slack group. Each one of our workshops and retreats has a dedicated Slack channel as well.

Focus on the social media platforms you are already familiar with and, more importantly, enjoy using. There are enough other things we have to learn and put energy into as authors without having to figure out TikTok.

DON'T BELIEVE EVERYONE IS ON SOCIAL MEDIA BY J. THORN

Confirmation bias. We all are susceptible to it, even if we don't know what it is.

I bought a Jeep Wrangler in the mid-1990s, and this was the first time I'd purchased any Jeep vehicle. But what I would find out is that people who own Jeep Wranglers belong to an unofficial club. As a side note, this happened to my dad when he bought a classic Corvette.

People driving Jeeps (and Corvettes) wave at each other in passing. The first few times this happened to me I wasn't sure exactly what was happening. I'd look at the passing Jeep in my rearview mirror, racking my brain as I tried to remember either the driver's face or the vehicle. After doing a quick search on Yahoo! (this was the 1990s, pre-Google), I discovered that waving at other people driving a Wrangler was a "thing." Same with Corvettes, school bus drivers, and bikers riding Harley Davidsons.

Before I'd purchased my Jeep, I hadn't noticed many Wranglers on the road or in parking lots unless they were tricked out or especially nice. But now that I had my own and strangers in other Wranglers began waving at me, it seemed as if everyone and their mother had been at the Jeep dealership. Two or three times on each way to the supermarket, I was waving at people.

"What are you doing?"

That was my wife, trying to figure out why this hardcore introvert was smiling and waving at random people driving by.

I saw old Jeeps, new Jeeps, Wranglers with a soft top, ones with a hardtop. Some had tow

bars, others had running board lights. New Wranglers had round headlights, and the older models had square ones. I started noticing not only the number of Wranglers on the road but details about them that I would have never seen before.

My confirmation bias was in full gear. It felt as though everyone had a Wrangler because I did.

It's easy to believe that everyone is on social media. And, it's even easier to convince yourself that if you're not leveraging every social media platform out there, that your author business is going to suffer. Readers won't be able to find you, interact with you, or know when you have a new book out.

The Big Blue and White Monster is the platform that makes you feel as if everyone in the world is on it. Let's face it, your grandmother is probably using Facebook. But what does that mean?

You can convince yourself that everyone is on it, that you're late to the game, or that you're not using the platforms to the best of your ability. But you have to remember that most social media networks are echo chambers, and therefore, you're probably only reaching the same groups of people, even if you are spending 5 hours a day writing pithy tweets or crafting that perfect meme for Facebook.

An echo chamber is when groups of people with similar values, perspectives, or opinions begin to interact in a closed environment. For example, if you're in a Facebook group with other independent authors, the tone of the conversations within that group will almost always reflect the group's shared values. Independent authors won't be in there talking about querying agents, slush piles, or getting placement on the front table of Barnes & Noble because those aren't concerns of independent authors. That echo chamber would not include traditionally published authors.

Social media works the same way. Any group of connected people will tend to gravitate around commonly shared values. If you look at your Facebook friends right now, you'll probably see that they are people in a similar demographic, liking the same things, talking about the same things. Echo chamber.

What does this mean for thriving authors? It means that it's difficult for you to break into these chambers unless you share the same values with the people inside of it. Therefore, finding a new audience becomes exponentially more difficult.

But even if you don't believe the social media echo chamber is a problem, you still have to face the reality that not everyone is on social media. I'm not sure Facebook would release the actual statistics, and even if they did, I don't know how long they'd be accurate, but there are literally hundreds of thousands—maybe millions—of fake accounts created every year. When you hear about how many people are "using" social media, what you're getting is a distorted view of usage. Many of those "people" are not people at all, they are accounts being created for or by bots, probably for nefarious political reasons.

Therefore, it might *feel* as though everyone is on social media, but that's not true. If you start asking around in your life, you'll understand that many people do enjoy social media, but they usually stick with one primary platform. Folks tend to love their Instagram, which means they're probably not on Twitter. And hardcore Facebook users are probably not anywhere else.

People's use of social media tends to be siloed, narrowly cornered in one sliver of the Internet. And even those people might not use social media in a way that benefits authors. Most people are on social media to be *social*. Times have changed, and we've become much more sophisticated users. Gone are the days of "buy my book" tweets or spamming Facebook with posts about your new book. Some people have even gone so far as to block promotional posts or advertising from their feeds with third-party apps. Even the people on social media might be tuning out all of your efforts to sell books.

That doesn't mean social media should be entirely abandoned by authors. However, consider how and why you're using it. Social media is great for connecting with other authors or engaging dedicated fans who want to hear from you. But believing that everyone is on social media and therefore, you should be, too, that's just not something thriving authors do.

BELIEVE THAT ALL READERS WANT TO INTERACT WITH AUTHORS BY J. THORN

It had come out of my mouth before I realized it. I was sitting on a panel at the Sell More Books Show Summit (now the Career Author Summit) in 2019, discussing different aspects of being an independent author. We had been discussing marketing, and inevitably, how social media fits into that paradigm.

"I have a secret," I said. I'm paraphrasing slightly. "I have a hunch that not all readers *want* to engage with authors."

Zach said he'd heard a gasp move through the venue. I had inadvertently touched a nerve—in what I think was a positive way.

The assumption has always been that everyone wants to engage everyone else on social media. If you try and place yourself back in 2006 when Facebook was becoming a thing, that was probably true. We'd had written letters for many generations—not exactly the most exciting or efficient means of technology. And then, for the past generation or two, telephones made it infinitely easier for us to connect and communicate.

The Internet didn't change that drastically with the advent of email, although it did change the way business was done. I remember sitting in the computer lab at the University of Pittsburgh in 1989, being instructed on how to type the green commands on the black screen to send "electronic mail." It didn't matter that I didn't know anyone who was able to receive my electronic mail, but I was now capable of sending one.

For at least a solid decade, email has been propelled by the network effect—the more people that adopt the technology, the more people use it, like fax machines. Even so, email didn't seem to truly invade our personal spheres the way social media would.

When it became clear that social media could fill the gap between our real-life encounters and those conducted over wires (phone and email), things changed. Rapidly.

By the early 2010s, Facebook had become a normal part of all of our lives. We all assumed everyone wanted to be part of Facebook except for the Luddites among us who would eventually get on board. I remember thinking that once you could get grandmothers on Facebook, the tipping point had been passed.

It's no coincidence then that Facebook became the first and primary tool used by the first generation of Kindle Direct Publishing authors. We rushed to set up a "wall" and then later, an "author page." Facebook was more immediate than email, especially with the Messenger app, which was now available on just about any smartphone to hit the market.

All of this demonstrates that we came about the assumption naturally and through a normal progression of the adoption curve. We rightly assumed that all readers wanted to interact with authors because they *could*.

But I don't think that is the case any longer. And for some segments of my reading audience, I don't think it was ever the case. I neglected my own behavior, which is often the go-to advice for customer development: you are not your customer. Well, I don't think that's necessarily true either.

It took me several years to realize that I wanted nothing to do with authors—as a reader. I've enjoyed reading dark fiction since I was a kid, and in the decades that followed, I never wrote a letter to Stephen King or Dean Koontz. Not one time. And once it became easy to join an author's mailing list, I didn't do that either. I'm only one person, but I'd later discover that thousands of people on my author mailing list were just like me.

Some genres and subgenres will have readers who want to engage in each and every way possible. These readers will follow their favorite authors on any and all social media channels, interacting as often as they can.

But not all. I have data to suggest that fans of postapocalyptic fiction aren't as interested. Sure, some will join Facebook groups and chat with other readers. Some will join an author's mailing list. But many won't. They want to read a good book. That's it.

Reading a book is a completely different experience than listening to one. I'm not placing judgment. One is not "better" than the other. However, those are different people. Readers (like me) who enjoy the quiet and solitude of reading with their eyes don't want someone else's voice inside of their head. They don't want to "optimize" their reading time by listening to a book while working out, or walking the dog and picking up dog crap. They want to savor the private and silent experience of reading without distraction.

And it's these types of readers who will not engage on social media. They won't join your list, and if they do, they won't ever respond.

The assumption that all of your marketing and promotional efforts should be designed to engage readers is a faulty one because it's not true. Some readers want as much access to you as possible, and some simply want to read a book.

You'll need to do the research, explore your genre, and talk to other authors in it. For some readers, not having a social media presence could be a costly mistake. But for others, it might be unnecessary at best or annoying at worst.

Not *all* readers want to engage with authors online, in email, or on social media.

Listen to your gut. Don't be afraid to examine your own behaviors. If you're not on social media or don't enjoy using it, you should seriously consider that approach for your business. If you're not into it, readers will feel that, and they won't be into it. I know because I've tried. And failed.

You might be your ideal reader, and so it makes sense to cater the reading experience to the readers in the way you'd enjoy it. It might mean you'll need certain elements of social media, or it might mean you can ignore them completely.

But one thing's for certain. In this day and age, the use of social media as a tool for reader engagement is not a given, and it doesn't apply to all authors equally.

PODCASTING

Podcasting is having a moment. However, it's going to be a long moment.

Since the early 2000s, podcasting has been on a steady increase until the mid-2010s, when the advent of the smartphone added fuel to the fire. These days, more and more people are consuming podcasts throughout their days and consistently from one week to the next.

But should authors have a podcast? Aren't we better off locked in a quiet room, hammering away at a keyboard?

There has never been a better time to enter the world of podcasting. The benefits are immeasurable, and there's no better way to gain a fan than whispering into their ears weekly.

In this section, J. Thorn explains why podcasting is unique, compared to other forms of content marketing and how authors can take advantage of this exciting and fun medium. With years of experience and well over 600 episodes under his belt, join J. as he discusses the nine things that thriving authors don't do when it comes to podcasting.

Here's a quick summary of the valuable lessons you can expect to learn in this section:

"Don't Quit a Podcast Before the Seventh Episode" – Seven can be the loneliest number. When you fire up the microphone and send out your voice onto the Internet airwaves, and nobody is listening, most podcasters give up. J. shows you how to develop a show that is destined to make it while not losing your motivation to continue.

"Don't Record Podcast Episodes with a Phone" – While you can record a podcast with your phone, thriving authors would never do such a thing. J. explains why a dedicated microphone is essential and why that little one at the bottom of your phone won't cut it. Get tips on what type of microphone is best for podcasting. And hint, it's not the one you think it is.

"Don't Record Podcast Episodes in a Coffee Shop" – J. approves of writing in a coffee shop, but never podcasting there. Room sound matters, and the last thing you want in your recording is the barista telling Franklin that his large soy latte is ready. Learn what it means to "treat" a room for optimal audio quality while creating a consistent recording environment that your listeners will appreciate.

"Don't Ignore Listeners Who Engage with the Show" – Although engagement is a buzzword in the world of podcasting, it matters. Beware the pitfalls of giving your listeners a place to interact with you but then ignoring them. J. explains why it's critical to read and reply to *every* comment posted on your podcast's website. For authors who want to use a podcast to create a client base, consistent, 100% engagement will build solid relationships for years to come. Yes, it's another thing to add to your to-do list, but it's not something you can afford to ignore.

"Don't Record Episodes and Then Never Listen to Them Again" – *Do I really sound like that?* Yes, yes, you do. Our recorded voice always sounds funny to us when we listen back to it. Get used to it. Becoming a professional at any skill requires deliberate practice. If you're not listening thoughtfully to all of your episodes, you won't improve and will be prone to making the same mistakes repeatedly. While it might not be enjoyable, a thriving author always listens to previous episodes to become better at future ones.

"Don't Ignore Podcast Analytics" – J. knows the importance of data, and he explains why podcast analytics are crucial to continually improving your show. A periodic review of podcast analytics can give you a sense of which topics or episodes are connecting with your audience, and which ones are not. More importantly, periodically surveying your listeners will ensure that you're delivering the content they need, content that is relevant to them on their journey to become a thriving author.

"Don't Start a Podcast Because It's Trendy" – "Podcasting to Market" is not a thing, and J. hopes it will never become one. Thriving authors don't chase trends when it comes to show formats or ideas. Discover how much energy it takes to produce podcast episodes regularly and how that'll feel if you're not completely passionate about the topic. Podcasting is a long-tail game, and if you're chasing trends, it won't be a game you'll be able to play for long.

"Don't Ignore Other Podcasts in the Same Industry or Category" – If you've never listened to a podcast before and you're reading this book because you want to start one, close it and get a refund. Much like writing, you can't be an excellent podcast host if you're not a rabid fan of podcasts. J. explains why thriving authors don't start a show without first being a fan of other podcasts in the same industry or category.

"Don't Expect to Make Fast or Big Money" – Podcasting is not a get-rich-quick scheme. Only a small percentage of podcasts generate any revenue, and thriving authors don't expect to make fast or big money. However, if you create a podcast that serves the needs of your audience, it is possible to earn money through patronage, ad runs, sponsorships, or all of the above. Strive to be a podcast star while keeping your expectations grounded.

Don't Quit a Podcast Before the Seventh Episode by J. Thorn

It seems like it's been a difficult few months for you. You're refreshing your sales dashboards in the hopes that the problem is slow reporting, but it's not helping—you're a victim of saggy sales. You've been reading the online message boards, posting in Facebook groups, and emailing influencers in the hopes of finding someone with the answer to the question you seek: What can I do to get my sales numbers up?

We've all been there. Paid advertising can be hit or miss, so you start to think about ways to reach people you know who would be interested in your books, whether it's fiction or nonfiction. I had to embrace the potentially Internet-sleazy term of "content marketing" before I could come up with a way to reach more people authentically.

Content marketing is a generic term that still gets a bad rap, even though the concept is proven and genuine if you do it right—create something of value for your ideal customer and give it to them for free.

In theory, the feeling of warm reciprocity you develop will inevitably result in a sale or a new customer because that person will be grateful for your generosity. Then, when their pain becomes so overwhelming that they're ready to pay someone to alleviate it, you'll be the first person they go to, assuming the content you gave them for free was high-quality information.

The reason that content marketing hasn't been viewed in the most favorable light is that often, the content creator doesn't create something of real value. Instead, the content is more of a tease designed to upsell the potential customer. People are Internet-savvy these days—they can sniff out that insincerity in an instant.

But what about paid ads? Isn't it easier and wouldn't it involve less work if you could just pay to get eyeballs on your books? In theory, absolutely. However, the ad platforms function more like casinos—the house always wins. Dashboards are clunky, reporting mechanisms are often archaic or inaccurate, and the developers use overly complicated technology to separate you from your well-earned advertising budget. Unless you spend hours each day experimenting with your ads, continually tweaking and refining them, you'll probably lose money.

Sure, there are influencers out there who will sell you a great course or book on paid advertising, and most of those people know what they're talking about. But unless you're willing to spend hours managing ads, you won't benefit from their teachings. Remind yourself: you're a writer, not an advertising account manager.

If we take paid ads off the table, what's left? Blogging? YouTube? Social media? Podcasting? Ninety-nine percent of your content-marketing options will fall into one of these categories. I could write an entire book on each one, but for the sake of brevity and your sanity, let's talk about why podcasting could be your best option.

Nobody reads blogs. Those people with successful blogs have probably been at it for years, if not decades. People don't go on social media to buy things, and users have become numb to sales pitches and paid ads, meaning that even organic social media reach is in steady decline. Yes, YouTube is an excellent option for content marketing, but only if your channel gets millions of views. Like blogging, starting a new YouTube channel is like whispering into a hurricane.

Podcasting (and audio in general) is on a continuing upward trajectory. You can Google the stats. Here's why: Podcasting is practically the only content that someone can consume while doing something else. The same can't be said of social media, or YouTube, or blogging. You can listen to a podcast while walking the laundry or doing the dog. Er, you know what I mean.

I'm not going to sell you on the value of podcasting because you've already purchased this book.

But here's the rub: Most podcasters quit before they reach the seventh episode. Why? Because it's a long-tail play. In other words, don't expect to see thousands of people flocking to your new podcast feed. Don't count on sponsors rolling up wheelbarrows full of cash to your front door. Growing an audience with a podcast takes time. A long time. If you don't love podcasting, if you're not an addicted podcast listener, return this book right now and slowly back away from the microphone.

Thriving authors who have been podcasting know that it's going to take a long time to build an audience. It can take months, even years, before you start to see measurable results. And with most new podcasters quitting before the seventh episode, you have an opportunity if you're willing to stick with it.

Over time, podcast listeners become some of the most loyal fans you'll ever have. You are literally in their ear every week (as of now, producing an episode a week is optimal). They feel as if they know you, that you're good friends. Plus, if your podcast is providing quality entertainment or useful information, these people will trust you when it comes time for them to pull out their wallets to solve a problem.

From May of 2014 through January of 2020, I've launched eight different weekly podcasts, recording and producing a total of 664 episodes. And that's with a 10-month hiatus during which I didn't produce a single episode, and that number doesn't include hundreds of guest podcast appearances. I currently have 4-5 different podcasts in production and nearly a million downloads since I first plugged in my microphone.

I'm going to share with you what I've learned on this long, strange trip—one that I'm still on. I love listening to podcasts. I love making podcasts. I love everything about podcasting.

If you remember nothing else from this book, remember that podcasting is a long-tail play. You must show up week after week, broadcasting to nobody for weeks or months before you start to see results.

But thriving authors don't give up after producing six episodes. Keep going, even when you think nobody is listening. Unlike traditional mass media, you don't need a following of millions. You don't even need a following of thousands. A few hundred dedicated listeners can help you sell books, build your platform, and eventually earn revenue from podcasting.

Turn on the microphone, put the earphones on your head, and let's crank podcasting up to 11.

Don't Record Podcast Episodes with a Phone by J. Thorn

You think you're technically challenged. You hate the computer, and you can't tell the difference between a hard drive and a hard hat. You were that person in college who paid other people to type their exam papers. Even the thought of doing a Windows update makes you break into a cold sweat.

According to some articles you've read, creating a podcast requires technical expertise. The posts are filled with abbreviations and acronyms that seem like a foreign language.

Folks with a particular skill set or who are members of a specific industry like to make others feel inadequate by using jargon to scare novices away, and that has certainly been true for podcasting.

On the other hand, you may believe that you can record a podcast with your phone, that the barrier to entry is low. Technically, you can record a podcast with your phone, but that would make you sound like an amateur who didn't care enough to create a quality experience for the listener. While the microphone and technology on your smartphone continue to improve, it cannot match the quality of a dedicated microphone operated by someone who understands how to use it.

You might think that recording a podcast on your phone would be smart because then you would save yourself some money. That is true, and to a certain degree, you wouldn't want to invest a lot of money into something if you're not sure it is an activity that you want to continue doing. However, most professional podcasts—the ones you listen to regularly—are produced and published with proper, quality gear.

Once you've decided that you are not going to use your smartphone to create a podcast, you are now adrift in a world of technical jargon, and you might not be sure which microphone or earphones you should purchase to produce your podcast.

The truth is that most of the recommended pieces of gear for podcasting will create an optimally produced audio file. But podcasting is a performance, and although the sound quality should be exceptional, your performance and technique are much more important. For now, let's focus on getting the least amount of gear possible that will create the best quality product.

Most podcasters will purchase a dynamic room microphone such as the Snowball or a Yeti. These microphones are usually USB plug and play, which means all you have to do is plug them into your device and hit record. However, for about the same amount of money, I'm going to make a recommendation you probably don't hear very often.

For years, I was the lead singer in a rock band. The Shure SM58 microphone is the industry standard for live musical performance because you have to get right on top of the microphone for it to pick up your voice. This is essential when you're on stage with a stack of blaring amplifiers and a maniac drummer because if the microphone is too sensitive, it will feedback. The 58 does not pick up anything that isn't right in front of it, and for that reason, I believe it's the most underutilized and under-recommended microphone for podcasting. Shure makes a USB version of this microphone, which means all you have to do is plug it into your laptop just like any other microphone created for podcasting. As long as you place that microphone close to your mouth, you won't pick up the dogs barking next door or the garbage man slamming your cans into the curb. The 58 is a world-class microphone that is relatively inexpensive, and if you listen to any of my podcasts, you'll hear the difference. I've used a Shure SM58 for almost every episode I've recorded.

So, what else do you need once you have a decent microphone? Honestly, not much except for a little bit of software.

Many podcasters like to use free recording software such as Audacity. This is a great choice, especially if you don't have any experience with audio editing. Whatever software you choose, you want the ability to set up templates before you record, edit, and produce episodes. An episode template already has the tracks created, the levels set, and any sound effects that you might have included in the episode, such as intro music or a call to action at the end. Once you've created a template in your software, it's as simple as editing the recorded tracks and then exporting as an MP3 file, which can then be uploaded to your podcast distributor of choice.

Although designed more for multitrack recording, I like to use Reaper. I've used the program for decades to record my bands, and I find it extremely powerful and easy to use. I've created a template for each one of my podcasts, and when it's time to record an episode, I simply open that template and hit record. When I'm finished, I trim the beginning and end of the recording and then export it as an MP3 file.

The microphone and the audio editor. These are the only two elements of podcast production that you absolutely must have. It's easy to go down the rabbit hole of research and create a wish list of all of the other gear and software you think you need to create a world-class podcast, but the truth is that a clean input through a good microphone and plugged into a simple audio editor is all you need.

If you want to practice podcasting using your smartphone and to send those files to friends for feedback, you should do that. But once you put your podcast into full-on production mode, it needs to meet the same standards as all of the other podcasts you're listening to on your platform of choice. In the same way that your book must compete with traditionally published titles on the bookstore shelves, your podcast must be able to stand up next to the others that are professionally recorded and mixed.

On the other hand, don't feel compelled to spend thousands of dollars on microphones and gear that is unnecessary because you believe it will somehow make your podcast better. What goes into the microphone is far more important than what comes out of it, but give yourself the best shot at success with a decent microphone and a simple audio-editing software package.

DON'T RECORD PODCAST EPISODES IN A COFFEE SHOP BY J. THORN

Now that you have the proper gear and you're somewhat confident in how to use it, the next question is where to record the podcast. Thriving authors don't record podcasts in busy public places or coffee shops.

Where you record, your podcast is dependent on the format of your podcast. If you are doing a solo podcast, then you can record virtually anywhere. However, if you are doing a podcast with a cohost or if you are conducting interviews, you will most likely need to record on a device with an Internet connection. For now, let's talk about the aesthetics of the room.

Many authors find it stimulating to write and work in a public place with the hustle and bustle around them to excite their senses and invigorate their brains. While I don't necessarily subscribe to this idea, I do understand why other writers can be productive in this environment. But when it comes to podcasting, quiet is king. You want to make sure that you minimize the amount of external noise as much as possible for as long as possible. Noisy podcast episodes can be distracting, and some listeners will unsubscribe if listening becomes too much of a challenge.

This doesn't mean you need to spend tens of thousands of dollars to create a professional sound studio in your basement. If you have enough room to sit inside of a wardrobe closet, you can create the best environment for podcasting.

When I first started podcasting, I took my laptop into the closet. Usually, closets are filled with clothing that will deaden the sound. Your goal with podcasting is to find a room or a space that does not have harsh surfaces because those are not optimal. Look for places where sound waves will be absorbed, such as a closet or a room with lots of soft, plush furniture.

Sound engineers do what is called "treating a room." They place baffles and other sound-dampening devices into certain parts of the room to keep the sound waves from reverberating. This is your goal when you are creating your podcasting environment.

Again, you don't need to have a dedicated space. Most wardrobe closets will give you the deadened sound that you're looking for.

Don't forget to tell your family, friends, relatives, or roommates that you are about to record. Radio stations have the "on-air" sign that lights up above the door when they are broadcasting. This is probably not something you're going to want to install in your apartment. However, whether it's a note on the door or a text message to your housemates, make sure everyone understands that you are recording. If you are doing a solo podcast, you will always be able to stop or edit out extraneous noise, but if you are conducting an interview or hosting a podcast with someone else, it is not always possible to stop. And even if you can edit it out, the flow of the conversation can be easily disrupted when those on the call are distracted.

If you have the room, standing up in your podcast space is preferable to sitting down. Many scientific studies explain why you should always stand when presenting to an audience and make no mistake about it; the audience might not be in the closet with you, but they are an audience, and you are performing for them. Make sure you have avoided consuming dairy products before podcasting (which is not beneficial for your vocal cords), that you have water on hand, and that you've attended to all of your biological needs before recording. Optimally, you want to record your podcast in one take because that would mean less editing to be done afterward, and it will begin to sound unnatural if there are too many edits.

Before you hit record on that first episode, test the room. Take your laptop and your microphone into the closet and record yourself reading one page from a book. Then go around the apartment or the house and do the same experiment in different rooms. As long as it's unoccupied, make sure you do this in the bathroom as well. You will quickly hear the difference between a live room and a dead room (sonically). The bathroom recording will represent everything you're trying to avoid. Because of all the hard surfaces, the bathroom is highly reflective and not conducive to achieving a dead sound. When you are finished, listen to the recordings, and you will hear the difference a room makes when it comes to the quality of your recording.

You might look cool sitting in a coffee shop with your earbuds and microphone, but nobody will be impressed, and the sound quality of your episode will suffer. Remember, a podcast is an intimate medium. Listeners are focused on the words that deliver right into their ears, so make them the most pleasurable listening experience that you can.

Finally, if you can record every episode in the same place, this will provide a consistent experience for your listeners. Every week, they will tune in, and they will listen and become accustomed to the standard of quality you set. Don't let them down. If you're recording in a coffee shop, that latte machine will drown you out.

DON'T IGNORE LISTENERS WHO ENGAGE WITH THE SHOW BY J. THORN

Now that you've started your podcast and have stuck with it past episode seven, you'll notice that people are listening to what you have to say. You might have checked your podcast analytics and seen downloads and listens increasing every week.

But what catches your attention is that listeners are beginning to leave comments on your podcast's website. This is significant for many reasons.

Most podcast listeners are doing something else while there listening to your show. So that means they're unlikely to take action while listening to an episode because they could be out walking, doing some type of physical activity, or driving a car.

So when you ask a listener to take action on your episode, and they do it, it means they had to make a note to come back to the website and take that action at a later time. As you can probably tell, that takes an enormous amount of dedication for someone to do. Therefore, if someone takes the time and the energy to remember to come back to your website and post a comment, you know they are genuinely enjoying your show.

It might be tempting to believe that the comments are a space for listeners to interact with each other, and while that is true, without a source of inspiration, your fledgling community might not grow.

I understand that it seems like yet another thing you must do as a podcast host. If you sit down and read every single comment and reply to those comments, it will come at the cost of doing something else. And let's be honest about it, nobody is paying you per comment that you reply to on your podcast's website. It takes time and energy and dedication to answer questions and comments left by your listeners regularly. For most of us, it would be much easier to let the listeners comment back and forth with each other while we watch Netflix.

At this point in the journey, your podcast is like a very delicate flower, and if you don't tend to it, the podcast can wither and die. Unless you are a show with millions of listeners and hundreds of comments per episode, you must engage and reply to every single listener comment posted on your website.

Do I mean every single comment? Yes, every single comment. You don't have to write a thoughtful and detailed response to every single person who comments. It is not necessary to write pages and pages of text in response to a question; in fact, you might not even answer every question. But what you must do is acknowledge the fact that someone who is listening to your podcast made a note to come back later and post a comment or question for you. Never underestimate or take for granted the importance of that small gesture in a world boiling over with distraction.

You build a podcast listenership one set of ears at a time. You must strengthen those relationships if you want to have a community or if you want your podcast to succeed. Some podcasts don't emphasize listener engagement, but those are few and far between. Less than 1% of all podcasts have an audience so large that they can afford to ignore it. Podcasts are not like mass media. NBC doesn't care if its news anchors are responding to Internet comments of people who watch their broadcasts because NBC generates revenue through advertising, not engagement. But podcasts are different.

I can trace almost every single client I've worked with back to a podcast episode. They heard me on someone else's show, or they're a loyal listener of one of mine. Over months and sometimes years, these people began to trust me and rely on the information I provided, so when it comes time to hire someone, they come to me first. I take this responsibility seriously because I understand that there are many people out there who can help. Most authors have a limited budget, and so, if they're willing to spend that money on my services, I want to do the best I possibly can.

And purely from a self-serving standpoint, if you don't engage your listeners when they are reaching out, they will find other show hosts who will engage them. Your goal is not to create the most unique podcast ever produced. There will probably be many shows just like yours. What will differentiate you from your competitors is how you treat the people who support you.

I understand how difficult it is to stay on top of things like Internet comments. In Facebook groups, you could spend an entire day doing nothing but replying to comments and answering questions. I recommend that you have a dedicated website for your podcast, a place where people can go to leave comments. It's vital that you own this real estate so that you can control who comments, the tone of it, and who gets to see those comments. If you build your following on someone else's platform, like a social media channel, and they change their policies or terms of service, you could lose your audience. This has happened before, and it will almost certainly happen again.

However, you decide you're going to handle comments, and you should create a system or process for it. Whether it's a daily check-in or batching one week at a time, get it on your to-do list or in your calendar so that replying to comments becomes part of your routine.

Because thriving authors who host podcasts never ignore their listeners.

DON'T RECORD EPISODES AND THEN NEVER LISTEN TO THEM AGAIN BY J. THORN

Your voice sounds funny. So does mine. Every person who has ever heard themselves on a recording or voicemail cringes at the sound of their voice. I will not go into the science or biology of why this is the case but simply understand that the voice you hear with your ears is different than the one the rest of us do. The good news is that over time, the more you listen to your voice on a recording, the more natural it will begin to sound to you until you reach a point where the voice inside of your head matches the one on a recording.

But let's be honest. It's challenging to listen to yourself. I can remember the first few episodes of the Horror Writers Podcast, and even though I haven't listened back to them in several years, I have periodically listened to a few minutes of those early shows as a way to measure my progress. No matter what you do, the first few episodes will sound terrible to you at a later time, no matter how good you think your performance is when you record them. It is just like a novelist who spends years on that first book and looks back later, realizing that even though it was as good as it could've been at the time, it's not nearly as good as a book written five years later.

Therefore, you have a choice. You can suck it up and listen to your voice, realizing how uncomfortable it's going to make you, but at the same time, allowing you to be analytical about it and improve your performance. Or you can move on and continue recording episodes without ever listening back to the ones you did, which would be like a professional athlete who refused to watch game film.

I'm often shocked by the number of podcasters who say they never listen back to their episodes. From the very beginning, over 600 times, I've gone back and listened to each episode I recorded before posting it. And, on some occasions, I will listen multiple times, with each pass evaluating a different aspect of my performance that I want to improve. While a vocal coach or speaking coach can help you improve your podcast delivery, you can get started simply by being analytical and deliberate when listening to yourself.

There are many things I'm listening for when I replay a podcast recording before posting it. The first and most obvious is that I want to make sure that it is technically perfect. In other words, if I had to make any edits or cut something from the recording, I want to make sure that I did so smoothly, so that the listener does not detect it.

I want to listen to the audio levels and make sure that I am maximizing the volume while not clipping the gain and causing distortion. If I'm recording with a cohost or if I'm interviewing someone, I want to make sure the levels are adjusted in such a way that the relative volume is the same. This isn't always possible, given the fact that the person on the other end—whether an interview or a cohost—does not have the same setup that you do, nor do they have the same room, and therefore, the tone of their audio will always be different. But the relative volume can be matched.

Also, I'm listening to my performance with regard to pace, diction, and dynamics. I want to make sure that I'm not using a lot of filler words like "so," "um," "but," and "actually." I'm listening to make sure that I'm not speaking too quickly or drawing things out too slowly. Quality control around diction is a challenge because if I mispronounce a word, it's cumbersome and awkward to go back and re-record it, especially if it's a conversation I'm having with another person. But I will make notes of words that I stumble upon or don't know, so that it doesn't happen again.

And finally, I want to make sure that my voice is dynamic. I do not want to speak robotically so that the performance sounds flat. Like diction, this is not necessarily something I'm going to fix in the mix but is a point of emphasis when I do future episode recordings. I want to make sure that I'm varying my tone, delivery, and the energy in my voice so that the listener does not become bored or fatigued.

As a lifelong educator and a teacher with decades of experience, I understand the power of deliberate practice. There's no better or faster way to improve your craft—no matter what it is—than analyzing one's performance. If you study the most prolific and successful people in any profession, field, or industry, you will notice they all have something in common, which is the ability to view and critique their performance to improve future performances objectively. Podcasting is no different.

Yes, your voice will sound funny until you get used to it. Yes, you will be embarrassed about some of the mistakes and stumbles that you make. But listeners understand the nature of a podcast. You are not presenting an inaugural speech in Washington, D.C. or reciting the Gettysburg Address after the Civil War.

Podcasts are mostly an organic and dynamic medium in which people have a conversation with another person or with the audience, and because of that, listeners do not expect perfection. However, it would be irresponsible of you as a podcast host and producer to ignore quality control.

Some podcasters seem to be naturally gifted in the medium. You hear them on other podcasts or watch them on YouTube, and their delivery seems effortless. And while this might be true for a small percentage of us, most podcasters got that way because they were willing to put in the time and effort to be self-critical of their performance in the hopes of improving it.

Thriving authors who podcast always listen back to their episodes so they can become an even better podcaster in the future.

Don't Ignore Podcast Analytics by J. Thorn

Thriving authors who run a podcast never ignore the analytics. Analytics is a term used generally that means statistics about your podcast or listenership, including the number of downloads or listens. Most podcast platforms, commonly called podcast hosts, will provide some level of analysis that you can use to make decisions about your show.

There is some debate in the podcast community about what constitutes a listen. There are differences in the ways that people consume podcasts on both the software and hardware side. Some people download episodes and listen to them offline while others stream them. Some people will listen to an episode multiple times, and depending on the platform, that can count as one listen, or multiple listens. Therefore, it's essential to take the analytics at face value and not put too much stock into what you see, but at the same time, there is important relative information you can leverage from these reports.

You might hear podcasters boasting about their number of downloads per month. Those analytics are not helpful to you. What you can do is look to see how some of your episodes compare to others you've published, and then make decisions about future topics based on that data.

It's easy to see yourself as an artist in much the same way that an author or a painter might. You might come to the microphone and know what it is you want to say and how you want to say it, and you're not interested in feedback from listeners. You might argue that as the creator of the show, you get to determine the nature of your intellectual property, and to a degree, this is true. However, your other choice is to pay attention to those relative numbers and make decisions about the content you want to create in the future, based on what your listeners want.

I've had episodes that I thought would be a tremendous hit with my audience, but they received minimal listens, while others I hadn't thought were that interesting have become some of my most popular episodes. The truth is, you will have a general idea of what your listeners want, but within that range, you'll find a wide disparity between what you create and what they listen to, and you'll ignore that information at your own risk.

It doesn't take long to scan through your analytics and begin to take note of which topics have garnered the attention of your listeners. In the same way in which we've discussed other tactics for podcasting, create a process or a routine that involves checking your analytics. What types of shows do your listeners prefer? What titles seem to have caught the most attention? Which episodes have resulted in the most listener comments on your podcast website?

But merely studying analytics might not be enough. Again, it's worth mentioning that the way those analytics are designed could create a false sense of security, and it's hard to verify that those downloads and listens are accurate. Therefore, it's imperative to take that data and use it to make your show better but do so with a healthy dose of logic and common sense.

Some of the most significant increases in downloads and listens have come after I sent my audience a survey. If you can ask people what they want to hear, you're more likely to create content that helps them. It's essential to recognize that even in a best-case scenario, you might only get a small percentage of your listeners to complete a survey, but that doesn't mean that data is not valuable. The people who do respond are most likely hardcore fans and dedicated listeners. These are the people who will tell others about you, who will create a word-of-mouth interest in your show, and therefore, paying attention to what they're telling you is critical to take your podcast to the next level.

A survey doesn't have to be and shouldn't be extensive. It can be as simple as asking two questions of your listener: What was your favorite episode? What is your least-favorite episode? And if you want to throw in an open-ended third question, ask them to create a title for what they believe would be their perfect podcast episode.

Even with only 5% of your audience completing the survey, you'll have a much better understanding of what topics resonate with your listeners and what episodes they skip.

A counterpoint to this approach is that you may end up taking your podcast topics in a direction that you don't want to go or is not of interest to you. This is a real concern and not something you should take lightly. However, there are ways to appeal to your audience while also creating the content that interests you.

Examine the survey results and begin to write down the episodes or aspirational titles that are of interest to your audience, and then brainstorm the topics you might be able to create that would fulfill those desires. By doing so, you will be creating content of value and interest to them while at the same time scratching your itch about the things you wish to talk about.

It doesn't mean that every episode is going to be in perfect alignment, and remember that just because you think it'll be a great episode doesn't necessarily mean it'll be received that way. But if you're being intentional and soliciting feedback from listeners based on pure analytics provided by your podcast host, you are in a much better position to continuously create episodes that connect with your listeners.

You take a considerable risk by not paying attention to both the analytics and the feedback provided by your listeners. Thriving authors with a podcast don't ignore the numbers or stick their heads in the sand. They don't stubbornly dig in their heels and produce content that doesn't appeal to the very people they hope to serve. You have access to data that the major broadcast networks would have killed for, decades ago. Use it wisely.

DON'T START A PODCAST BECAUSE IT'S TRENDY BY J. THORN

Audio is all the rage right now, and everything you read is saying that the trend will continue as people consume more on cheaper and more ubiquitous devices. You see double-digit growth in all reports, and it seems like everyone and their mother has a new podcast.

Authors behave like a herd of scared cats. Once one person starts something and can prove even a modicum of success, others quickly join in until whatever tactic or strategy that once worked is so saturated that it no longer does.

But you'll be different, and you'll be the exception to the rule. Imagine what would happen if you don't capitalize on podcasting at this very moment? Imagine how intense your fear of missing out would be? You scan the top of the podcast section on iTunes and see so many new and hip shows that you know you'll find success doing the same thing.

This scenario will most likely lead to a significant decision you must make before you go any further in developing a podcast. You must decide what it is you are going to talk about. Are you going to chase a trend and try to cash in on what's happening right now, or will you dig deeper and look for something within yourself that can be of value to other people?

This is not an easy decision. I know because I've done both, and at separate times, have been right and wrong.

I created 100 episodes of a podcast that I started because I felt it was trendy. That's not to say I wasn't true to myself or that the podcast was inauthentic. In fact, at the time I produced the podcast, it was the closest thing I had to writing a diary in public. Nevertheless, part of me wanted to capitalize on a trend and maybe more so than what I wanted to admit.

In another circumstance—also a show in my podcast graveyard—I started one based solely on who I wanted to be and where I wanted to go professionally. That podcast survived my solo effort as well as two different cohosts before it also ran out of steam.

The ugly truth about podcasting is that you will lose interest or run out of things to say for the majority of the podcast ideas you generate. Whether it's because your topic is too trendy or timely, or simply because you've said all you could about a particular subject, the majority of podcasts have a shelf life. You will almost certainly quit some and start others. There is nothing wrong with this approach as it is a natural evolution for many in the industry who have started or currently produce multiple podcasts.

But your decision is one you should not make lightly because, unlike your show's artwork, or the format, or the way you make the show notes, you can't change the reason you're doing the show. Once you start down that path, there is no turning back.

If your goal is to start a trendy podcast and possibly use it as a lead generator for a business that happens to be in high demand, then following that trend might not be a bad idea. For example, if you had a Christmas tree business and decided to start a podcast in August about Christmas decorations, the seasonal trend might pay off six months later when your audience is in the Yuletide spirit. Although I've never started a Christmas-themed podcast, I would imagine that downloads and listens probably tank in January and February.

If you're doing this for the first time, you should think hard about what you offer the world and develop a theme or topic that is close to your heart. Podcasting can be a thankless endeavor. Sure, you can look at your analytics and see how many people are listening or downloading your episodes, but chances are, you'll never hear from the majority of them. Every time you podcast, you'll feel as though you are sitting in a room talking to yourself. And in many ways, that's precisely what is happening.

It takes time to build your audience, and for the first several months, you will be talking to yourself. Therefore, you need to be intrinsically motivated to sit down week after week, planning, recording, and producing your episodes.

Will it pay off? Possibly. Even with the most detailed research, there is no guarantee that people will connect with your podcast. You can book the most amazing guests, hire the slickest postproduction audio editor, and create the most fantastic intro music, but none of that can guarantee dedicated listeners.

But for thriving authors who want to become podcasters, the best approach is always to play the long-tail game. Focus on your expertise and what you're passionate about, and that will give you the best chance of attracting others who are like you. You can chase trends, and you might get lucky, but more often than not, you'll lose at that game.

DON'T IGNORE OTHER PODCASTS IN THE SAME INDUSTRY OR CATEGORY BY J. THORN

You set your alarm for 5 a.m. You climbed out of bed and walked to a dark corner of the living room, pushed the cat off your chair, and sat down to force yourself to type words through bleary eyes before the rest of your family gets up to start their day.

You go to work and spend eight or ten hours pleasing your boss, hitting your sales projections, filing the reports you're being paid to write. When you get home, you've got family responsibilities, you've got to pay the bills, take the dog for a walk, clean up the kitchen.

Now the day is done, and maybe even you've done some marketing or advertising work. What do you do next?

So, you say you want to start a podcast? How many podcasts do you listen to weekly? How many podcast subscriptions do you have in the app on your phone? When was the last time you emailed a host of a podcast or commented on the show's page?

If at the end of the day you sit down on the couch to binge Netflix or immerse yourself in video games, there's nothing wrong with that. However, if you want to become a podcaster, you must listen to other podcasts.

I've often heard writers say that they don't have time to read any longer, and that statement always makes me sad. I don't understand how you can be involved in the creative industry and yet not consume the very product you are creating. Imagine a chef who did not eat at other restaurants or a personal trainer who ignored the trends in personal fitness.

If you want to be a podcast producer, you must first be a podcast listener.

You should listen to a wide variety of podcasts. First of all, identify the two or three shows that best represent the type of show you want to produce. If you know you want to podcast about the publishing industry, you should be listening to several shows focused on the publishing industry by people you know and trust.

Also, subscribe to other podcasts outside of your industry but make them ones you enjoy. Maybe it's the production value, or the storytelling, or the host's personality? Whatever the reason, it doesn't matter. Just make sure you know why you enjoy those podcasts because those are the elements you are going to want to incorporate into your own.

I know what you're saying. By the time I get to that point in my day, I'm not in a mood to listen to my spouse, let alone podcasts. I'm exhausted. I just want to go to bed. That's a legitimate concern, but there are ways around it. For example, you could listen to podcasts on your phone during the breaks in your day. Maybe it's during your commute, or on your lunch break, or perhaps when you're walking the dog? Those ideas are obvious because podcasts are made to be consumed while doing other things as opposed to video or reading, which requires 100% of your focused attention.

One way you can take advantage of the medium is to adjust your listening speed. No, it doesn't make the host sound like a chipmunk. The technology in most podcast players has improved tremendously, to the point where you can speed up without distorting the quality. Up to a point.

Start by slightly increasing the playback speed. Normal playback speed defaults to a setting of 1. Pushing it to 2 means the speed is doubled. Therefore, start by bumping your playback speed from 1 to 1.2 or 1.3. You'll barely notice the difference, and then, your hearing will acclimate to that speed. Each time you feel as though you've adjusted, bump up your playback speed another decimal point or two, and you'll be surprised how quickly you can get to 2 or 2.5 times normal playback speed and still be able to understand and retain information in the episode. This will give you double (or more) the amount of time to consume podcasts in the same number of minutes.

Don't feel obligated to listen to every single episode of the show, even if you've subscribed. Depending on your podcast player settings, if you are subscribed, then the episode is being downloaded, and the host is getting credit for the listen, whether you finish listening to the episode or not. Either way, your time is precious, and if a particular episode is not resonating with you, then you should feel free to skip to the end or leave it unfinished. Just like a good book, there are so many podcasts and so many podcast episodes that you don't want to waste precious time on ones that don't inform or entertain you.

Like a young guitarist learning blues scales, you'll eventually incorporate what you like from the podcasts you listen to into your new version. There isn't a new podcast format that you are going to pioneer. Like the blues, your podcast format will be a derivative of something that already exists, which is fine because people want something that they know but with a unique twist, which is where you come in. You can bring your voice and personality to the show, and even though you are saying things that other people are saying, you will be saying them in your own way, and that is what listeners desire.

Although it should go without saying, if you are not a fan of podcasts, starting a podcast is probably not a good idea. Furthermore, you need to be listening to other podcasts that are like the one you want to create so that you understand what people are looking for and how you can develop and deliver it in a unique way.

You can still watch Netflix and play video games, but make sure you are turning yourself into a podcast fan before you pick up your microphone.

Don't Expect to Make Fast or Big Money by J. Thorn

Book sales are slumping. You've checked all of your dashboards, and the news isn't good. Royalties are down, and that big plan you had for the nine-book series is looking much less viable than it did when you were planning it. You still have to pay your cover designer and your editor. You have multiple subscriptions to essential services to run your publishing business. With ongoing expenses, can you afford to invest in a podcast?

Can you generate revenue with your podcast? You're listening to some of the most prolific and accomplished podcasters in the industry. You can see that they have corporate sponsorship or a healthy pool of patrons, and they seem to be making money from their podcasts.

Is it that simple? Can you start a podcast and simply flip the switch to make money? It might be possible, but it is not something that is going to happen as soon as you upload your MP3 files.

The great thing about being an independent publisher is the ability to create your revenue streams. Yes, we all want to make enough book royalties to make a living, but that isn't always possible, and it changes over time. Therefore, many authors subsidize their income by doing other things such as freelance work, ghostwriting, author services, and podcasting. With the current lure of podcasting, that might seem to be the best choice if you are looking for ways to create more revenue.

On the surface, the ROI of a podcast is quite grim. As we've already seen, most podcasts don't last beyond seven episodes, and those that do take months or years to build a sizable enough audience to generate revenue. And for those types of podcasts, the revenue is indirect as opposed to direct. Podcasters use the show as a lead generator, or the top of the sales funnel where they are selling products or services to their audience. This is legitimate, and because podcasts are free, they can be some of the most effective content marketing that you can do. But expecting to draw a direct line from podcast production to revenue is not realistic.

There are several ways to monetize a podcast. The most direct method is a listener-supported podcast. Using a platform like Patreon, podcasters can ask for continued patronage from their listeners. This is usually set up as an automated monthly contribution in exchange for some kind of extra value that podcasters deliver to their patrons because the podcast itself, in most cases, is free. Therefore, patrons will receive bonus episodes or exclusive downloadable materials created exclusively for them by the podcaster.

Another way to monetize a podcast is through corporate sponsorship. The barrier to entry for sponsorship is higher than it is for a patron-supported show because businesses and companies want to see evidence of your audience. It is common practice for podcasters to share their download and listener analytics with a potential sponsor. The sponsor wants to know that their ad dollars are targeted at their ideal customers. The good news, unlike more traditional media advertising or sponsorship, is that you don't need to have numbers in the hundreds of thousands or millions. Women who tune in to the "Female Knitters and Cat Lovers Podcast" will buy loads of yarn, so if you own a yarn company, this podcast would be a great one for you to sponsor. The sponsorship spots are not being broadcast like a commercial to the general population. Instead, the product is being shown only to the people who regularly use it or one like it.

Ad placement is a third way to monetize a podcast. Unlike sponsorship, which would require the host to provide some sort of testimonial or real-world experience with the product, ad placement functions in much the same way as commercials do on broadcast television. Whether it's static or dynamic ad placement, an ad service will pay a small percentage of revenue to the podcaster or in exchange for running ads at the beginning, middle, or end of the show. Often, the service is aggregated, and the company that runs the ad platform will decide which spots run and where. As a podcaster, you have less control over the commercial messages shared with your audience than you would with a more traditional sponsorship situation.

Using your podcast as a way to generate business is acceptable, ethical, and done all the time. Whether it's a book, a course, or a service, you can offer it to your audience, and once you have earned their trust, you will also earn their business. There are entire books written on how to sell to your podcast audience, and once you decide on the medium that suits you best, you should do your research on it.

In an ideal world, you could maximize all of these revenue-generating ideas for your podcast. You might not necessarily do them all at the same time, and you probably wouldn't try monetizing your podcast as soon as you launch it. Still, the long-term opportunity for revenue generation can be quite significant if you stick with it long enough.

My good friend Joanna Penn makes good affiliate income from her podcast, which has been running for ten years. It might not take you that long to begin making a profit, but you should not expect to instantly monetize a brand-new show.

Take it slow and focus on being an excellent podcaster who serves an audience that needs help. If you continue to do that regularly and you put your best effort forward, you will eventually build an audience. And once you have an audience, you'll have an opportunity to monetize your podcast, whether that is directly or indirectly.

But do understand that the immediate ROI of the show is going to be negative. You are going to invest quite a bit into your podcast for a long time before it starts making you money. But that shouldn't stop you from working toward that goal. There is no reason why you can't authentically serve an audience and make money while doing so, which is the very definition of a successful small business.

Have big dreams for your podcast, but make sure those come with realistic expectations.

MARKETING

In this section, Daniel Willcocks explores the topic of "Marketing," identifying nine core things that successful authors don't do.

Here's a quick summary of the valuable lessons you can expect to learn in this section:

"Don't Mistake 'Marketing' for 'Sales'" – Marketing and sales have a lot in common, however, one is a mindset and one is an outcome. Dan guides you through how one does not preclude the other, and how marketing should be the umbrella over your entire author business.

"Don't Buy Book 'Art'" – The moment your reader places eyeballs on your product, there's a very short amount of time in which they'll decide to buy or leave. Dan discusses the difference between book "art" and book "covers" and how crucial it is to ensure that you're spending money on the right product. After all, despite the old adage, people *do* judge books by their covers.

"Don't Break Reader Trust" – Trust is the bond that connects reader with author. Trust is the glue that holds the process together and helps you to build a sustainable career. Dan examines the pitfalls of breaking readers' trust while providing tangible methods to ensure that your readers love you from the bottom of their hearts and never give up on you.

"Don't Think of the Short Game" – The true secret to a successful author career lies in sustainability and longevity. Rome wasn't built in a day, and that goes for your author career, too. Dan explores why short-term thinking is dangerous and will actually take you more time to achieve your dreams of living in a cabin and writing all day, while also taking a dive into common mistakes that authors make early in their journey.

"Don't Care About Vanity Metrics" – We all know that numbers mean something important—scientists explore data on the daily—but too many of us pay attention to the wrong statistics. In a world saturated with social media platforms begging for likes and follows, as well as terms like ACOS, CPC, and impressions, how do we sift through the muck and find the diamonds that will push us further ahead? Dan breaks down the metrics that mean zero in your business, and those that will have an impact on your sales and growth as an author.

"Don't Rush Launches" – A launch can have the same nervous excitement as New Year's Eve. The promise is unlimited, the way ahead is uncertain and thrilling, yet far too many authors squander what is arguably their greatest shot at reaching readers and activating the algorithms. In this modern age, artificial intelligence is king, and we have to respect the robots. Dan discusses the importance of your launch and ways to ensure that you give your book your best chance of success.

"Don't Forget the Fans" – What are authors without their readers? How many authors are aware of the layers of fandom? Are you serving the right readers? Looking after those who *adore* you? Dan believes that too much attention is paid to recruiting new readers, while not enough attention is focused on maintaining readers and nurturing the superfans, too.

"Don't Hide Their Wallets" – The world has changed, and now, you must pay to play. It's not just advertising, either. It's covers, it's editing, it's doing whatever you can to ensure that you've got the most professional, high-quality product to offer to potential readers. Once upon a time, writers could find thousands of readers with just a sprinkling of pocket lint. Dan believes those times are gone and he prepares you for the road ahead.

"Don't Stagnate" – The world moves faster every day. Not physically... Though, maybe it does. The technological world does, however, and the onus is on you to keep up. Perpetual learners and those who can adapt to what life throws their way are the ones who are thriving. Just because a marketing method worked a year ago doesn't mean that it will now. Dan helps you to navigate this fast-paced publishing world and encourages you to ignite your curiosity about... well... everything.

DON'T MISTAKE "MARKETING" FOR "SALES" BY DANIEL WILLCOCKS

Ah... Marketing. The duck-billed platypus of the author business world. We know it exists, we love what it can offer to the menagerie of strange and exotic professions that spring from the Internet, but few of us actually know the truth behind this enigmatic creature, choosing instead to simplify what can fit our narrow worldviews.

"A platypus is just a beaver."

"It's a furry duck."

"It's nothing more than a wet cat."

But what *is* marketing?

When an author thinks of marketing, they likely visualize sales spreadsheets, social media platforms, and pretty pictures. I should know. I worked in corporate marketing for over half a decade. We were affectionately called the "Art and Sales Team" by everyone else who worked in other parts of the business.

That did not make me happy.

Not because we didn't do those things. We had an art team, we had copywriters, and we had analysts looking at the bottom line of statistics to ensure that we were bringing in income, but the range of skills of the marketing team went far beyond that.

You may be asking, "What does any of this have to do with my author business?"

My answer is, "Everything."

Marketing is a core fundamental facet of the thriving author lifestyle. The milking stool of your author business consists of:

- your product (books and affiliate properties)
- finance (income and expenditure)
- business strategy (systems, procedures, targets, goals, etc.)

You may notice that marketing doesn't exist as one of those three legs of the milking stool.

That's because it is not a standalone leg of the business.

Marketing exists within all three of those branches of your business. Marketing funnels into sales (finance), it encompasses author brand and product message (products), and uses statistical evidence to inform the direction of your business and any development of your author strategies (business).

This does not make marketing greater than the rest. In fact, it's symbiotic with the others. Without marketing, you'll struggle to unite the elements of your business and understand its drive and purpose. Without a product, business strategy, and financial plans, you've got nothing to market. Without marketing uniting these three prongs, you've got chaos.

Unrectifiable chaos.

When it comes to sales, we need to understand that these are a key measure by which to evaluate your success, and many authors (rightly) use the overall annual income of their author business as a benchmark to aim toward future, more profitable targets, but thriving authors think bigger than that. Thriving authors know that sales aren't the only indication of success. Nor are they the be-all and end-all of their marketing strategy.

When building a business, no matter what your core strategy is, you have to keep in mind the overall image of your business. The publishing industry term is "author brand." How are you being perceived by customers? What message are you trying to send? What do you have that transcends the mere act of writing books? A few years back, author brand was simply known as your "reputation" as a business. What is the common theme tying your books together? Why should people buy and read your works? What is your why?

Try and put a sales figure on "reputation." You can't. It's hard to quantify.

When a soccer player scores a goal, the fans go wild, and they celebrate the goal. For a moment, both player and spectator are bound together in the joy of the sport. However, it takes a hell of lot of other components to get a soccer player, basketball player—whichever sport you play—to score in their chosen game. Players train, they study their competitors and their tactics, they ask questions, they rest, they recover, they push the boundaries of their sport.

Being a thriving author amounts to the same thing. Those sales of your book may feel great, and knowing that your work is being read is a euphoric feeling, but what about all of the work that goes before that? What about your market research into your genre? What about all of the effort that goes into positioning your book so that it stands its greatest chance of success? How about studying the algorithms of the major publishing platforms? Quizzing your readers? Asking for feedback and reviews?

All of this and more goes into marketing that book. Marketing is about building trust with your readers so that they come back and want more of what you're offering. You may look at your annual net sales and feel satisfied, but the hidden currency is really the trust that readers have offered in taking the gamble to spend time with you and your words. They didn't have to pick you or your book, but they did, and that's likely because you've done something right along the way with your marketing.

There's a whole mega-mash of marketing tactics that we could go into, but that's highly individualized, and that could be a whole book in itself. Marketing is more than simply reducing your advertising platform to a post on Facebook or Instagram. It's more than sending a newsletter once a month. Thriving authors understand and embrace the truth behind marketing, recognizing the many-headed hydra and taming it, one head at a time. Thriving authors know that they have to keep trying new things, and playing with different platforms in order to ensure that the books sell in the long run.

To market effectively is to bring this all together with the "RACE" acronym, understanding the reader journey in depth.

- R=Reach

- A=Acquire
- C=Convert
- E=Engage

To market is to *Reach* new readers and find ways to bring them into your writing ecosystem. To market is to *Acquire* those readers and bring them closer to you as they turn into curious potential fans. To market is to *Convert* those potentials into genuine sales, nurturing those who have taken a chance on you. To market is to *Engage* your current readers, and ensure that they keep coming back for more.

Thriving authors know that marketing, once fully embraced, is the most powerful tool they can brandish. Marketing is the story behind the story, the journey the reader takes. Marketing is an adventure that you take with your customer, one step at a time.

"There is no sale without the story." – Gary Vaynerchuk

Thriving authors know that sales are just a metric, marketing is the combined effort of smart tactics, an agile mindset, and delivering value and delight to your hungry consumer base.

Don't Buy Book "Art" by Daniel Willcocks

"Cover art serves one purpose, and one purpose only, to get potential customers interested long enough to pick up the book to read the back cover blurb." —— Larry Correia

The cover of your book is *the* number one conversion tool that you have in your thriving author's tool belt.

The journey to getting a reader to your book's sales page is a long one, and for every reader, it's different. They might have seen your book on a friend's Facebook page, they might have spotted one of your sponsored adverts, your book might have ranked on the best-seller charts, or you could have been featured on a podcast. Perhaps they liked your vibe. Whatever the reason was for clicking through to the sales page and pressing the buy button, we all know how difficult it can be to get readers to even notice your book. But if you've done your marketing homework, the first thing they are going to notice is your book cover.

If your cover doesn't meet their expectations, it's, "Bye-bye, Felicia."

There are a number of reasons why a book cover wouldn't convert a potential customer into an avid reader. Thriving author know that there is a psychological component to book covers (not that you need to have an MSc in psychology to understand this). Readers become familiar with the look of book covers that reflect stories in their favorite genre. They recognize the appearance of covers of the types of books they like to buy most. The cover art themes in their preferred genre led to previous positive reading experiences, so they might purchase something that looks similar. If their attention is grabbed by a book cover that practically demands, "Pick up this book, now! It looks amazing!" they might not even know why it appeals to them. But thriving author know. It's like they spotted a familiar face in a crowded room of strangers. That's the marketing appeal of a well-strategized book cover.

Finding the right book cover to wrap around your book is the fundamental difference between a book that rakes in the dough, and a book that does not. A bad book cover or one that does not resemble any from their familiar genre may still sell your book to *someone*, but a thriving author wants *everyone* who is interested in their genre to buy the book.

"Good cover design is not only about beauty... it's a visual sales pitch. It's your first contact with a potential reader. Your cover only has around 3 seconds to catch a browsing reader's attention. You want to stand out and make them pause and consider, and read the synopsis." —— Eeva Lancaster,

Marketing with book covers starts with the design process. Thriving authors know the difference between a book cover and a piece of art. A book cover is a design that is specifically crafted to communicate the book's theme, genre, and feel to a reader. It should be a promise to the reader of what's to come. It shouldn't be an accurate portrayal of a particular scene within the book (with a few exceptions). It should be *designed* by a *designer* who specializes in cover *design* for your genre, and it should convert to sales.

A piece of art is a pretty picture that may please the eye, but it does little for the reader. Slap the Mona Lisa on the front cover of your fantasy book, and it might sell, but boy, will your readers be pissed.

We all suffer from this in the beginning of our author journeys. In the early days, it's easy to find a striking image on the Internet and think that slapping some text over the top will sell books. It's cheaper. It does the job. And, hey, it looks fantastic.

Right?

However, as time wears on and we strap on our thriving author boots, we realize that there is far more to design than the average writer can understand. We may forego hiring the pro designer because of financial constraints. Or we may think we can do better than the masterpiece covers that they've created, but let me ask you a question: Would you let a cover designer write your story?

This may seem like an extreme example, and this isn't to disparage those designers who also write, but it illustrates the point. The reason that great designers can earn upward of $300 for their designs is because they produce great work. They sell. They have spent years honing their craft, studying the placement of text, trawling through databanks of fonts and stock images, and refining their process until they can create something powerful that speaks to the reader.

Likewise, you've spent years honing *your* craft, studying writing processes, researching story, and putting fingers to keyboard until you reached the point that you can hit publish. Why go through all of that effort to fall at the final hurdle with a piece of art that doesn't sell?

Thriving authors find professional book cover designers. They pay the necessary costs to ensure that their book catches the right eyes and makes back their investment tenfold. They understand that you need to spend money to make money, and that there are no corners you can cut with art and book cover design. Your book blurb, sales page, keywords, and categories may be perfect, but if the book cover is subpar, it's just not going to sell.

Trust me.

If you're struggling with finances, you can still attract prospective readers with pre-made covers, as long as they come from a credible source. While custom covers are always better, a pre-made cover can be snatched up for less than $100. It doesn't *have* to be expensive (though the better designers often charge more for good reason), but if you can find the right recommendations from readers within your genre, you may be able to hire an up-and-coming designer while their covers are still affordable.

As long as you're working your way into the best possible situation for your current circumstances, that's progress. Start with a pre-made cover and move on later to a full custom design if and when you can. But remember that to make this a sustainable business, you need to deliver the quality that your readers demand. That quality starts with the best book cover that you can afford at the time. The book cover will be the first thing the readers see of your book, and remember, you have three seconds for that visual pitch.

Don't Break Reader Trust
by Daniel Willcocks

"Relationships are built on trust. Trust drives revenue." — , INC.

It's widely underestimated how much value comes from earning a reader's trust in your product. Many authors get swept away in the pageantry of writing, of basking in the reviews, or diving into gold coins like Scrooge McDuck. They make promises to their readers that may later get cast aside because another opportunity glints and catches their eye and they don't follow through.

The thriving author secret to consistent, regular sales comes from keeping readers happy, and the number-one way to keep readers happy is to deliver on your promises.

Think about your favorite TV show, or maybe a podcast or radio segment that you live for each week. Choose something that comes out weekly, or monthly, that you just *have* to tune into.

I'm certain there's something that springs to mind.

Now imagine that that show changes its schedule without warning. Imagine if *Game of Thrones* decided to just not broadcast that week, and instead waits another three weeks to show episode seven with no communication or valid explanation. Imagine if your 5 o'clock drive-time radio station ditched its comedy segment in favor of a death metal medley without so much as a warning.

I'd imagine that you'd be somewhat annoyed. If you're like me, you'd look to fill the time you reserved to enjoy that particular show with something else. Something reliable and familiar. There are a thousand forms of entertainment out there in the world, why stick around for something that's only going to let you down?

Attention and trust are the greatest currencies in the world. That's what every filmmaker, podcaster, writer, reader, journalist, ad agency—you name it—are fighting for. We're not just fueled by gold coins and green notes anymore, the world is fighting to grab our attention.

And, therein, is the battle.

Thriving authors understand that, once you've hooked a reader, you fight tooth and claw to keep them. If you promise to deliver a book in a month's time, that's what you do. If you tell your readers that there'll be six books in this series, they'll expect you to live up to that promise. Readers don't care what's going on in your personal life (for the most part), they just want the goods. If they don't get it, well there's a whole ocean of media ready to take them away and treat them the way they should be treated.

That's not to say that you have to commit to rapid-release schedules or push yourself further than your limits allow. The key message here is that the cleaner your communications with your reader are (from initial discovery of you and your work, to their first purchases, to engaging with you through social media, or newsletters, etc.), the greater the chance you stand of making your business successful. It's empowering. You are still in the driver's seat, you've just got to plan your promises carefully.

Every step of the reader journey brings with it a new promise of the story you're presenting, and of your brand.

Think about it. When you go online to buy a book, the first thing you'll likely see is the book cover. The book cover tells a story; it details the theme, the feel, the genre, maybe it also gives you a peek at the characters inside the book, or the world, or the power dynamics and struggles. You look at that cover, and you think, "Yes. This is a story I can get on board with."

The reader then looks at your book blurb and investigates the story further. Already, we are looking at cohesion of your journey, hoping that everything lines up. Does the book cover match the blurb? Does your book cover show dragons, and yet, the blurb doesn't mention dragons at all? The reader will be looking for these things. If these two don't match, you've already broken the reader's trust, and they're on to new and better things.

Lying gets you nowhere in this game. Thriving authors know that one of the main paths to success is to play the game. To ensure that your book cover matches your blurb. To make sure that your blurb gives a realistic view of your story. That your story fits the genre and theme and feel that you promised from the moment your reader set their hungry eyes on the book cover. That your book fits the right categories and follows the correct genre tropes.

If you can lead a reader through that journey and leave them satisfied, then you're on to a winner.

Every step of interaction with a reader can either push them closer to your inner circle of superfans (which we'll touch on later) or shove them back toward the ledge where you'll fall off their book radar forever. Simple things can gain reader trust—and keep it. From remaining consistent with the quality of your stories, to writing in the same genre, to sticking to your deadlines and delivering on your promises, thriving author keep their promises.

The key across all of these facets is to underpromise, but overdeliver. Wow your audience with the consistency of your prose. If they liked one of your books, there's no reason they shouldn't enjoy another one. Only by drawing in those regular readers who look to you and rely on you to entertain them can you truly make this a career. Repeat customers are key — they are repeat customers because they trust you.

Trust is one of the hardest things to gain, even outside of writing, and it's incredibly easy to lose. Break that trust, and your readers are gone. If you had your pick of every single chocolate bar in the entire world, and you tasted one that you thought you liked, but it turned out to be sour and filled with fungus, would you just move onto something else that would satisfy your palate?

Netflix, Amazon, Apple, Google, HBO, Nook, chain bookstores — all of these companies and organizations are vying for your readers' attention.

Cheat on them, and they'll cheat on you—without ever turning back.

"Cover art serves one purpose, and one purpose only, to get potential customers interested long enough to pick up the book to read the back cover blurb." —— Larry Correia

The cover of your book is *the* number one conversion tool that you have in your thriving author's tool belt.

The journey to getting a reader to your book's sales page is a long one, and for every reader, it's different. They might have seen your book on a friend's Facebook page, they might have spotted one of your sponsored adverts, your book might have ranked on the best-seller charts, or you could have been featured on a podcast. Perhaps they liked your vibe. Whatever the reason was for clicking through to the sales page and pressing the buy button, we all know how difficult it can be to get readers

to even notice your book. But if you've done your marketing homework, the first
thing they are going to notice is your book cover.

If your cover doesn't meet their
expectations, it's, "Bye-bye, Felicia."

There are a number of reasons
why a book cover wouldn't convert a potential customer into an avid reader. Thriving
author know that there is a psychological component to book covers (not that
you need to have an MSc in psychology to understand this). Readers become
familiar with the look of book covers that reflect stories in their favorite
genre. They recognize the appearance of covers of the types of books they like
to buy most. The cover art themes in their preferred genre led to previous
positive reading experiences, so they might purchase something that looks
similar. If their attention is grabbed by a book cover that prac-

tically demands, "Pick up this book, now! It looks amazing!" they might not even know why it appeals to them. But thriving author know. It's like they spotted a familiar face in a crowded room of strangers. That's the marketing appeal of a well-strategized book cover.

Finding the right book cover to wrap around your book is the fundamental difference between a book that rakes in the dough, and a book that does not. A bad book cover or one that does not resemble any from their familiar genre may still sell your book to *someone*, but a thriving author wants *everyone* who is interested in their genre to buy the book.

"Good cover design is not only about beauty... it's a visual sales pitch. It's your first contact with a potential reader. Your cover only has around 3 seconds to catch a browsing reader's attention. You want to stand out and make them pause and consider, and read the synopsis." —— Eeva Lancaster, *Being Indie: A No Holds Barred, Self-Publishing Guide for Indie Authors*

Marketing with book covers starts with the design process. Thriving authors know the difference between a book cover and a piece of art. A book cover is a design that is specifically crafted to communicate the book's theme, genre, and feel to a reader. It should be a promise to the reader of what's to come. It shouldn't be an accurate portrayal of a particular scene within the book (with a few exceptions). It should be *designed* by a *designer* who specializes in cover *design* for your genre, and it should convert to sales.

A piece of art is a pretty picture that may please the eye, but it does little for the reader. Slap the Mona Lisa on the front cover of your fantasy book, and it might sell, but boy, will your readers be pissed.

We all suffer from this in the beginning of our author journeys. In the early days, it's easy to find a striking image on the Internet and think that slapping some text over the top will sell books. It's cheaper. It does the job. And, hey, it looks fantastic.

Right?

However, as time wears on and we strap on our thriving author boots, we realize that there is far more to design than the average writer can understand. We may forego hiring the pro designer because of financial constraints. Or we may think we can do better than the masterpiece covers that they've created, but let me ask you a question: Would you let a cover designer write your story?

This may seem like an extreme example, and this isn't to disparage those designers who also write, but it illustrates the point. The reason that great designers can earn upward of $300 for their designs is because they produce great work. They sell. They have spent years honing their craft, studying the placement of text, trawling through databanks of fonts and stock images, and refining their process until they can create something powerful that speaks to the reader.

Likewise, you've spent years honing *your* craft, studying writing processes, researching story, and putting fingers to keyboard until you reached the point that you can hit publish. Why go through all of that effort to fall at the final hurdle with a piece of art that doesn't sell?

Thriving authors find professional book cover designers. They pay the necessary costs to ensure that their book catches the right eyes and makes back their investment tenfold. They understand that you need to spend money to make money, and that there are no corners you can cut with art and book cover design. Your book blurb, sales page, keywords, and categories may be perfect, but if the book cover is subpar, it's just not going to sell.

Trust me.

If you're struggling with finances, you can still attract prospective readers with pre-made covers, as long as they come from a credible source. While custom covers are always better, a pre-made cover can be snatched up for less than $100. It doesn't *have* to be expensive (though the better designers often charge more for good reason), but if you can find the right recommendations from readers within your genre, you may be able to hire an up-and-coming designer while their covers are still affordable.

As long as you're working your way into the best possible situation for your current circumstances, that's progress. Start with a pre-made cover and move on later to a full custom design if and when you can. But remember that to make this a sustainable business, you need to deliver the quality that your readers demand. That quality starts with the best book cover that you can afford at the time. The book cover will be the

first thing the readers see of your book, and remember, you have three seconds
for that visual pitch.

Don't Think of the Short Game by Daniel Willcocks

"I've learned that the long-game is the shortcut." —— Richie Norton

A thriving author is a marathon runner, not a sprinter.

In the beginning of your author journey, it's easy for desperation to sweep you away as you try to peddle your books to strangers and climb the rankings ladder. You hop onto Twitter for the fiftieth time that day and shout into the void, screaming about your book and trying to think of a creative way to get someone to buy a copy. You spend $200 on a Kindle so that you can give it away and collect email responses in return, but you pay no mind to the types of readers you're acquiring as your list goes from 0 to 1,000 in a matter of a month. You pester more-successful authors to blurb your books, to give you advice, to show you the way. Everything's about you.

And that works. For a short time.

In your first few months, you may sell a couple of hundred books. You may receive a few kind responses from other authors. You may build a four-digit list in record time. Wow, you made $100 on your books? The journey is starting...

There is a problem, though. Every action you make has a knock-on effect and may, in many cases, slow your progress.

When your next book release rolls around, you hit your four-digit list with a news blast and tell them how amazing your book is and why they should buy it. You eagerly wait by the computer and watch for the sales, but only a handful trickles in. You go away, make a coffee, come back, and there is no movement. The needle is still.

You can't understand it. What about those 3,000 people you emailed about your book? They're on your list. Why don't they love you? Why won't they buy the book?

There could be myriad factors going on here. Maybe your cover isn't up to snuff, or perhaps your blurb isn't great. Maybe you've priced the book too high, or too low.

My guess would be that your list isn't as great as you think it is. When you gave away that Kindle and got a surge of people adding themselves to your list, you didn't pick readers who gave a damn about you. They wanted a chance at a free Kindle. Who wouldn't? A chance at a $200 e-reader in exchange for subscribing to a mailing list, I'm in!

There was no vetting process. You offered a prize to anyone. Your list could be full of romance readers, sci-fi readers, Western readers, erotica, horror, thriller, any number of readers who didn't care about the first book in your epic fantasy trilogy. There could be people on that list who only wanted to win a free prize so they could give the e-reader to their son or niece. They didn't care about you.

They didn't want your new book.

You wanted the numbers, but you didn't think about the quality of the people joining that list. It's these kinds of quick-fire, (sometimes) desperate decisions that burn out authors. Why put in all of that work, and spend all of that money for a launch promotion, if you're not going to get anything back?

And what about all of those authors you messaged for advice? Why won't they help you? You log onto Twitter or Facebook and find that you've been blocked. You shoot them more messages and they don't reply. You can't understand why they won't help you, even though you've given them nothing in return; all you've previously done is hounded them until they responded.

Thriving authors know that every decision you make has a long tail. Lists often take time to grow. Marketing strategies last for years at a time. Your reputation (author brand) is one of the slowest things to build, and you want to be damn sure that you're making it the strongest you possibly can.

Despite all of the courses selling shortcuts, and the marketers who promised overnight success, for most indie authors, the reality is different. A career in writing takes time to cultivate. You keep watering those seeds until the field yields its crop, in its own time. You don't chuck a seed in the soil and dig it up the next day, you wait until the growth process is complete. *Then* you harvest.

A thriving author knows that the best way to secure success is by consistently putting out quality books into the market. A thriving author knows that his backlist is a valuable asset. A thriving author understands that a completed series will, in most cases, sell better than a series in progress. A thriving author knows that building a strong author brand is crucial to their success.

All of these things take time. Sales take time to grow. Oftentimes, the path to indie success is exponential, so don't spend all of your creative energy making rash and expensive marketing decisions in the beginning, just to shift a few books.

Be deliberate, think of the long game, and make sure that you're not starting your career by setting yourself up for failure later on the journey. Quality and intention are the keywords here. If you write horror, find the communities where the readers gather and become a part of that community. It all takes time, and the ones who turn the hobby into a true career are the ones who prove that they're in this for the long haul.

DON'T CARE ABOUT VANITY METRICS BY DANIEL WILLCOCKS

"Just because you *can* measure everything doesn't mean that you *should*." – W. Edward Deming

Ah, the scourge of the world of marketing.

In the years before the Internet, it used to be difficult to measure the success of campaigns and marketing efforts, outside of simply looking at the bottom sales line. This brings us back to why many used to think of marketers as salespeople. Everything they did was measured by currency.

Fast-forward several decades and technology exploded, giving us the Internet, unbelievably fast computers, and a whole array of methods to track and monitor the activity of our projects. If we share a video with our Facebook fans, we have a dozen different metrics to access: everything from likes, to engagements, to overall time spent by individuals watching the video.

We're inundated with possible methods to measure our success. Our Amazon ads include ACOS (average cost of sale), impressions, clicks, and more. Facebook ads offer a similar dashboard. We can use tracking links to find out where people are finding our books, we can measure the engagement on our mailing lists to see how interactive our audience is.

In this world of numbers, data, graphs, and charts, is it any wonder that we can so easily become overwhelmed by trying to work out the best ways to find out if what we're doing is working?

"Vanity metrics" is a relatively new term, and one that a lot of people aren't familiar with. However, a thriving author knows that vanity metrics are any measurements of data that may seem satisfying but offer no real value in the grand scheme of your business.

Here's an example, and one that may strike a chord or that you may find eerily familiar. An author posts on their Facebook page, sharing the fantastic news that they've just released a new book, and that it's now available to buy. This author has 10,000 likes on their Facebook page, and they're waiting for the sales to roll in.

The sales trickle. It's nothing to write home about.

They log onto their dashboard to investigate the data and they can't understand it. Thanks to their boosted post, they've reached over 32,000 people on Facebook. That's incredible! They've spent months building their Facebook base and recruiting people onto the page, so why the hell aren't the sales converting?

It's a similar story on the AMS (Amazon Marketing Services) dashboard. The ad has had 100,000 impressions, which is fantastic! 100,000 impressions is amazing.

Add to that the 15,000 followers on Instagram.

Add to that the 3,000 followers on Twitter.

The 8,000 people subscribed to their newsletter list.

No doubt, up until the point that they tried to sell a book, this author believed themselves successful. They have social proof of tens of thousands of followers across a number of platforms. Many may look from the outside at this author's profiles and label them a success.

But what does it all mean if it's not making the sale?

When I was back in the corporate world, I was once given the task of proving to a colleague that her weekly vlogs to our customers weren't working. She vehemently disagreed, thanks to the 3,000 views that hit that video every week.

I went into research mode, I studied the data, I looked at the value of that particular video and what it meant for our communications. The final picture was not good.

Although the video regularly received around 3,000 views each week, the statistics showed that the average watch time of that six-minute vlog was 10 seconds.

The introduction to that video alone was 20 seconds.

No one made it to the call-to-action at the end. No reliable evidence indicated that people were taking action because of that video.

This proved that, although people were clicking the video, they were not engaged. They didn't want to watch past the introduction. Add to this evidence the additional fact that there were less than five active engagements each week (likes, comments, etc.), and the real story was revealed. The overall views of the video were a vanity metric. It was revered by my colleague because the numbers were high when, in reality, the three hours she spent each week putting the video together to communicate her messages weren't working. No one cared.

It's a harsh reality, but thriving author have to trust the numbers and put their ego aside.

Let's bring this back to our "super popular" author example, and the similarities can easily be drawn. Sure, they have the likes and the followers, but how many fans are engaging with them on a regular basis? If a person with 10,000 followers on Instagram collects a handful of comments and likes per post, are they really successful? If those posts don't convert somewhere down the line to sales, is it worth it at all?

There are a million paid services that offer the chance to buy followers and 10X your social media account overnight but think about the quality of those followers and fans. What's it all worth if they're not actively engaging with you? We live in a social media era where algorithms decide what content your fans will view. If they show no initial interest in your pages, your posts will not be seen by your intended audience as paid ads and trending content may overtake your offerings.

By paying attention to metrics that matter, a thriving author knows that they can accelerate their success. A thriving author knows which data matters and ignores those that simply provide a short-term ego boost with no long-term reward.

DON'T RUSH LAUNCHES BY DANIEL WILLCOCKS

"If you don't have time to do it right, what makes you think you'll have time to do it over?" — Seth Godin

The day that your book launches may just be the happiest day of your life. All of those hours of blood, sweat, tears, and cursing have culminated in the lawful birthing of your book baby into the world.

Launches can be exciting, they can be exhilarating. Launches can brighten your week and instil a sense of euphoria that carries you through the rest of the month.

When they're done right.

A thriving author knows that the book launch is one of the hottest moments of marketing you'll have with your new book because it's the day when all of your pre-work comes together, and you can finally begin to measure its success. It's also what will determine the next steps of your book-marketing strategy, allowing you to dodge, duck, dip, dive, and dodge (hands up if you get that reference) to maximize your success.

Book launches are intense, but they are critical. A book launch can often be the make-or-break event that positions your book between a meteoric rise in the charts and a total flop of nightmare proportions, particularly if you're an indie. The vast majority of online retailers have stepped up their game over the last few years in order to maximize their income and ensure that they're selling the right products to the right customers.

These publishers *want* your books, but they don't *need* them.

These publishers want their customers, *and* they need them.

The bottom line of business states that money needs to be coming into the organization to continue its functional operations. Online stores of all kinds now employ sophisticated algorithms to determine what is worth showing to a potential customer, based off the likelihood of that item selling.

If an online clothing store shows a customer a tank top or a jacket that the customer is not interested in, they lose the customer's attention, and they lose the sale.

If they show the customer a pair of shoes that they're certain will have some impact and lead to a sale, they make the money, and the corporate heads smile gleefully down upon their minions.

It's exactly the same with books. It's easy for authors to think that it's all about simply pushing the sales to whoever will buy the book (family, friends, colleagues, distant relatives), but a thriving author knows to be deliberate in who they're targeting, and the strategy they're employing to reach the right customers as early on in the process as possible.

Let's talk a little about algorithms.

The moment your book goes live online, the algorithms kick in. The minute your book publishes, the cyborg gremlins living inside your online retailer's machinery start using your keywords, book description, and genre to determine the right place to display your book to prospective readers. If you have a surge of sales, you get placed higher in the charts so that more people will see your book, and the sales will keep rolling. The thriving author knows that's a great place to be. Hell, Aunt Agatha knows that's a great place to be.

However, while your book is accelerating up the charts, the gremlins also know that they need to find the right place to store your book if the sales taper off. If you're a horror writer, and you discover that you've made it to #1 in the Sci-Fi > Alien Invasion categories (yes, I'm talking from experience), then you're in turbulent waters. While your book may appear successful, is your book really in the category where it truly belongs? What happens when the hype dies and the reviews come in, slighting the book for not having any mention of aliens or otherworldly goings-on?

The thriving author knows that you have to actively engage the right audiences in order to correctly index your book. They also know that launch day is the single-most important day to impact how many copies of your book you shift over the initial 90 days of sales—commonly known in the business as the 90-day cliff.

Digital bookstores are hungry for new books; they know that readers love brand-new, exciting things. The entire economy is built around new book releases and promotions of what's to come. Except in very rare cases, those initial 90 days will drive the highest number of organic sales to your book, thanks to the hype juice that fuels your book rocket as it hopefully begins its ascent to Millionaire-moon. That single day brings together the culmination of your previous marketing efforts and accelerates you to where a thriving author should belong. High in the charts and ready to ride the wave, baby.

Think about a time when you discovered that your favorite author had a new book on the horizon. Remember the anticipation leading up to that book launch? Remember racing through the pages on the day when you finally got your hands on a copy? That's the kind of hype you want to capitalize on, because every day that passes by and a reader doesn't buy your book, you're already competing with tomorrow's chart-toppers.

While there is always the option to remove and later re-launch a book further on down the line if you fail at your first attempt, a thriving author knows that they only get that one chance to make a true first impression.

Don't waste it.

DON'T FORGET THE FANS BY DANIEL WILLCOCKS

"[D]iehard fans will drive 200 miles to see you sing; they will buy the hardback and paperback and audible versions of your book... [...] If you have roughly a thousand of true fans [...] you can make a living." — Kevin Kelly

Driving a new reader into your own personal corner of the Internet is one of the most difficult challenges to overcome.

We have our techniques and methods, sure, but let's go back to the customer journey of your average reader.

No doubt, your soon-to-be reader already has a roster of authors whom they love and will give anything to read a copy of their latest book. They'll have their favorite genre, they'll have their favorite author style, and they may likely have a specific shelf in their room reserved for their favorite books.

They have a little bit of time to spare until that author releases their next book, so they go browsing online. Although they aren't always aware of this, they're already looking for something similar to what they've read. Something that will give them more of that dopamine hit that keeps them reading. They browse the first page of the charts and are immediately bombarded with a barrage of book covers.

They wonder which one looks the most interesting. Will any of these books deliver on the promises that are kept by their favorite author? They spot your book cover and maybe, at first, they open the free book sample in a separate tab to examine later.

Maybe they buy your book straightaway. What's more likely is that they'll scroll on by and continue searching without actively clicking your book, but the reality is that just seeing a glimmer of your book cover creates a little imprint in their mind. Your name logs somewhere in their brain matter for later.

The next time they visit the store, they see your name again. They don't consciously remember your book, but having seen the cover before, something triggers them to open that sales page and look through the blurb. They add the book to a mental "maybe" pile or might even add it to their wish list. If you're lucky, they hit the "buy" button.

Assuming that they haven't bought the book, maybe they're browsing Facebook a few days later and they see a sponsored post with your name on it. Maybe they're scrolling Instagram and they see your book cover yet again. Perhaps a friend mentions your book in passing, a friend who they trust because they read the same genre.

Now you're beginning to earn their interest. Out of the millions of books and authors online, you're starting to find your way into their conscious mind.

They log your name for later and check out your website. They visit your product page again, debating the possibility of actually taking a chance this time.

This cycle repeats infinitum, until your book is bought. On average, a customer requires 7 interactions before they consider buying your product.

"The Marketing Rule of 7 states that a prospect needs to 'hear' the advertiser's message at least 7 times before they'll take action to buy that product or service." — Kathi Kruse

Fantastic. Great. You've sold the book. Now you move onto the next thing...

Not so fast.

Your part in this journey is far from over. A thriving author knows that the sale isn't the end of the customer experience. Your reader is reading the book. That's a huge step, and you'll have a few extra bucks in your bank account because of it. But if you truly want to make this a sustainable, long-term career, you have to engage that reader and drive them down the last segment of the sales funnel.

Let's recap our "Race" acronym.

- R = Reach
- A = Acquisition
- C = Conversion
- E = Engagement

By the time your reader has bought your book, they're somewhere between stages A and C, but it's in stage E that the magic truly happens, and you can start cultivating what Kevin Kelly coins, "True Fans."

A thriving author knows that their true fans are the staple of a long-term author business. While their competitors spend hours on end plugging Facebook ads and Amazon ads to drive new customers to their books, a thriving author is looking after those who have shown interest and want more. Steps to converting readers to fans include mailing lists, private groups, any kind of communication in which you take them beyond the book and get them to buy into your author ecosystem.

Kevin Kelly argues that you only need 1,000 True Fans in order to make a living from your art. He believes that if 1,000 fans spend an average of $100 on you per year, you are essentially guaranteed a salary of $100,000. (Besides conventional online sales, Kevin Kelly mentioned on his website that he used Kickstarter crowdfunding to publish to his true fans.)

In most businesses, there is not enough attention paid to maintaining and cultivating fans. Businesses like the vanity metric of reaching new customers, while offering little loyalty to those who offer it back. But if you have a solid, stable base of readers who will buy your books every time you release something new, you can make it in this business.

A thriving author knows that the fans are the magic, and they're relatively easy to engage with. Communicate regularly, give them special treatment and advance news, pull their names out of a hat and feature them in a story—the possibilities are endless. Underpromise, overdeliver.

Pay attention to those readers who are paying attention to you. Nurture the relationships you already have and combine this with a campaign that also reaches new readers and brings them into your funnel. It's a delicate balance of the two but looking after your fans pays dividends.

A thriving author also doesn't forget that not all true fans are vocal. A lot of readers don't reach out to authors. That doesn't mean they're not your fans, so combine your knowledge of your sales numbers with those true interactions online in order to get the full scope of who is in it with you for the long haul.

It makes the writer's journey that little bit less lonely, too.

DON'T HIDE THEIR WALLETS BY DANIEL WILLCOCKS

"Pay now, play later; play now, pay later." — John C. Maxwell

Welcome, dear author, to the world of "Pay to Play."

We indie authors have had a good run of it. Since the advent of the Kindle, we've been blessed with the gift of being able to publish our fiction and nonfiction for... well, virtually nothing.

If you wanted to upload a hastily edited manuscript with a thrown-together cover, you absolutely could. There are no restrictions. Kindle publishing is free, but the cost of publishing is time. There are no barriers.

When the first Kindle released in 2007, and authors ran to the KDP dashboard, there was a flurry of success stories borne out of the early adopters. Authors who had been batting their heads against the walls waiting for yet another rejection letter from a traditional publisher suddenly had an audience. Algorithms were in their infancy, and the only thing that mattered were the download numbers. "Free books" were where you initially launched your books for higher visibility and thrilling download numbers to hopefully get the book to chart as a number-one best-seller (before you increased the price), and the funnel was king.

Over the years, the algorithms began to evolve. Amazon experimented with different formats and methods to sell books as the markets only continued to grow. More readers turned to e-books, while more authors than ever were fighting to get their books read. Newsletter promotional sites were at their cheapest and their conversions were the highest they may ever be. Many authors called this the "Kindle gold rush," and as all things in the past are viewed with rose-tinted glasses, they may have been better times.

For some.

For the thriving author, though, it's a new age. The thriving author knows that, while the easy route to success has dissolved into the past, there is still a clear route for those who can brave the obstacles. The thriving author knows that one major problem in the past was the quality of the final product that was delivered to the reader. Anyone with a bank account and the ability to hit the "publish" button could throw together a story and make some money. Over time, algorithms have grown sophisticated enough to let these low-quality works sink to the bottom of the lists, while quality, well-written, well-marketed fiction rises to the top and is seen by the masses.

The funnel is still king, although the market is considerably more crowded than it once was, and therefore, the thriving author knows that the old adage is true: "You have to spend money to make money." Promotional sites thrive on the competitive nature of authors who attempt to outbid each other and fight for visibility on their respective platforms and charts. While there are still some free options out there, the thriving author is aware that a percentage of royalties that goes into your pocket must lead to a percentage of money that goes out.

As with many of the previous essays, let's flip this on its head. If you were an advertising company with an ever-expanding platform, and you had the chance to increase your profit by upping the cost of your services, you'd take it. You'd be stupid not to. If there's demand, you capitalize on that audience and you boost your business accordingly.

Welcome to capitalism, friends.

It's the same for thriving author. If we have a demanding audience, we may increase the cost of our books over time to generate more income. Why not? It's up to the customer to choose whether they want to pay the higher price, so let the audience speak for itself. If the demand starts to drop, then drop your prices. It's a classic stock market strategy.

The thriving author accepts this pay-to-play economy as a reality and doesn't simply bitch about the way things are. To play the long game and to engage readers and maintain their trust, you have to invest. Your wallet should not be a place to store your gold, it should be a veritable transaction machine. Good business dictates that investments should earn back what you spend to produce and publish a book—first and foremost—but you'd be kidding yourself if you think you can make a career in this business without investing some of your hard-earned currency into marketing.

The boundaries of marketing investments do not stop at advertising and promotions, either. The thriving author recognizes that marketing begins from the moment you put the first words on that clean white page. It starts from the story you're writing, to the editors you choose to clean up your work and make it sellable. It extends to the proofreaders who promise a smooth experience for the reader, and straight on through to your creation of the blurb and a book cover that will catch the eye and bring everything together on the sales page.

The thriving author is prepared for all of these costs. We are blessed to work in an industry in which start-up costs of the business are incredibly minimal. If you wanted to start a coffee shop, you'd need to rent a storefront and purchase the machines, the tills, the ingredients, the advertising and marketing promotions, cleaners, staff, as well as pay gas, electricity and water bills, arrange garbage collection, and more. If you wanted to begin work as a bricklayer or electrician, you'd likely need a van, and a whole assortment of tools and parts so that you'd be prepared for any job that might come your way.

What does an author need? A computer, electricity, and an Internet connection.

That's it. That's how lucky we are. So, when it comes to making a sustainable career from this industry, it doesn't seem so bad that the average thriving author spends a minimum of $1,000 on the costs of a single book before they hit publish, does it? That's, of course, not taking into account the costs of advertising and promotion after the book has published, as it begins its journey into the publishing river and straight on down to the sea filled with readers.

The thriving author is prepared to spend. They invest money in the right pieces of the puzzle, and they ensure that they earn back every penny. They understand that you could sulk and look back at the gold-rush days with glossy eyes and a heavy heart, but the true path to success will always lie ahead.

The thriving author is prepared for the journey, using the cash they've spent on marketing as stepping-stones to the top of the best-seller rankings.

DON'T STAGNATE BY DANIEL WILLCOCKS

"The only constant in life is change." — Heraclitus.

The world spins on its axis. Every day we lose the past and gain the present. Insects are born and die, rivers carve new paths as they erode the ground around them, shorelines adjust to the constant bashing of the waves.

And every day, my father yearns for the good ol' days and their swift return. Only, nothing ever stays still, does it?

The last two decades have seen some of the most rapid and dramatic changes in history. Technology has advanced beyond what sci-fi writers could ever have dreamed of in the 1970s. We are constantly connected to everyone, smartphones are now a part of people's bodies, and we can video chat people in the blink of an eye, talking to our friends and family from across the world.

With these technological advances, a distinct rift has grown between two types of people. Those who adopt changing technology, and those who won't. My nan didn't want to surrender her VCR for a DVR. She didn't want the channels to all turn to a digital service. She liked sending Pam her letters.

Well, while she hoped the world would stay the same around her and her bubble would never pop, everything changed. Digital TV became the norm, and any other service expired. Videos and films are no longer released on VHS tapes. She can still send a letter to Pam, of course. But that mailed communication can take from 4-12 days (depending on the delivery service). I can send an email to J. Thorn in three seconds, and he lives on another continent.

All of this is to say that it's very easy, no matter what industry you're in, to yearn for the times when you had things figured out and life seemed simpler. The thriving author understands that that's not the world that we live in. Every year, we are blessed with a new service that allows us to easily connect with readers. Every month, a new expert discovers a secret hack to convert our ads. Every day, new authors are making their mark on the book business and shaping the path ahead.

The thriving author doesn't stagnate. Stagnation will be the death of any business in this day and age. Marketers often refer to the word "agility" to describe their strategies and how they respond to change. Most businesses project a 5-year forecast, but the reality is that every month it is tweaked to respond to the changes in the world.

You *cannot* control the way that the world changes, but you *can* control the way that you respond to it.

The thriving author is prepared for the challenge ahead. They know that, while Wattpad was considered a joke by "true professionals" five years ago, Wattpad.com has since established the careers of dozens, if not hundreds, of new authors who found fame by delivering fan fiction to readers, and who now make their living through writing. They know that, while traditional publishing houses spent years denying the advent of the e-book, choosing instead to stick to their typical publishing schedules, the e-book economy has caught up to them and is fundamentally changing the way they work. Why would a customer want to pay $12.99 for an e-book from a traditionally published author when they can receive the same quality from a hundred other independent thriller writers for $3.99?

The customer speaks, and the customer dictates the market. Your survival in this business is reliant on your ability to respond to ever-changing consumer demands. The businesses that rise to the top are the ones that are prepared for change. They're the ones that are ever-learning, watch the markets, keep an eye on competitors, and push the boundaries to try new things—even if they fail sometimes.

We've seen it time and time again. The High Street consumer experience once denied the online shopping revolution. While thousands of businesses kept their prices high and ignored the birth of Amazon, Jeff Bezos pushed ahead, knowing that he could offer cheaper, more convenient service for the world's customers. Now, 90% of UK shoppers buy on Amazon, with 40% using a Prime subscription. If you had a brick-and-mortar store that sold homeware and your traditional foot traffic was 2,000 customers a day, you've already lost 1,800 of your customers to Amazon.

I may be simplifying this a little bit, but you get the point.

Over the last two decades, I've watched businesses slowly cast their "Clearing Out" sales and hang up their "Closed for Good" signs. The taxi industry has been taken over by Uber, which offers cheaper, faster, more convenient service. Netflix crept up and took out Blockbuster and other video stores with an easier and cheaper way for the world to consume media. Netflix even offered for Blockbuster to buy their service, but the stale giants were so stuck in their ways, stagnating, that soon they couldn't afford to keep their stores open. There are a thousand examples of these cases, and in each one, the common denominator is simple.

The business got comfortable. They didn't build their systems to adapt to change.

Even McDonald's is feeling the effects of this strange new world. After vehemently denying takeaway services to their UK customers for years, recently they have changed their tune. They became agile in the face of adversity, offering a service that can compete with the likes of Domino's, and every Chinese, Cantonese, and Indian takeaway service, even though it's still through a third-party business. Convenience is king, and you don't get to decide what the market does.

The thriving author doesn't stagnate. The thriving author keeps their ears close to the ground and is prepared to change. A dozen times in the last decade, Amazon has changed the way they sell e-books and pay royalties, sometimes to the chagrin of authors who don't earn what they once did during the Kindle gold rush.

Amazon is still experimenting with and tweaking different programs, such as pay for page views, free book promotions, paid ads, and Kindle Unlimited subscriptions. Various programs, such as Kindle Worlds (licensed fan fiction), have come and gone, and the print book service has changed, too, as CreateSpace gave way to KDP's paperback printing service.

As long as its customers are satisfied and treated fairly, and as long as their profit margins are clean and growing, Amazon continues to charge ahead with innovations, as well as make changes that sometimes perplex thriving author who must rise to new challenges caused by those changes.

If a revolutionary change occurs in the book industry that fundamentally affects your earnings and your work, how prepared are you to survive?

There are solutions, of course. The thriving author understands that the way to a successful business that can outlast the competition is diversification. Find multiple revenue streams to feed into your business, and don't rely on one giant conglomerate to feed you.

Consider going wide with your books and e-books on other sales platforms (if your books are not contractually subject to exclusive distribution). Think outside the box by transforming your books into audiobooks, videos, podcasts, and other media that diversifies your product into even more products so that you can add those new revenue streams from different income sources.

You may be feeding off the shark's scraps right now, but what happens when that shark gets greedy?

Market your books like a thriving author. You'll be glad you did!

Personal Finance

As you start reading this section, you might be suppressing a groan... You want to be a thriving author, you want to sell books, but you know that means earning money and dealing with the business side, the—sharp intake of breath—numbers.

Yes, as thriving authors, no matter what path you've taken into this life, at some point you're going to have to deal with "the numbers."

You can't have a career without the money to support it. As authors, too many of us shy away from the numbers and the business side, preferring to focus on the words and the art. Yet, those who choose to embrace money—the thriving authors among us—find it flows faster and in the right direction.

Money isn't a dirty word. You don't have to hate it or be afraid of it. You can embrace it, you can earn it, in fact, you can learn to love it. You have our permission.

In this section, J. Thorn and Sacha Black identify nine things that successful authors don't do when it comes to money. So grab your wallet, brace yourself, and open your mind as we discuss how changing your mindset around money can help you to become a more profitable, financially stable thriving author.

Here's a quick summary of the valuable lessons you can expect to learn in this section:

"Don't Take on Excessive Debt" - Sacha explains why debt will be the death of your business, especially if you're in the red before you've even started. She also shows you why you need to be debt-free before you start your full-time author career.

"Don't Buy Frivolously" - Sacha calls you out. We've all bought expensive gadgets and gizmos. We've all spent money on things we end up never using. She goes on to explain why you have to be honest with yourself and work out whether the item you want will truly help save you time, money, and efficiency in your business or if it's just something you want and can really do without.

"Don't Use Personal Accounts for Business" - This essay discusses how it's an easy mistake to make, but one that over time can be costly both for your reputation as a professional, for your time (having to sift through thousands of statement lines for tax returns), and for your mindset.

"Don't Ignore Cash Flow Planning" - Cash flow planning usually provokes an eye roll, but Sacha explains why it's one of the most important and fundamental tasks a thriving author can do. It's the difference between surviving a financial crisis and kissing goodbye your author dreams. She'll show you why you need to budget and plan for your business's future.

"Don't Ignore Retirement Savings" - We might want to live forever, but our time on this planet is but a fleeting yawn for Mother Earth. This essay discusses why there's always an excuse not to save or invest your money for the future, but it's a fatal error. The essay also explains why you need to shift your mindset and see yourself as an employee. All good bosses treat their employees well and that means saving for their future.

"Don't Focus Only on Books" - Sacha challenges the myth that to be a real author you can only earn money from book sales. She explains why that way of thinking is redundant not only for your personal identification but also because it threatens the financial security of your business.

"Don't Mix Up Passive and Active Income" - This essay explains the difference between active and passive income as well as the times you might need to earn each. Sacha also covers why it's essential to get the balance between the two right, especially early on in your author career.

"Don't Ignore Professionals" - Here we discuss the reluctance so many indie authors have to delegate and outsource work to other professionals. Yet, if you want to continue to grow your financials, then it's essential that you not only seek an accountant, but when you reach financial stability, you seek advisors and wealth managers to help you grow your wealth long into the future.

"Don't Hate Money" - Sacha talks about the poisonous and negative stigmas that many of us grow up with around money. She also delves into how we're taught the wrong mindset from an early age and that hating money only leads us to an impoverished lifestyle. This essay shows you why it's time to open your mind and stop the self-limiting beliefs. It's time to earn and become a thriving author.

Don't Take on Excessive Debt by Sacha Black

There are two types of lessons in life: the ones we learn growing up: manners really do go a long way, don't eat yellow snow—it won't taste good and will probably give you a belly ache—and 1 + 1 =2.

And the other ones—the plethora of other lessons that our parents and loved ones *try* to pass on, but our inner rebels refuse to play student.

Things like, you don't have to wear shin pads to play hockey—but if you don't and you get hit, you're gonna know about it. Or that, yes, your twenty-one-year-old self *can* drink a liter of Southern Comfort in one evening, but you can be assured that you'll puke for a week and will probably need to see a doctor—was it just me who learned that one?

Moving on... These "other" lessons are the kinds of lessons our families *try* to impart on us. But more often than not, we're too stubborn to listen to their advice. Instead we have to learn through the classic "school of hard knocks."

For the vast majority of people, taking on debt is one of those lessons.

Growing up, my mother was militant with money. She was necessarily frugal but that ensured we had luxuries like a holiday every year. Right from first toddling, I learned a money mantra: *save a third, spend a third, use a third.* But it didn't stick. Sure I knew the principle of good money management, but unfortunately, the society I grew up in, and worse, the society my child is growing up in, doesn't foster good money-management skills.

This isn't a political statement, it's a personal observation.

For the kids who want an education all the way up to college, we saddle them with tens or hundreds of thousands of dollars' worth of debt. Society has ushered in a materialistic culture where we need the latest sneakers now, now, now. Oh, and that shiny gadget that costs five hundred dollars is a must, even if you don't have the cash in the bank. Who cares? Just slap it on your plastic and deal with it next month. That's future-you's problem. Present-you wants the "thing."

Somewhere along the lines, something went very wrong.

I know it did for me. I learned the hard way. Education debts piled on top of a car loan, which piled on top of fertility treatment debt. When you're in a $40,000 hole, that thriving author dream feels really far away. And realistically, it is.

Thriving authors know that in order to leave their day jobs they have to reduce their outgoing expenditure as much as possible.

If you owe tens of thousands of dollars, then you're going to have to pay off hundreds of dollars a month.

Let's say you take home $2,000 per month. Your bills for rent, food, and the gym, etc., come to $1,200 a month. But you have debt, and that debt is costing you $800 a month. In this situation, before you could even consider leaving your job, you'd *need* to consistently earn $2,000 from your author business each month. That's at a minimum. There's no change in there, no wiggle room for emergencies or book covers that need designing.

If you left your day job in that kind of financial state, you'd be placing extreme pressure on your creative business to earn money. Earning that kind of cash instantly as an author is a tough job for anyone starting out.

Let's flip this on its head. What if you didn't have debt? Instead of *needing* to earn $2,000 from your writing to cover your bills and debt, if you had no debt, then in that situation, you'd only *need* to earn $1,200. That's a helluva lot easier to achieve than $2,000 a month. It's less pressure, more wiggle room, and no stress because you don't owe anyone anything.

The problem is, debt is so very easy to accrue.

Personal debt

Ever thought, "Oh, I'll just book the family holiday and put it on the credit card and we'll pay it off before we go?"

I know so many people who've done this, and only a small percentage pay it off before they travel. Why? Because they forgot they needed "spending money" for the actual holiday. So, they frantically save spending money, but fate gives them a flat tire. Now, the $100 they scraped together for the flights has to be spent on new tires, and on it goes.

How many of us have had our car spontaneously break and need a new clutch? Who's had their boiler go pop at Christmas? And you can be assured that the month the boiler goes is the month your child's feet grow two sizes and their trousers become ankle-swingers. Before you know it, the holiday debt is suddenly holiday debt, plus clutch debt plus boiler debt, plus, plus, plus.

Paying it off isn't just difficult, it feels impossible.

Company debt

Writers are in the fortunate position of not needing much overhead to set up and run a business.

You need your brain and creativity—both free. You need some kind of writing device, preferably digital—okay, not free, but you can buy cheap computers these days or secondhand ones for less. Or, failing both of those options, go to your local library and use their computer for free. There are some publishing costs along the way, but for the most part, we're pretty lucky when it comes to both start-up and running costs.

Zach Bohannon tells an awesome story about his friend who launched a coffee business and had to shell out $25,000 on equipment and supplies before he could sell his first bean. I spent less than $700 on publishing my first book. It's a colossal difference.

The point is, if you don't *have* to take on debt to start your business, why would you?

Here's what debt is: it's a virus, an insidious parasite that burrows into your business, eating it cell by cell until there's nothing left but a shattered dream of what could've been.

Thriving authors know two things.

1. You don't leave your day job until you're debt-free or in a stable financial situation.

2. You don't put your business in debt unless it is 100% unavoidable and necessary for its survival.

Above all else in this book, this lesson is the most important.

Thriving authors are here for the long term. This isn't a career of debt. You don't build a career by digging a financial hole. Thriving authors take their time growing their business. They save up for the big spend, buy only what they need, and when they do, they do it with hard-earned cash. Thriving authors don't put covers on credit cards, they don't borrow money to pay for edits. They save up, plan for the outlay of cash, and make sure they stay in the black.

DON'T BUY FRIVOLOUSLY BY SACHA BLACK

"Too many people spend money they earned, to buy things they don't want, to impress people that they don't like." – Will Rogers

You know what I love? A new gadget. What's better than a shiny piece of tech or a sweet piece of software that's going to help speed up my publishing process? Or how about the latest pair of Louboutin shoes? I've always been a fiend for heels. But, I'm a thriving author, and I had to get a grip on my desires in order to safeguard my career.

For a lot of people, consumerism is a real problem.

Sure, we all have our secret weapon—willpower—to stop us from shelling out on frivolous purchases. But advertising isn't a multibillion-dollar industry for nothing. And over the course of a day, we wordsmiths make thousands of decisions. Do you want the fajitas for lunch or a liquid mojito? Do you need to email Boris back or Jasmin first? Should you take the deal or leave it? Can you use the small white envelope on your desk, or should you get up and find a bigger brown one?

Each decision uses up a little piece of your willpower. Hell, even boredom wears down willpower.

Which means, at some point, you're going to cave. Whether it's for a new pair of trainers, a new fruit-branded laptop, a 10-book splurge for your To-Be-Read pile, or a creamy bar of chocolate, eventually, you'll splash out on something.

I can hear you screaming, "But, but, but... I needed to buy that formatting software, I had to get the program that scrapes for keywords so I can run ads, and the shoes were a treat because my launch went well. And yes, there are going to be times when you do need to splurge on these things—though perhaps not the shoes.

Investing in both yourself and your business is an essential part of running a company and a necessity if you want growth. I'm not suggesting otherwise.

But we both know that isn't what I'm getting at.

For me, I'm talking about the $490 Instagram course that I may have purchased a year ago and only studied half of—and if I'm honest, I've lost the login details and worse, I've not implemented any of the lessons I learned.

For you, I might be talking about those $300 trainers you've worn once and have since found a forever home in the back of your overfull wardrobe. Or what about that sickeningly expensive Magimix you've used three times before your baking frenzy wore off?

The problem arises when you have a little spare cash. The phrase "money burns a hole in my pocket" means something, it's a real phenomenon. See, you *could* save the money. You could store it in a spare business account for those days when the cash flow gets tight. Or perhaps add it as an extra to your pension fund. But where's the instant gratification? Where's the tangible "thing" you can hold for the time and effort you expended to get that cash?

There is none.

There's just some distant promise of a not-so-impoverished retirement—and that's IF you even make it to retirement. How are you supposed to say no when there's that gorgeous sparkling thingamajig wafted under your nose? When the alternative is a vague promise of a potentially easier time—if harder times hit. It's all so distant, so intangible, so boring.

And yet, what good are the expensive trainers to you if you're laid off? Or what if your sales tank? Secondhand goods might get you some spare change if you sell them during tough times, but it will be a far cry from the wad of dough you had before you spent it recklessly.

Look, I'm not saying you can never buy anything or that you can't treat yourself to the occasional nice toy. Of course, you can. Life is about living and enjoyment, but what do you want more? The trainers or a life as a thriving author? Because that's the real question. That's the question that thriving authors ask themselves every time they face a new shiny object they want to buy.

You're not on your own in this plight. We're all facing the daily onslaught of marketing temptations. Hell, as writers, we're responsible for some of it. And that's the point, isn't it? Marketers are good at crafting enticing ad copy—it's their job to sound convincing. It's their job to persuade everyone they need the new toy from the latest fad.

But do we?

Do you?

Do you really?

You have a choice.

You need to stop and ask yourself, do you *want* this item, or do you actually *need* it? There's a huge difference. Do you want it because it's cool and would be fun for five minutes? Or is it something that's going to improve your business?

Thriving authors are able to see through the nonsense and rose-tinted marketing spectacles. Thriving authors write ad copy themselves. They teach themselves to recognize when the marketing wool is being pulled over their eyes and when something new is going to make a difference to their business.

You have a choice. You can spend the five hundred bucks on something that's probably going to last three minutes, or you can save it and invest it in your business when you really need it. Thriving authors know that every dollar you waste by spending on gadgets and things is a dollar less you can spend on your business. A dollar less that you're investing. The less you invest, the less you make.

Some won't like hearing this and probably because they love their precious games console, shoe habit, insert whatever purchasing habit you have. You know why else they won't like hearing it? Because being a thriving author means taking away your instant gratification.

Like it or not, at the heart of a thriving author's strategy is the long game. Books take time to write, a back catalog takes time to create, another income stream takes time to build, a reputation... you guessed it, takes time to grow.

Every small business—author or otherwise—has cash flow issues, until they've done the hard part of not buying all the gizmos and business toys. Every business needs to act like a squirrel and store away cash for a rainy day, only buying the items they really need until their business is not just stable but sustainable.

Over time, saying goodbye to frivolous buying habits will help your business prosper. Remember, no one's saying you can never treat yourself or buy something for your author business.

You just have to ask yourself the important question: is it going to help you sell more books? Is it going to help save you time so you can work on producing more words? Is it going to make one of your business processes more cost effective? Or is it just a frivolous treat?

Your answer is the difference between an amateur and a thriving author.

Don't Use Personal Accounts for Business by Sacha Black

There are mistakes—oopsies and whoopsies—and then there are *mistakes*—the *oh,* "insert a choice word here" this is going to cost me big-time mistakes.

On the surface, using your personal checking account for business seems like the former. Perhaps you forgot your business card, left your wallet at home—easy mistakes to make. Perhaps you're only doing it for a few months until you're making more and can justify the account fees on a business account.

But in reality, and over time and persistent perpetration, this mistake definitely becomes the latter. There are three reasons why you should never use your personal bank account for business.

The first is that regardless of where you live, at some point your government is going to come sniffing around your business for tax money. You can't earn for long before the hungry mouths of our government overlords appear. That's just how society works.

When the tax man or woman appears, it's a painful enough experience handing over hard-earned cash. Do you really want to make it any harder on yourself by having to sift through lines and lines of bank account transactions?

Thriving authors want to spend their time creating. Whether it's books, services, and products, companion novels, character art, or something else entirely, they know their time is best spent creating. This means they have to streamline every other business process.

Especially the finances.

If your personal costs are buried between lines of business ones, mixed in with income from invoices and travel costs, the amount of time it will take you to separate the business lines from the personal lines is tripled. Thriving authors would rather spend that extra time writing and creating, not using financial tweezers to pull out the transactions needed for tax returns.

Trying to calculate your taxes is hard enough as it is, especially—and yes, I'm generalizing—for the word-preferring creatives. For a lot of writers, numbers aren't really our thing, words are. So why make the experience of dealing with numbers any harder?

The second reason you need to have a separate bank account for your business and personal finances is the fine print.

Let's be real, does anyone actually read the 48 pages of terms and conditions when they set up their bank accounts?

Didn't think so.

But when it comes to your personal bank account, the chances are, that buried somewhere deep in those waffly lines of bureaucracy is a key phrase you shouldn't ignore: "For personal use only."

When you break your terms and conditions, the bank can do just about anything it wants, including closing your account. Then you lose your personal account, which also happened to be your business account. Where would the royalties go next month? And believe me, having recently changed business banks, you don't want to have to do that unless it's a necessity.

Of course, the chances of you being caught and the bank closing your account while your business is earning small amounts of revenue are slim. But what's your game of risk like? How big is your appetite for uncertainty?

I assure you, once you start to bring in four and five figures a month, the bank starts to notice. You might become eligible for more products or for special treatment. Irrespective of whether you're a bank or an author, it makes good business sense to treat your bigger customers (or readers) well. If you've been using your personal account for business, that's not going to impress them.

Lastly, and in my opinion, the most important of all is the mindset reason. If you treat your business like a hobby, that's all it will be: a hobby. If you treat your author career like the business it is, then it will become the business you want it to be.

Act like a business and you'll be seen as a business.

Besides, how would you feel if you came to pay for a $1,000 book cover and instead of paying "Book Covers Ltd," you're asked to pay "Mr. Jonesy McJonesFace?" If that were me, I'd be raising a few eyebrows and frankly, I'd probably refuse to pay. How do you know Jonesy McJonesFace is legit? What's to say it's not a fraudulent account? There's nothing to indicate that Jonesy creates covers. Instantly, my back is up as a client.

It makes the business look unreliable and worse, unprofessional. I know I'm not alone in thinking that way. Lots of people prefer paying into a business account. It gives the impression of professionalism and professionalism breeds trust. You might not like it, but appearances count, first impressions count, professionalism counts.

Thriving authors know they have to treat the business side of their career with the respect and professionalism it deserves. With the respect and professionalism both the publishing industry and their readers will expect.

You can get away with rebelling on a lot of fronts as an indie author. It's our prerogative to break the rules and do things our way. But this is not one of those times. There's no room for excuses or laziness or ignorance when it comes to your business finances. Having a bank account that's purely for your business is a basic foundation for any self-employed person.

Thriving authors take responsibility for creating both the products their businesses sell, and the financial structures supporting those sales. Thriving authors don't accept ignorance as a reason for messing up the important or legal stuff. If you want to sustain a career as an author, you need to get the business basics right, ideally from the start.

And this is truly one of the most basic of business foundations.

DON'T IGNORE CASH FLOW PLANNING BY SACHA BLACK

I don't know about you, but when I hear the phrase "cash flow planning," I get this innate, carnal desire to either fall asleep or let my eyes roll out of their sockets. But you—and I—need to fight the yawns. Use smelling salts if necessary. There's important stuff going on here. Stuff that will save your business and keep your writing career dream alive.

In business speak, cash flow planning is:

When a business owner looks at their assets and their income over a period of time and then balances those against their current and future liabilities.

In other words, what do you have that will make you money? How much have you made over time? And what potential costs or bills do you have coming up in the future?

While this particular essay is about preventing you from having a business with a negative bank balance, it's about more than just income and outgoings. This is a mindset shift. It's about looking ahead, ensuring both your business' future and your ability to write.

I like being positive, but there's a difference between being positive and being in denial.

There have been enough financial crashes over the years for you to know there's always another one sniffing at our financial heels. And sure, no one wants to think about that. I know I prefer to look at the positive opportunities than the negative what ifs. But the reality is, financial crashes happen—and frequently.

A thriving author knows this, and they plan for it. A thriving author knows the consequence of ignoring cash flow planning. Not paying attention to their income is dangerous, including the potential for debt accrual and the end of self-employment. They also know this is the grunt work, the hard graft of cultivating a business.

No one *wants* to crunch the numbers instead of spending time writing words. Everyone wants to ignore the hard stuff and leave it for a different day. It's so easy to put off reading the tax forms for another day? And when you get there, perhaps you'll do it tomorrow. After that? Well, you have a writing deadline, so you'll do it next week.

A thriving author doesn't put off the hard stuff because they know having financial security means their future writing time is protected.

Through careful cash flow planning, a thriving author can ensure one bad sales month won't force them to jump the self-employment ship and swim back to the rat race. The benefit of having a flexible business is the ability to pivot during financially difficult times—and part of that equation is about good cash flow planning.

But of course, you need to know how much you're going to get paid in order to plan your cash flow.

We're lucky as authors. Some industries have very few ways to predict their income, and while we don't have a legitimate crystal ball, we do have a lag between the month a sale occurs and the month we get paid. A pain in one respect as we have to wait for what we're owed, but it also gives us at least some cash flow planning ability.

At the time of writing, Amazon, for example, has 60-day payment terms. IngramSpark has 90-day payment terms. That means if you make 100 sales during March, Amazon will pay you the royalties for those 100 books at the end of May and Ingram at the end of June. This enables you to plan and recognize at least two months out what money you'll have, what bills will be easy to pay, and if you might need to dig into your savings.

Over several years of sales, you'll be able to pattern-spot annual fluctuations.

For example, with my nonfiction, I'll often see a sales spike with little to no advertising in December because paperback writing craft books make for excellent festive gifts. Likewise, January is often a good month because everyone starts a new hobby and that leads to sales of books related to their new hobby.

These pieces of knowledge help me to plan and budget and choose the most effective months to spend advertising budget. But I wouldn't know that unless I was actively looking for the patterns. Thriving authors spend time studying their finances and the ebb and flow of their cash so they can continually tweak and improve their systems.

Excel spreadsheets are mythical creatures to me, I understand them about as well as I do Dynamical Mathematical Systems, which is to say, not at all. But, with a bit of Googling or help from an Excel whiz to do some wizardry, you can get a spreadsheet to take your sales figures from March and project the cash forward into May—the month you're going to get paid, so you can see what's coming and when. If you prefer software, then there are plenty of systems out there that can help for very little cost.

Thriving authors know that cash flow planning and budgeting is vital for their survival. They also know going into debt to cover business costs is a no-no. Which is why—no matter how reluctant they are—they do the hard work. They budget and plan for impending costs.

A thriving author knows if they're planning to publish a book in June, then they're probably going to need an edit in May (or before) which means, from January they need to save for editing costs. A thriving author will do their research and find their editor ahead of time so they can plan the approximate editing costs they'll incur. Then they budget for the cost. They do the same with book covers and launch costs and more. Some thriving authors have their covers designed ahead of time, so the costs don't hit them in the same month as editing bills—that's cash flow planning.

The means and methods don't really matter. It also doesn't matter whether an author uses a simple spreadsheet or a complex accounting software. What matters is that a thriving author looks to the future, they hope for the best, but plan for the worst.

The result? Their businesses, and therefore, author careers, can weather any financial storm.

DON'T IGNORE RETIREMENT SAVINGS BY SACHA BLACK

When we're young, we spend the vast majority of our time blissfully unaware of the realities of growing old. My six-year-old son thinks his grandmother—a spritely young thing at 56—is, and I quote, "an old lady."

That's the thing about reality, it's built from the bricks of perspective. What's old to a six-year-old is frankly middle-aged to me. Old age might seem like a distant beacon practically an eon away to a twenty-year-old. But to Mother Earth, 90 years is barely a breath, less than a single inhalation.

I have this theory that everyone stops aging before they reach thirty. At some point, cognitively, you stop. Sure, you continue to gain a wealth of experiences. You definitely make better decisions. But how many older people do you know who confess to still feeling like they're 18, or 23 or 28? I'm betting most of them.

I like to think of this as the universe playing silly buggers with us. It's a wondrous juxtaposing magic trick that warps reality and perspective. Age really is but a number. Our bodies wither and crumble, but our minds—unless we're unfortunate enough to suffer with a brain-degenerating illness—stay young. It's a strange paradox: an aged brain as young as it was in its prime.

But what's that got to do with writing and a career as an author?

Employment is a nanny state. Thinking about old age and retirement is done for you. The burden of worrying about your later years is swept under the carpet in taxes, 401ks, and company pension plans. You don't have to think about it because you get given what's left of your salary, your retirement pennies safely stowed away for later days.

But when you work for yourself, you don't get the luxury of ignorance. If you don't face the ugly mirror of old age, no one else will face it for you. This isn't Kansas, Dorothy. There is no yellow brick road, no glittery slippers, and no Toto. When you're a thriving author, no one builds you a cushy retirement fund. That's scary. It's also reality.

Do you know how you're going to pay for retirement? Do you know how you're going to fund a care home, or nurses, or heating?

Burying your head because old age feels like a lifetime away isn't going to win you any prizes. The harsh reality is that ignoring old age while you're young wins you one prize only: a terrifying retirement in ice-cold conditions, sickness, pain, and starvation.

Retirement funds are the ultimate test of delayed gratification. And here is our old friend—the long game. Are you noticing a theme yet? Are you seeing how important delayed gratification and playing the long game is for a thriving author? It's a pattern, a theme, a constant mantra that you need to sing to yourself.

"Play the long game. Play the long game."

"Play."

"The."

"Long."

"Game."

Save now for that distant Never Never Land. You don't know if you'll make it, but here's hoping you hit the big 100. As morbid as it sounds, that's the truth. No one knows if they'll make it past 50, or 75, or a century. So, I get why retirement saving seems pointless. If you don't know if you'll get there, why worry? You might never make it anyway. Remember Mother Earth? Our life might seem endless while we're young, but the elderly have a different perspective. Nothing is limitless.

Retirement seems far away. It seems like you have forever to save for it.

But you don't.

Not really.

Because there's always something trying to stop you from saving. A kid, a medical bill, a new car, a holiday, redundancy. And what if the economy crashes? What if, what if, what if?

There are a million reasons why you *could* put off saving for retirement. Fewer reasons for doing it.

But if you want to be a thriving author, you have to behave like a business. Especially when it comes to money and your employees. If it helps, split the roles. You be you and play with characters. Let the other you be boss.

Ultimately, you are your own employee.

You need to be a good boss. You need to look out for your staff's future. Your staff is far too busy playing make-believe with dragons and longboats. Someone's got to do the hard work of protecting them. I'm looking at you, buddy.

Thriving authors know that temptation is a super villain; it wins most of the time. So they make it easy for themselves and set up automatic savings. They take away the hard part of *having* to choose to save by removing the need to choose at all. They talk to the professionals, they liaise with accountants and financial experts to help them set up funds and accounts and direct debits and standing orders or whatever the similar mechanism is in their respective country, and they make the process as streamlined, automatic, and easy as possible.

Thriving authors know they're not alone. There are experts out there who can help them set up retirement funds. And it's not all bad. There might even be tax breaks for your conscientious saving.

Thriving authors don't let the excuses creep in and steal their retirement. They don't let the holidays or cars or "wants" of now overtake the needs of the future.

Thriving authors are knights, and warrior women, they accept the pain of saving now in order to let future-them live pain-free.

Don't Focus Only on Books
by Sacha Black

Writing full-time is a bit of a misnomer. I know writers who argue that if you earn *any* money from another source, you're not a real writer. You can't be a full-time author if you spend even an hour of your working time on another project.

Utter baloney.

First, it's your business and your life. As an indie author, you get to choose what you do in your business. I happen to like podcasting and teaching and speaking. How you (or I) define "full-time" is no one's business other than our own. That's the whole point of quitting the rat race.

But second, it's an extremely bad business decision to rely on one source of income. Did James Dyson settle after he made his first Hoover? Or did he make cordless ones and upright ones, and fans, hair dryers, and an array of other products?

See, even the authors who only have books as their single source of income don't "just" write. They have to deal with accountants, freelancers, the media, some form of marketing, business admin. Even Stephen King—who admittedly does write for a large portion of his day—still has to engage with his readers, do interviews, and be the face of his novels.

Writing full-time, in its pure form, is a lie. I'm going to make a wild assumption here, but I think that lie is one of the biggest culprits for so many authors not creating multiple streams of income.

What do I mean by multiple streams of income?

Multiple streams of income don't mean having a paperback, ebook, hardback, and an audiobook. Though those things are extremely sensible to have. Having multiple streams of income means you generate money from entirely different sources.

For example: affiliate sales, Patreon, editing, consulting, speaking, merchandise, courses, and events (digital or in-person). But the sources don't have to come just from writing-related avenues. They could be from an Etsy store, cake baking and selling, consultancy back into a day job, a second property rented out as an Airbnb, stock market investments, Uber driving, or any other way you can imagine. The "what" of the income doesn't matter. What matters is that it comes from a different source than your books.

It's all good me telling you that multiple streams of income are the way forward, but what's important is to explain why they're so crucial.

Here's the thing: Only having one source of income, even if you're a mega bestseller, is dangerous. It's no different than having a single day job where you're vulnerable to the whims and fancies of your boss. As an author with one income stream, you're in the same position—at the whims of your readers or worse, the likes of Amazon and other book retailers. If one retailer (let's use Amazon) suddenly slashed royalties, and chose to give you 30% while they kept 70%, what would you do?

Don't answer that because there's nothing you *can* do. It's their sales platform and their prerogative to choose the royalty rates. And it's not like you can march into Bezos' office with a placard and chain yourself to his desk until he flips the royalty rates back.

The real question is: What kind of damage would that do to your business?

Let's put it into perspective. If your royalties were slashed to 30% instead of 70%, your business would lose 43% of its income *overnight*.

Could you survive if your boss slashed your salary by that much without warning? Hypothetically, if you earned $2,000 a month, you'd be going home with $1,140 instead. Could you survive if that happened to you?

Didn't think so.

Neither can most people.

And that's why having multiple streams of income is so vital. I learned this lesson the hard way. When I was still in a day job, I worked for local government. They allowed some key worker staff to rent properties from them at a discounted rate. So, being the bargain-loving woman that I am, I jumped on the opportunity as I knew it would help me to get rid of student and car debt faster. It was a great idea at the time.

Aren't all ideas?

A couple of years into living in that house, the British government was facing unprecedented cuts. Inevitably, those cuts trickled down to local government, meaning we had to make financial cuts, too. That meant job losses, redundancies, and many of us fighting for our jobs.

But you see, I wasn't just fighting for my job, I was fighting for my house, too. If I lost my job, I lost the house. Never had I felt the need for financial and physical independence more starkly than I did in that moment.

I was at the start of my writing career, and in the following two years, I faced redundancy or layoffs three more times. I still remember the closest call I had. In the middle of the restroom, my boss told me there wasn't a job for me and that I had a month to find another job and house—like a cockroach, I survived that day, too. I also swore I'd never be put in that position again.

My question to you is, how safe is your writing business?

Thriving authors know they have to build a stable foundation under their words. Thriving authors shy away from that age old adage, "all your eggs in one basket." They know that one of anything isn't going to sustain a career. One book, one dollar, one series, one income stream. One of anything isn't enough.

I'm not saying you have to have 5,000 arms to your business. Nor am I saying that thriving authors have to build business empires with hundreds of employees and a gazillion products.

What I'm saying is that to protect yourself, your business, and your financial health for the long run, it's sensible, nay, essential, to have a financial backup plan. As much as I'm loath to talk about it, the global pandemic in 2020 and subsequent lockdown is the perfect example of why diversifying your income is so important. Aside from the thousands of businesses in immediate financial jeopardy, there were hundreds of writers in the same position.

A thriving author knows that they need more than one income stream. They know that earning income from another industry or source creates the flexibility for them to choose whether they want to write for eight hours a day or fill their time with a multitude of different work.

Multiple streams of income is oxygen for your business. It's safety, stability, and sustainability; more than anything, it's a career.

DON'T MIX UP PASSIVE AND ACTIVE INCOME BY SACHA BLACK

In an ideal world, we writers would sit by a log fire sipping our poison of choice and brooding over our characters—or if log fires and gin don't float your boat, then insert your writing paradise of choice.

No matter whether you're an indie author, a traditionally published one, hybrid, or something in between, to get to that point, you have to secure your financial health.

It's a nice dream, but no one can pick up their laptop and disappear into the sunset without some kind of financial backing behind them. Not unless you like sleeping under the stars and eating Witchetty grubs for dinner.

So how do you get to that mythical financial freedom point where you can say no to freelance work, you can sack off the speaking gigs, and avoid all the jobs you hate? Other than becoming the one in a billion to hit a zeitgeist and smash all the bestseller charts, it's hard work, hard savings, and having a good financial strategy.

Behind all of those strategies are two types of income: *active* and *passive*.

Active income is the day-job model. You work for a month, then you get paid for that month's work. The key is that you don't get paid for the work you did in that month ever again. It's a one-time only deal.

Active income includes work like editing, consulting, baking, cleaning, office work, or whatever else requires you to use your time in order to receive payment. The upside of this type of income is that it's an instant injection of cash. Something we all like now and then.

Passive income, however, is a different beast altogether. Purists might argue that there is only one form of income: active. At some point, even the things you create to sell and resell require you to put "active" time into their creation. To the purist, I say, nonsense. There's a clear distinction, and it all comes down to the good stuff: money.

Passive income occurs when you earn repeated income from something you created once.

I earned my first passive income at sixteen. I'd acted in a TV show a year or so before and one of the producers sold the show to a station in some obscure country. I had no idea what passive income was until that point. I realized very quickly as I stared at a healthy-looking check—that I'd done precisely nothing to receive—that this was the kind of income I wanted for the rest of my life.

We writers are lucky. Passive income is the stuff our careers are made of. Once you've created a book, so long as you're selling copies, you're earning royalties.

Likewise, if you create a course, or if you set up a YouTube video with affiliate links, or perhaps you're renting out a second home, or maybe you're earning interest on an investment portfolio. Passive income is powerful because it's your route to freedom. It's a pension, a future, it's generations of income for your children's children and their children after that.

Simply, the two main differences between passive and active income are:

1. Active income you earn once, passive income you earn over and over again.

2. Active income is typically a larger quicker injection of cash, where passive income is slower to build but continues long into the future.

Of course, every thriving author's journey to full-time life is different, but there are some strikingly familiar patterns.

When you first leave your job, most writers take a pay cut. It's inevitable. If you've spent any kind of time in your day job industry, you're leaping from a position of authority to a fledgling business. As much as the overnight success myth continues to permeate, it's not even close to true—everyone knows it takes years to create a successful... well, anything!

This leaves many of us in a predicament—a drop in cash and a need to spend on advertising, covers, editing, etc. Many authors who are starting out in their full-time careers use active income to generate enough funds to bridge the gap between the passive income they're currently earning and whatever their business needs.

This is a great solution. It's also a dangerous one.

Breaking out of the rat race once is hard enough. Diving headfirst into freelance or active-income generation is dangerous for a number of reasons. Everyone loves cash injections. Money talks for a reason. Having cold hard cash wafted under your nose is tempting to say the least. Cash pays the bills. Cash buys pizza and holidays and cars.

But a lot of people fall foul to temptation and then can't get back on the bandwagon.

Look at dieting across society, look at addiction and hobbies. How many fall off and never quite make it back? Too many. And herein lies the issue with active income. Spend too much time working on active-income jobs and suddenly, you no longer have a passively earning business. Worse, the passive generators you've created languish in rankings and sales, making it doubly hard to bring them back to where they were. At this point, that white sandy beach, cocktail, and book-penning under an umbrella is further away than you'd like.

Getting back on the independence bandwagon is hard.

Here's another issue: cash, as delicious as it is, runs out. That's the purpose of generating passive income, it keeps on giving. If you focus on generating active income, you'll forever be caught in the cycle of needing to spend time working on the immediate cash cows and never quite having enough time to work on the passive generators.

It's a problem. It's a paradox. It's a perennial pain in the butt.

A thriving author knows that the art is in balancing the two.

To begin with, every thriving author will probably need some kind of instant cash buffer they can generate quickly. That's cool. We have to do what we have to do to create enough cash to buy the time to create books and products. But thriving authors also know that to gain true financial freedom, they need to create products they can sell time and time again.

Either way, it's an opportunity cost. Work on passive income and you're giving yourself less to live off in the short term. Work on active income and you're doing detriment to your future self.

There's no right or wrong way to do this.

Whether you take 1 year or 30 to create enough passive income, you can live off it for the rest of your days. *Creating it* is the point. Thriving authors know that, which is why they fight for every day, hour, and minute they can get to write books, create products, courses, or anything else they can muster from their creative loins to sell time and time again.

Here's something else a thriving author knows: active-income generation is the easy way out.

If you want to take your time back, you're going to have to make some sacrifices. At some point, you'll have to take less instant money, so you can use the time you've gained to generate passive products.

How much time you need and how much you have to sacrifice to get that time is entirely up to each individual author. If you can't afford to sacrifice much of your current income, it doesn't mean you won't finish books, it just means it might take you a little longer.

Maybe you're lucky and can afford to go part-time immediately. Either way, a thriving author knows the most important type of income they can generate is passive. The fun is in the rollercoaster of how you earn it.

DON'T IGNORE PROFESSIONALS BY SACHA BLACK

We all get arrogant sometimes. I mean, I've read a book on the lost art of tadpole capture. Surely that makes me an expert catcher?*

No?

But I have so many opinions...

Okay, I'll back away from the tadpoles...

When Aunt Ethel—who only reads one erotica book a year while donning her tiger-print spandex pants—tells you that you don't need to bother paying for an editor, it makes you twitch, right?

Ol' Aunt Ethel knows the square sum of diddly-squat when it comes to publishing. You, as the thriving author, have poured hours, weeks, months, years even, into studying the industry. You've spent eons of time learning everything you need to build a sustainable career.

You're a professional. You know your industry, you know you need an edit. You know you need good covers and good blurbs to entice readers to part with their cash.

Aunt Ethel is not a professional.

She knows she has a penchant for erotica and that's about it. Someone needs to tell Ethel to get back in her box.

I don't know about you, but when someone raises their sniffy eyebrow at me and asks why I didn't "go the traditional publishing route," I get a little irked. Not because there's anything wrong with trying to pursue traditional publishing—there really isn't, I'm sure I'll pursue it one day, too.

No, I get irked because it's disrespectful.

Like many thriving authors, I make a good income from what I do. I know the industry and I pay my bills from the work I do. More to the point, after years of working at this, I know what I'm talking about. Like so many other indie authors, I *chose* this route after careful consideration.

So then, why do we, as professionals, ignore the other professionals? Part and parcel of the professional mindset is knowing when you're best placed to do something and when it's really time to farm out that work.

We indies like to harbor our controlling natures like they're a dirty little secret—I hate to break it to you...

whispers

Everyone knows.

It's in our blood. It's why many of us become indies. We want to retain control over our creative assets. But, there comes a point in every thriving author's journey when they realize that not only is it okay to delegate, it's a necessity.

Shocking revelation aside, thriving authors know it's positively essential to delegate, particularly when they're not an expert in the area.

We're words people, right?

I'm sure, someone's now going to send an angry email to me claiming they're an accountant and an author, well, good for you, buddy... You can get back in the box with Ethel.

The majority of writers specialize in writing. We entrust our book cover designs to expert cover designers. You wouldn't build a conservatory or extension on your property unless you were a builder.

Professional accountants, professional designers, professionals as a whole, place their business in the hands of their reputations. As consumers, we trust those professionals because of their reputation.

So, I've never understood the reluctance to trust professionals with money. My granddad used to store hordes of cash in gentlemen's socks. My father-in-law used to store it in frozen pea bags in the freezer.

Now, of course, all thriving authors eventually get an accountant because their finances either get too complicated or it becomes more effective to pay someone to do it because their time is more valuable spent doing creative tasks.

You should have an accountant and probably sooner rather than later. But if you become a company then it's a necessity because your accounting books are no longer simple. But having an accountant isn't really what I'm getting at.

You don't get to be a thriving author without having made your company work for you. Once a thriving author reaches the point where their business is generating surplus income, they know it's time to invest in the help of a professional. Most thriving authors start small, upgrading to professional financial software and to accountants.

Just as a thriving author made their business work for them, so, too, do they make their money work for them.

Being a thriving author is about making your career and your money work for you over the long term. It's about maximizing and optimizing your creative assets to produce the best outcomes for your business now and long into the future.

There's an important distinction here.

Some authors might think financial advisors and wealth managers are for other people; the rich and the successful. But a thriving author knows otherwise. They recognize when they need professional help, they recognize when their knowledge of savings and schemes has reached its limit. They know when their money can do more, make more, and be put to better use. So, they enlist the help of financial advisors and wealth managers.

They spend a little on professional help to ensure that what wealth they've built makes them even more. Thriving authors aren't afraid to see their success and reach for more. Financial advisors aren't for other people. They're for all of us and they're for authors too. A thriving author knows this because they have the money mindset.

*I have not, in fact, read a book about the lost art of tadpole capture, but I'm sure there is one out there and I'm equally sure I wouldn't be an expert after having read it. But that's not really the point.

DON'T HATE MONEY BY SACHA BLACK

Rich Dad Poor Dad

This was nearly a completely different chapter. But I realized that regardless of the "don'ts" in this book, there's one don't that rises above all the others.

It's here that I want to leave you with what I believe is the most important lesson of all: The Money Mindset.

As I approached the end of my first year of working for myself, I took the opportunity to write down and share the lessons I'd learned. To my surprise, I discovered that half of them were mindset related. Half!

Going into the exercise, I assumed most of the lessons would be about business and strategy and productivity. But in reality, half of them were about shifting my mindset and the continuous work that goes into improving it. But perhaps that shouldn't be such a shock. We construct our realities and those constructions stem from our minds and mindset. So of course, the final and most important essay should be about your money mindset.

I think society has money all wrong.

Too many of us are given a stigma around it before we can toddle. We're taught the scarcity principle. Money is hard to come by, we have to work hard for money, it leaves us too easily, borrowing is a necessity, there's not enough money for everyone.

We've got it all backward. Money as a concept barely exists anymore as we're moving toward a cashless society. When we arrive, money will just be a string of ones and zeros in another intangible digital system.

I love Robert Kiyosaki's quote because it cuts to the heart of this issue. I have a Post-it on my computer screen with the same quote to remind me to keep my mindset in check.

What about you? Would you rather have too much money or too little?

Thriving authors know there's enough money for everyone because they take responsibility for their mindset around money and they decide it's so. You can decide the same, too.

I had a chat right before I quit my job with someone I highly respect in the industry. This person said two fundamental things that radically changed the course of my money mindset.

I'd made it clear that my goal was to be a six-figure business owner. But I'd absentmindedly said, "Oh, I don't really want to tip into the higher tax threshold because then I'll have to pay more tax." She, rightly so, called me out. If I want to be a six-figure business owner, then I should *want* to pay more tax because that means I'm closer to my goal. I can't get to my goal of having a six-figure company unless I'm in the higher tax bracket.

I was looking at my goal from the wrong angle. I was self-sabotaging before I'd even started. If I want to earn six figures, then I'm going to have to pay a higher tax rate. Telling myself I didn't want to pay more tax was self-limiting. I was stopping myself from earning it before I'd even tried. This is a pattern common to so many indie authors and so many new authors. We haphazardly make statements without thinking about the words we're pouring into the universe. It's a dangerous game to play.

Sure, no one "wants" to pay more of any kind of bill, tax or otherwise, but that's besides point. It's the self-limitation we instill in our reality when we make statements like that that's the issue. Thriving authors don't self-limit themselves when it comes to money. They constantly work on their mindset, their affirmations, their beliefs. They embrace money, they let it flow into their lives. They don't stop it before it can arrive.

The second thing that rocked my world was the statement, "Don't be romantic about where your money comes from." It kind of blew my mind.

I was quitting my job because I wanted to sit and write books for the majority of the day and so I'd assumed my income needed to come from, well, books. But that's nonsense.

Are you seeing a pattern yet? It was another self-limiting belief that needed busting. By limiting myself to only earning income from book sales, I was making it harder for myself to do the very thing I wanted to do. If I created multiple streams of income, they'd pay for the time I wanted to write. Who cares where I earn my money if it means I get to spend the years I have on this planet doing the thing I love most?

No one is saying you have to jump on the FIRE (financial independence, retire early) bandwagon and live on pennies for a few years so you can quit work and retire at 25. And equally, no one's saying you need to be an unscrupulous meanie ripping off everyone you encounter in order to make your millions. There's a path out there for all of us.

But, and here's the clincher, thriving authors don't find their path, they carve it. They don't hate money, they embrace it.

Thriving authors have a vision and a financial mission, and they actively drive toward it. They aren't romantic about money. They open their arms and their mindsets, and they let money flow toward them. They definitely don't let money flow the wrong way and they don't get into debt.

Thriving authors don't set limiting beliefs and they don't self-sabotage their income-earning potential. They set up the financial foundations of their businesses correctly, they lean on professionals when they need them, and they expand their income streams into multiple layers that support both their current careers and their relaxed retirement days.

CREATIVE NOMAD

Want to buy experiences instead of things and work for yourself while traveling? Many authors search for more time to write and want to work toward financial freedom. If you're thinking about having a creative life on the road, this section offers the lessons that Janet Kitto discovered when faced with changing her story from an aspiring writer to a thriving author.

Janet was on the road from July of 2018 until May of 2019. During that time, she was homeless, meaning that she was without a mortgage and without a large portion of the things that had made up her life until that point. Janet traveled with her husband as far south as San Diego, CA, from Sooke, BC, in Western Canada, and then from Sooke, across the country, to Pictou, NS, in Atlantic Canada.

Janet and her husband sold their home to live in a 20-foot RV trailer. They stayed a few nights here and there with friends and family, or in a hotel, but lived in private RV parks for most of the journey. They bought a house on the opposite coast with money they made on the sale of their home in Sooke, never guessing that would be where the road took them. They remain without debt, and Janet now writes full-time, enjoying the freedom that travel created for her.

Here's a quick summary of the valuable lessons you can expect to learn in this section:

"Don't Be Like Everyone Else" - Maybe you've started asking yourself if you need to change what you're doing as a writer. Janet shares why she started her life on the road, and what she did to get there. It's not an easy choice if you want to travel, but you still want to hold on to what everyone else has.

"Don't Choose a Life You're Not Invested In" - It took Janet months of travel to decide what she valued and what she believed about herself. If you're searching for the freedom to write full-time, get a backpack ready.

"Don't Stay at Home" - Many aspects of your day-to-day living can fit into a life of travel. Janet built a solid financial base to go on the road, then worked on her craft while she traveled.

Whatever your life looks like, you don't have to wait at home for the perfect time to take a leap.

"Don't Have a Uniform" - There's a noticeable difference between dressing for comfort and cutting costs in your travel budget. You're the director of your publishing empire, so dress like a boss.

"Don't Work Empty-Handed" - After adjustments on the road, it's time to master your creative life. Janet works out what else she had to let go of and what she needed to keep writing.

"Don't Practice Social Distancing" - In a changing world, we need to stay connected, looking for new ways to reach out instead of hiding inside a carefully crafted online presence.

"Don't Need a Desk" - Thriving authors don't give up. Janet shares the system she adapted so that she was always moving forward and writing every day.

"Don't Rush the End" - Not only can you repurpose your content while you travel, you can discover more about yourself before the journey ends. Freedom, like the song says, is just another word for nothing left to lose. Don't run, take the time you need.

"Don't Travel without a Home Base" - All travel eventually brings you home. Janet was ready to have the RV trailer parked after a dash across Canada to her new home on the east coast. Recharged and changed by the miles covered, travel is still part of Janet's life.

DON'T BE LIKE EVERYONE ELSE BY JANET KITTO

This probably isn't the first time. You're thinking about leaving home. Maybe you're wondering if a creative life on the road will be cheaper and easier than the life you have maintaining a house. You're also questioning if your mortgage is keeping you tied to a job that you want to leave. Have you been spending a lot of time thinking that a better life is out there somewhere? You feel stuck where you are. Building a business like every other entrepreneur has you wearing too many hats.

If a creative life on the road was just about living cheaply, we'd all consider taking the leap. But it's not cheap, and it's not easy. If you're searching for a new identity as a thriving author, consider what your writing life might become if you change how you live.

When my husband and I sold our house in 2018, our goal was to eliminate all of our debt and experience financial freedom. We decided to leave the life we had, to say goodbye to family, to give up regular paychecks and routines that were keeping us too busy to travel. I also decided to let go of a lifetime collection of stuff.

We chose to downsize and sell what we could to fund our travel. I was emotionally attached to every book, every box in the garage, and a mindset that I had to live like everyone else. I started my journey as a thriving author by wanting to have financial freedom.

Before we hit the road, my priority was client work, then my own writing. I was spending a lot of time managing a house full of things that had an overwhelming weight.

Together, my husband and I made a choice to let go of who we were. Choosing to become an author after becoming an empty nester meant that the home I had built, the comforts that I had known, the services that had made my life easier, would no longer serve the person I wanted to be.

Why want a new identity? We all write. You wouldn't be reading this book if you didn't plan to go full-time as a writer or are already identifying as a thriving author. Do you need to change what you do?

I did. This is the journey I mapped out with my partner.

First, my husband and I paid off our mortgage and cleared all of our debts. We dropped the jobs where someone else was making the decision about how we spent our time. We met with a financial advisor and planned how to pay ourselves while we traveled. I put my laptop into a backpack and clothes into the RV we had parked in the driveway.

Up until that point, I had felt afraid to fully let go. I was afraid of losing everything because I had worked hard to have what everyone else had.

I started writing a memoir. In that early draft, I uncovered the root of all my sadness. I didn't publish the memoir, but I decided that grieving family life and a home was part of my thriving author process.

The next step was the big one. We moved out of a two-bedroom house into less than 100 square feet of living space in a travel trailer.

Once we were homeless and on the road, the place where I slept every night, a slightly undersized queen mattress, became the place where I also read, occasionally ate, and often wrote. Same for the passenger seat in the truck that pulled our little trailer from site to site.

While my husband drove us around the country, I wrote in a travel journal and worked on getting a website and blog running so I could post weekly updates and understand, in greater detail, the new life I had chosen.

Not every writer is going to want to leave the life they have, or feels compelled to trade their house debt for an unknown adventure. Getting out is not easy, and there were three years I lost because I convinced myself that this was true, that adventure was not for me.

The only way I could get out of what I had was to change who I was. I was done with hoarding china, paper, photographs, and art. A grade-school report card reminded me that my best grades came from creative expression.

Once I decided how I wanted my creative life to look, that I wanted personal wealth, and to discover what was beyond my status quo as a mother, wife, and daughter, a new identity on the road became mine.

Do you want to change who you are? Have you tried changing what you do? Your journey will transform you and your identity as a thriving author.

DON'T CHOOSE A LIFE YOU'RE NOT INVESTED IN BY JANET KITTO

Imagine the perfect future. You sit down and write, the words flow into a workable structure, and you earn more than you could have ever thought possible. The only thing missing from that dream is the place where that writing will happen, and you finding more time than you have to focus on all those ideas floating around in your head.

I had more time than I knew what to do with, once my husband and I were living in our RV. Not having a home to manage, just a tiny living space on the road, I looked at what I'd become, but I didn't yet see myself as an author. All of the planning and the steps to get this far meant that the perfect future was now at hand. I had more time to write than ever before in my life.

I wasn't a new parent with young children. I was past the days of starting my first career. I'm old enough to be a grandmother, now that my daughter has passed the age of 26, the age at which I had her.

I told myself that one day I would write a series of books and become a thriving author. Here I was in that new world, and I was not creating.

Choosing to become a thriving author means choosing a lifestyle based on who you want to be. You believe you can write, you can travel, and that you can improve your life. I was on the road with the mindset that I wasn't ready, and I was confused about what to do next.

If you go on the road to chase down your dream while traveling, do you know what the next move is? Planning to write when a good idea strikes won't make your travel easier.

There are always distractions like shopping and laundry that will take up more time than you expect. The weather may keep you inside, or you'll want to take a bike ride or a walk while the sun is out. You might need to pack up your rig when you first wake up, or check out of the B&B or hotel before breakfast. Every day may look different.

Will you stick to a routine when you never know when you'll have the time to write?

It took me months of travel to decide what I valued and believed about myself. I wasn't sure what to write, but I never went to bed without getting something written. Those words mattered. If I hadn't done the work then, I wouldn't have something to write about now.

My backpack contained all of the necessary tools so I could write whenever it was near. I chipped away at each project throughout the day. I used templates to make sure that I was writing what I needed to write, even when I didn't know what to express.

I was okay with not living how everyone else was living. I was okay with finding out what we needed as we went on our journey. I suffered through the discomfort of not knowing what was next because I knew why I was doing it.

I was going on the road to become an author who lived on revenue streams from writing. I had a list of questions that I answered every day to shape the content I hoped my journal would hold once the trip was complete.

The chance to live in the moment, to do nothing but write, that's where I was. I intended to reflect on why I hadn't yet been able to write and publish a series of books.

Being a thriving author means building a life around what you value, around working as an author, and earning a living from your writing. When you're on the road, you have more freedom to be self-aware, to do self-improvements, to be mindful. You have more time to do what makes you happiest, even if the work is tough. You have time to ask why you want nothing else but to be a thriving author.

Don't Stay at Home by Janet Kitto

Some moves take years of contemplation before they play out. Just like writing a novel, there are necessary steps to plot, but that doesn't mean you have to have everything figured out before you start writing.

Calculating how much you want to earn as a thriving author is one piece of having a creative life on the road. I spent a few years doing the math and putting myself in the best place I could financially before I was ready to write full-time. For me, it was like playing a game, positioning myself for "someday."

If you're waiting to feel ready, or waiting for perfect conditions, you might be playing the same game.

Decide how much time you need (and want) for travel, and what kind of travel you want to do. I wanted to have a period to write without needing to sell books. I wanted to write every day. I needed living space that was comfortable.

I desired privacy with a few comforts of home. I had a kitchen, a bathroom (with a tub and shower, as small as it was), and a bed. The truck that pulled our trailer was another quiet space I could retreat to, and did. It may depend on how you're wired, but I needed a bubble to separate me from noises, smells, and social interaction while I worked.

There were a number of decisions I had to make before the house sold.

What furniture did I want to keep in storage? What did I want to donate? How long did we need a storage unit?

I struggled to see myself earning enough for the travel to extend more than a few months. I didn't know how to earn a living as an author, and I guessed that our expenses would be relative to the life we were leaving. I can tell you now that our monthly expenses were never predictable.

The excitement of a different lifestyle will have you looking at what kind of huge leap into the unknown you're capable of making. Why stay in one place when, as a creative, you can take your work on the road?

Many things can fit into a life of travel. You can bring your kids, your pets, and your keepsakes. However, you can't leave home without something shifting. Travel is a shift from one place to another. Do you know if you're ready?

Routines change on the road. If you're trying to make everything perfect before you even leave your driveway, you won't be ready when it's time to go.

Conditions on the road are not static. Connecting to Wi-Fi at a coffee shop or at a library might be an option for you, but what is your plan when you have no way to connect? I learned to keep a keyboard and a notepad handy wherever I was, plus I switched back and forth between a number of projects.

Leaving old habits behind, those ones where my writing didn't take priority, I took time to reflect on my life. I enjoyed sunsets by the ocean, and I walked in the afternoon heat of the desert.

I had a new mindset that kept me healthy, positive, and working toward the goals I had as a writer. I kept my accountability partners while I traveled, and I found new opportunities to expand my network.

I also worked on my craft. I used my time like a gift to find out what I could accomplish. You're not just writing on the road, you're building a place to work in smaller spaces, often working at different times of the day.

You don't have to be empty nesters to do this, or have a pension, or money in the bank.

I went in search of an author life. There wasn't a right time for me to make the leap. There were events I planned, like selling the house and buying a trailer to travel in, but I had to trust that my decision was the right one because I wasn't ready. I went on the road anyway.

In taking the leap, you get a chance to see, experience, and learn more about yourself. I learned quickly what I couldn't do.

At home, I sorted through physical stuff I could hold onto, and beliefs I was ready to leave behind. I struggled out on the road, but I don't regret my decision. I did what was right for me.

There isn't a perfect moment to change your life. There aren't any rules so if you want to start with small trips and then work your way up to longer times on the road; trust yourself to do that.

There's going to be a void that will attract your old habits and debt back into your life, but once you leave your comfort zone and create financial independence, you'll discover that home on the road has everything you need.

Don't Have a Uniform by Janet Kitto

You're behind a closed door, or the blinds are shut tight. You dress to be comfortable.

Maybe on social media you are a fashionable dresser, but what have you been wearing for the past three days when no one was looking?

On the road, with a limited wardrobe and infrequent access to laundry facilities, you might be wearing the same thing for days.

When I don't get out to see other people, I admit that I give less thought to what I'm wearing. I like to dress in what makes me happy, and especially on the road, my travel clothes are less professional.

There was one point, after three months of travel, when I looked at my reflection in the shiny side of one of the truck door panels. I didn't recognize the woman staring back. Nothing I wore matched. Everyone could see that I wasn't looking after myself. At least I was changing my underwear regularly, but the faded sweatpants had to go. Not in the wash, though. Those ten-year-old comfy pants needed to be trashed.

When I went on the road, I was trying to use up old items of clothing before replacing them. I thought I could stretch my travel budget farther. That wasn't a good strategy. I would have been better off investing in a good pair of walking shoes, shorts, and t-shirts that fit properly. Having better layering options for different climates would have been smart, too.

There's a need to keep your bags light when you travel. You don't want to have five different pairs of shoes with you. The rule of one in, one out will work better than having a collection of anything you might have if you were set up at home.

You might need one formal outfit "just in case," but don't pack any items you wouldn't put into a communal washing machine. There are horrors in the dankness below—hairy, sticky, smelly horrors in those tubs. You might have towels and bed linens that you'll need to wash. To avoid having my laundry coated with animal or human fur, I invested in a small portable washer to hook up to a hose and power at our site. It had a spin and soak cycle and did a great job, albeit tiny loads. I gave more hours to laundry by using a smaller tub but kept my sanity from being lost in a sensory overload of sights, smells, and textures.

Travel can be an escape. You might be running away from something that needs attention. Whether you're reflecting on what you're putting out into the world, or looking inside yourself to measure what you are capable of doing, it's essential to pay attention to how you're dressed.

Even on the road, work clothes for writing are necessary. If a comfy hoodie and shorts make you the director of your publishing empire, that's great. Let me sound maternal here for a moment, please. The shorts are okay as long as they fit, and as long as you wash them regularly.

Travel is not just about discovering what is out there in the world, it's about finding what is inside of YOU. Changing your life, just like changing your underwear every day, is a choice. If you're traveling, there's probably a reason why you left the comforts of your home.

There are ways to make travel cheaper. You might want to consider your options, especially if you're making less money along the way. Take your creative life on the road to find freedom. Freedom buys time to write more, explore and see more, and practice a different lifestyle.

If you have limited time and limited Wi-Fi resources on the road, be ready to work when you can work.

Having a simple wardrobe is a great idea. Make sure you don't look like you need to beg for money on the street corner. Be inconspicuous, but not odd. Be professional, but not uptight. Letting something like personal hygiene go is too easy to do.

Don't lose touch with your markets, your audience, or the next big thing in the publishing world.

I took my creative life on the road because I couldn't let go of my past, and travel shifted me into a new world. I took myself away from the weight that had burdened me all my life.

Whatever moves you to travel, remember that you might not be able to upload or download on any particular day. You may not have a quiet place to work when you need to write, or you might be low on supplies and can't find a suitable place to live.

Still, if you've found the right lifestyle as a thriving author, the clothes you choose can fit even when you get out of your comfort zone.

DON'T WORK EMPTY-HANDED BY JANET KITTO

The search for adventure has taken you out of your house. You've escaped from a place where creating was difficult, so why doesn't the writing feel any different?

Heading out on the road requires constant adjustments. Externally, and internally. You won't always have the right amount of space, or be in control over your environment.

You wouldn't send a character into the forest without having the right weapons to end the story. You're the hero now. Think about what you need for your journey, and be ready to make constant adjustments because you will be faced with choices at every step, and you aren't going to be right about everything you need.

I packed office supplies—index cards and sticky notes, pens and pencils, colored markers, highlighter pens, leather notebooks, a laptop, phone, iPad, and even a good microphone for online meetings. I never used the microphone, but I covered that what-if.

What I didn't worry about was backups. I overpacked, thinking I needed everything, not trusting that I could find the tools on the road. Experience taught me to protect my most-valuable assets, the ideas I had daily. Those ideas didn't always get uploaded safely, or get filed in more than one place.

The bigger point here is to be distraction free, i.e., no Wi-Fi while you're working. You can research later when you get near a hotspot or you can use your own data. You don't need to be connected to the world when you're in the process of creating.

Anything you're working on can be broken into small travel-size chunks. Don't get trapped by thinking that you can control every detail. It's better to be a problem-solver.

If you have a mailing list with regular updates from you for the past year, when you go on the road, you'll likely have to write emails ahead of time to maintain that schedule, or detail current events and report them at a later date to your readers.

Have systems in place to keep your mailing list going and stay connected.

Having digital files is the easiest way to save copies and protect your work. Research what you'll need before you leave. Don't go on an adventure without being prepared. Have a Plan A and Plan B, and have a Plan C if all else fails.

I love to ask myself questions and then bust out my journal:

- What if you don't earn what you need to cover your budget?
- What if equipment breaks and you have to replace it while on the road? Can you find what you need? Can you get it shipped to your location?
- What if weather or some other event keeps you from taking the next steps in your travel? What if you get sick and can't work?
- What if you're enjoying what you're doing on the road but there is a good reason for you to return home?
- What if you need to be in place A, but you have to return to place C? You don't know if you can do place B again to get to place A. What do you do then if you're in the middle of a big project?

There are so many things out of our control that having a thriving author mindset for the road is invaluable.

That means don't forget about your craft. Keep learning, keep reading, take classes, and work with a mentor. Don't neglect to make improvements to yourself while your energy is consumed by the daily changes of life on the road.

When I needed to be creative, I'd first take a walk through a forest or a museum, even a small store would open the window to a new world. I reached out to family members, or connected with my writing community.

Before I left home, I also took care of my health. I visited my doctor, had my annual exams, and I even scheduled one at the halfway point of my travel before crossing the border. I reviewed all of my subscription services and paid for them before I left, but also eliminated anything I didn't need or wouldn't be able to use while I was away.

Next time I go on the road for an extended period of time, I'm going to write myself a letter or record a voice memo, to document something I can open in an emergency and remind myself that I'm going to be okay.

Think about a message that you know you'll need to hear when you're having an awful day. Write it as if you're the friend called upon to help. Be honest. What will you need to hear when you are ready to quit writing? What is the belief you need to remind yourself of as a thriving author?

Maybe this isn't so obvious, but don't plan on taking your laptop to the beach. There'll be glare on your screen, you'll get sand everywhere, and you won't get the work done that you think you will. Instead, take a walk on the beach. Dictate your thoughts into your phone. Do the work when you find a nice restaurant or coffee shop to hang out in, or when you're back in your vehicle or Airbnb for the night.

Get used to dictating notes, scenes, and blog posts. You'll find yourself inspired at all the wrong times when you're on the road and you don't want to lose those travel-induced ideas, as I sometimes did.

The road is a good place to learn to let go. You can't travel with the burdens of the life you wanted to leave. You're going to find things that you want to carry with you when you travel, and maybe you can't keep these things as long as you'd like.

So learn to let go, to be creative without anything to hold you back.

Don't Practice Social Distancing by Janet Kitto

I don't like isolation.

Even as an introvert who recharges while alone, I wouldn't say I like distancing myself from others. Exchanging ideas with writers and readers is necessary. I have a daily routine of talking with friends and family.

When I went on the road, I felt separated from my loved ones, but even more from other creatives.

The frustration I felt came from not having done enough planning when it came to staying connected.

I made sure to downsize and eliminate debt (to have financial freedom), but I didn't think about the scope of the travel we were doing. Not only were we trying to find ways to earn as creatives, my husband and I were also trying to find a place to settle down and live.

We drove to a new destination every few weeks, sometimes every few days, and finding a routine and the best place to work often pushed the idea of socializing far away.

The plan when I left home was to become a thriving author. I didn't know enough about my craft, about tech, about the future that was coming.

One day during our travel, we were stopped on the highway for hours while a large truck full of hay burned down to its tires. I was able to write that day, but not to focus. Life on the road is imperfect, and that forced me to change what I believed about working and traveling.

When my husband and I were on the move, we didn't have a date for the end of the road. We dashed for warmer climates in the fall, flew for the border in the spring, and then raced across the country to look for a new home.

I didn't have a plan for the frustration and isolation, just a need to discover more about myself.

I couldn't always be ready to write in the morning at the same time each day. There might be takedown (to pack up the trailer) that would start as soon as we woke up so we could drive to the next location.

Additionally, I might not be able to start making noise until my husband woke up. Our bed was also my office space. Some days, I might go for a walk in the morning because that was the best time and the best weather for my husband and me to go.

I worked around both of our schedules. While I wasn't under contract or earning anything from book sales at that time, I allowed my schedule to be flexible, often to my regret because I knew I was forcing myself to work under conditions that weren't great, and I wasn't doing my best work.

I didn't do any of the driving. I turned those hours into work time.

I knew when my butt was in the passenger seat of the truck that I could be writing. I had a laptop table behind my seat, and my backpack was always ready with everything I needed.

In our trailer, I converted the coat cupboard, a space less than a foot wide but a few feet tall, into storage for books, notepads, and all of my electronics. Those dedicated spaces were vital. I might be working in the truck in the morning, on the bed inside the trailer in the afternoon, and the next day, I might be set up at a picnic table. I needed to know where everything was, and there were times when I needed to have my bags and books out of sight so I could enjoy other parts of my day and recharge.

In a healthy world, being able to look at each other, hang out, talk, laugh, go deep into conversations about the publishing business, and have a shared human experience is essential.

We can't spend all of our time alone in front of a screen. Even though it might be scary to step out from behind pen names and our online presence, and allow another writer to see outside of the box we've curated, we need to share what we have below the neck. We need a creative community.

If you're thinking about travel on the road, how can you make that experience more significant than the one you're having at home?

It's not enough to listen in on a podcast conversation or to build a friendship through an email or a message on social media. Thriving authors don't go on the road to avoid people. Thriving authors stay connected because we want to get our books published.

We need support, and we need to bond together in person.

Don't Need a Desk by Janet Kitto

The lawn chairs are set up in a semicircle with one only a few feet from your open window. Remnants from last night's campfire are evident. There are ashes inside the pit. A dog is trying to dig a hole beside one of the lawn chairs. The family pet didn't want to be left behind. Digging is the only way he can deal with the separation stress. Until he starts barking.

This is one of the days when you planned to write because you heard that your neighbors were going sightseeing for the entire day. You thought it would be quiet at camp. You don't know your neighbors, but it's easy to hear almost everything they say because the sites are close together, and RV walls are thin.

There's a lake you can see if you go outside and stand at the back of your unit. Bird songs woke you at sunrise, the trees full of colorful species, but now, all you can hear is the cacophony of motorboat engines on the water.

The paradise you dreamed of for your life on the road is actually a huge distraction.

But you're a pro. You've got noise-canceling headphones and a keyboard set up at your dinette table. You plan to take your backpack with you later to a coffee shop and upload your files to the cloud. First, though, you need to write a few scenes. The bathroom inside your unit is off-limits while you work. No one is allowed to drop their guts on your work shift because a lingering odor is all it will take to make you leave your writing for another day.

The routines I created at home didn't serve me on the road. My life kept moving, taking me farther and farther away from how I came to the page.

I tried to bring elements of my home office with me to get into the writing. Without a proper chair, my posture over the keyboard tired me quickly. Food got on my notebook. How much energy was I wasting trying to figure out a space to work? At least 17 different thoughts would barge into the creative ideas I was wrangling with each passing minute.

I enjoyed tweaking my system, setting targets for the day, and checking in with accountability partners each week. I planned projects for when I knew I'd have larger blocks of time to write. I broke down each project into smaller units, so when I only had a few minutes and no Wi-Fi, I could still get work done. I had to write more because this was now my full-time gig. If I gave up, I would never discover the life of a thriving author.

Changing your lifestyle will make you creative. You think that once your decision is made, you'll expect this to happen, so it will happen. I wouldn't bet on it happening that easily.

I wrote more on the road, but I didn't make or save money. I simply changed my environment so I could see if I was capable of the change I desired.

I didn't need a desk or a fancy office or a block of time during the day to work. I didn't have commitments to anyone but myself to build a new life and find readers to build an audience. I had to write when I was tired because each day had unique challenges, and my writing process took longer than I thought it would.

On the road, I got to know my strengths. Travel was my way of running from failed attempts to publish.

Life on the road isn't the place to give up or get lost. Life on the road is where you discover who you really are.

The reason I came to the page was that even when the dogs barked and the constant distractions pulled me away, I wanted to let go of the idea that I couldn't be successful. With no more excuses to stop me, I said, yes, I can write today. Every day, I said, yes, I can do this.

Don't Rush the End by Janet Kitto

My husband and I tried to get outside and walk whenever possible because, in our little space, we could walk from one end to the other in less than 10 steps. We needed the downtime away from our trailer and we didn't think twice about walking for an hour to get a loaf of bread.

We explored each town where we stayed on foot, looking in the store windows on main streets. Sometimes, we walked to small coffee shops and talked to the owners.

Before I had a creative life on the road, I was working for the convenience of not having to cook for myself every night. Now I had the freedom to shop for fresh ingredients and connect with local people, cultures, food, and music.

I thought about, and wrote about, the impact I was having on small businesses. I considered the sustainability in these communities and made sure I didn't ruin what they had built. I stopped thinking about every detail and my plans for each day. I began enjoying the meaning of my own story as it unfolded in front of me.

I watched the desert turn green, saw what bare fruit trees looked like as they started to bloom. Later, I watched the trees bear fruit. I wanted to experience the seasons in a different climate. So I did.

Depending on what you write while you travel, you can create additional assets with a travel blog while writing your next romance novel. Study the landscape and sell stock photos while researching the next zombie apocalypse. Thriving authors find ways to repurpose their content.

Get a better understanding of who you are as a creative, instead of focusing on smaller details of your trip. Experiment with how much time you can write. Push yourself to write outside of your dedicated workspace.

Staying longer in each of your destinations lowers your transportation costs and cuts down on exhaustion. You also get better rental rates. Staying with family and friends and getting your laundry done is another consideration. Slow travel gives you opportunities to upload finished blog posts, articles, and book titles to every retailer.

Even using public transportation can be a way of economizing slow travel. Take a train, a ferry, or a bus. Explore historic attractions and write them into a post or use them as settings for your book or series.

Think local wherever you go.

See more, write more. Write in a journal. Take photos and document your travel through a story of pictures, just for yourself.

Draw in a sketchbook. Be mindful. Give yourself a chance to experience what is happening in the moment and let yourself heal and grow.

You'll be a better person, have more money left to write, have experiences to write about, or have done your research to create new worlds. Maybe you'll find connections to places and people that will last a lifetime.

Slow travel is not about the speed you move about in the world.

Support the local economy, eat local foods, stray off the beaten path. Make it an opportunity to learn more about your country and help out communities where loss is significant. Get out and find other thriving authors to share your story with.

Decide how intimate you want your slow-travel excursions to be. You hit the road for more freedom. Decide what that freedom can do for you.

Have you ever sailed? No? Then travel on a waterway. Enjoy being off the grid and see what your creative senses experience.

Never traveled by bicycle? We had folding bikes with us. In San Diego, we could ride for miles along the ocean, away from vehicular traffic. We could hear the birds, feel the sun on our faces, but cover great distances and enjoy our individual introvert bubbles to think.

Instead of trying to write a novel as you cross from the west to the east or from the north to south, take a scene from your current project and dedicate more time in one place to that story. Consider getting off the major highways and interstates. Get out of the noise.

Find an audience along the way. Do your books feature small towns? Feature one of the small towns you travel through in your books and convert the locals. Put your books in small bookstores across the nation.

Take time to plan a new series. Spend more time writing and less time looking at the map of where you can go next.

Do whatever will energize you. How immersive do you want this period in your life to be?

Make your newsletter links more clickable with a guidebook that correlates with your time on the road. Have this experience as authentic as you dreamed you would.

Even if you know what the ending is going to be, why rush it?

DON'T TRAVEL WITHOUT A HOME BASE BY JANET KITTO

Eventually, all travel brings us back home.

When I was near the end of the road, after 9 months of living in an RV, and before that, 6 months of downsizing all of my belongings to sell a house, and then, 3 months of researching and making a decision to relocate, I wanted a home base.

I wanted to take a long, hot shower in a bathroom with a big-enough mirror to show me more than what I was from the neck up. I wanted to taste life again from a kitchen that had a countertop spanning more than a foot and a half. I was ready to stare out of a window larger than the windshield of our truck.

A home base doesn't have to be a home you own. It can be a family home where you connect with siblings or parents, or a friend's house, or a location that always recharges you. It's where you have a comfortable chair to sit your butt in to write. It's where you can do your laundry, have good Wi-Fi, and use more than two squares of toilet paper (to keep your RV pipes from clogging up).

When we set out, we didn't think we'd see as many provinces and states as we did. We brought a little of everything for the road, not realizing we didn't leave enough space to live.

Our storage unit back on Vancouver Island was packed with tools for a cabin we thought we'd be constructing on a little plot of land. That plan fell through right at the start of our journey.

I now love to travel. I discovered how to live and move about in the world as a minimalist. Ten months was long enough on the road for me to be ready for a change.

There's going to come a point when travel loses its appeal, and you'll want to stop. If you've given up your mortgage and other debt for financial freedom, and you think that you'll always want to live in your RV and vehicle, leave space in your life to make the next move.

No matter how much you plan for travel, you can't control the conditions.

I had tried to chase indie authorship for years. There was no business reason not to, even in another country, except that I wasn't yet comfortable wearing an entrepreneurial hat. Instead, I worked on story structure and scenes.

I left my home before I knew where my home base would be. While I was away, I would see a flash of my previous life, which was good because it drove me to figure out what I did NOT want anymore.

By the end of our journey, my husband and I had different perspectives on why we were stopping. If I'd known that it was okay to take a job somewhere and keep writing, or that it was okay to stop and prepare for another season of travel, maybe I would have found a familiar driveway to visit.

Still, we decided together to settle down on the opposite coast of Canada. That way, we could still enjoy going to the beach, but we'd be reaping the benefits of a lower cost of living. Our income doesn't have to be six figures if we don't want it to be.

We decided to come back and find a home base because I was ready for family life again. I changed WHAT I was doing because I couldn't change everything about WHO I am.

MINDSET

As you start this section, you'd be forgiven for thinking it was all about anarchy. And while I do believe there's a little bit of anarchy inside of everyone, this rebellion isn't *just* about flouting authority. This is about empowerment, freedom, and creating a life you truly want to live.

Creating a business is one thing, but being a thriving author provides you with freedom and independence that most people only dream of. But in order to get to that freedom, there are a million pieces of resistance you have to fight… or "rebel" against. Whether it's your own mindset, a lack of support from family, having to take terrifying leaps of faith, or choosing to go against the grain to carve out the path you really want, they're all tiny acts of rebellion.

Being a thriving author sets you apart from the crowd, you shouldn't have to conform or apologize for your uniqueness and career choices. You have our permission to rebel.

In this section, J. Thorn and Sacha Black identify nine things that thriving authors don't do when it comes to rebellion.

So buckle up, whip out your sass, and brace yourself as we discuss how changing your mindset around rebellion can help you to shape your career, have a healthier, more kickass attitude, and get you closer to your author career.

Here's a quick summary of the valuable lessons you can expect to learn in this section:

"Don't Have a Fixed Mindset" - Sacha acknowledges that mindset is a huge part of working toward an author career, but more than that, mindset is a continual work in progress. She also draws attention to Carol Dweck's fixed and growth mindsets and why you need to have a growth mindset to succeed.

"Don't Say Yes to Everything" - Saying yes is par for the course when you're starting out. But as your career develops, you have to reserve time for the essential work. Saying no is always a small act of rebellion but one every thriving author has to learn.

"Don't Suppress Their Obsession" - Obsession is often seen as a dirty word. But Sacha calls out that error, arguing that the most successful people in history have all used their obsessive passion to further their careers and that thriving authors should, too.

"Don't Try to Be Part of the Crowd" - Being part of the crowd is the easy option. It's comfortable, safe, "normal." But no thriving author is normal. Thriving authors have to choose to rebel against the norm, against what's expected, and carve their own paths.

"Don't Stick to the Rules" - No one's saying you have to break the law to be a thriving author, but you do have to break some rules. They might be work rules, family ones, genre rules, or perhaps writing and publishing rules. To truly break out of the rat race, you're going to have to break some rules along the way.

"Don't Take on Expectations" - It's one of the hardest parts of being a thriving author. There are expectations everywhere from families, society, friends, the industry, even ourselves. While Sacha acknowledges how hard it is to break expectations, she also explains why the consequence of accepting them can end an author's career.

"Don't Refuse to Leap" - The biggest leap you'll ever have to take is leaving your day job. But the leaps of faith don't stop there. This essay explains that leaping is terrifying and full of risk, but something every thriving author has to get... well, perhaps not comfortable with, but at least accept.

"Don't Ignore What They Think and Fail to Speak Up"- It's hard to speak up, especially when all of the advice and helpful opinions of loved ones around you are saying something different. But thriving authors have to get comfortable in their decisions. They have to have enough self-belief that even when friends and family are clamoring for them to "stop now," or "just wait," they know they're doing the right thing.

"Don't Think There's Only One Way to an Author Career" - It's an easy mistake to make, looking at the big indies with cash rolling in and assuming that their way is the right way. But Sacha explains how no two authors have reached "thriving author" status in the same way, and how your path will be different.

DON'T HAVE A FIXED MINDSET BY SACHA BLACK

Mindset is one of the hardest elements of your business to get right. When I reached the end of my first year of self-employment and reviewed the lessons I'd learned, I was shocked to find that half of them were mindset related.

Thinking about it, it makes sense. You have to get your mindset right in order to work through the grueling "day job," bit of your journey. But once you've quit, the work on your mindset doesn't stop because you've achieved full-time status. If anything, the opposite is true. Working on your mindset becomes even more important. Vital even.

When you're going solo, it's so easy to let the insidious doubt-devil creep into the corners of your mind. It's a parasite, a persistent virus that will eat you up from the inside out. The only way to combat it is to constantly work on your mindset. A thriving author knows this.

Carol Dweck is famed for her work on fixed and growth mindset. She explains that a person will have one mindset or the other: fixed or growth. Those with a fixed mindset view intelligence as static. They tend to avoid challenges, give up easily, see putting in the effort as pointless and ignore useful, but critical feedback. The result of this mindset is that many people plateau or fail to achieve their full potential. Another result is that they will often see the world from a deterministic bent.

For an author with a fixed mindset, reading a bad review first thing in the morning could ruin their day and knock them off course. Having a bad sales day could result in them not bothering to write for the rest of the week because, "What's the point if I can't sell books anyway?"

A growth mindset then, is the exact opposite. They see intelligence as flexible, something to be grown. They embrace challenges and persist despite the setbacks. They see effort as a mechanism to aid them in their goals, they learn from criticism, and I'm sure you can see where this is going. The result is that they achieve or even overachieve their goals, and they also have a greater sense of free will.

For an author with a growth mindset, reading that same bad review might spur them on to prove the reviewer wrong, or to write a better book next time, or they may just view the reviewer as one person with one opinion. That bad sales day? No bother, they choose to work harder on their ads. They research a new type of ad and examine the ads they have running to see if they can make them more effective.

Having read both of those, I'm sure you recognize which mindset a thriving author has.

The successful leaders in the world all have growth mindsets, they embrace the challenges life throws at them and happily put in the effort to grow and learn and get better.

No one's saying this is easy, no one is expecting you to crack this mindset from day one. And I'm certainly not expecting you to have your mindset mastered day in, day out. We all have bad days, it's okay to have them. And just because you do have it mastered most of the time, that doesn't mean that a bad review won't punch you in the feels and knock you off course for a few days. It will, and you'll have to pull yourself back up again.

Thriving authors aren't cyborgs. It's okay to feel like poop on occasion, and hey, if you need a day to wallow, fill your boots.

What matters is how you pick yourself back up and soldier on. What matters are the choices you make following those setbacks. That's the difference between having a fixed mindset and a growth mindset; it's the difference between thriving authors and amateurs. Thriving authors might allow themselves a bad day or two, but they don't let bad reviews take over their lives or stop them from writing. They rebel against the wallowing, they stand up to their fixed mindset, and they fight on.

It's easy to look at the successful indie authors and think their success came overnight. It didn't.

Okay, everyone can name the odd lightning flash who wrote a book in a month and earned six figures. But 99% of indies didn't.

For the rest of the world, they wrote crappy books and edited them, edited them again, and published, published, published. They had bad days, bad reviews, bad launches, and bad series, and they carried on anyway. They faced plot problems, financial difficulties, and a lack of support from loved ones, and guess what? They carried on anyway.

Thriving authors look at their weaknesses and embrace them, choosing not to be crushed by problems but to seek help, learn more, and improve. Thriving authors don't seek approval from others, they prioritize growth and learning instead. They also focus on the process and not the end result. Yes, we want to hold the physical book in our hands, but once you've got it, that's it, the project is over and finishing one book doesn't create an author career.

The process is your foundation. A solid process that you can repeat enables you to write book after book, and that creates an author career.

This mindset stuff is hard. None of us get it right 100% of the time. Even industry giants like Stephen King and Judy Blume, who are decades into their writing careers, still talk about doubt and the fear of editorial criticism. It's natural.

But as you face these obstacles, you have a choice. Thriving authors choose to embrace the criticism, embrace the hard slog of editing, and use it to improve their craft and business. That's what builds sustainability in your writing business.

Being a thriving author isn't easy, and as much as I hate to say it, it will continue to be challenging. But that's why having a growth mindset is so essential, because when you have one, you carry on despite the obstacles.

The only person in the way of your goals is you.

A thriving author knows this and gets out of their own way. They choose to have a growth mindset because as much as they know the hard days will come, they also know they'll fight through them. They see the obstacles, setbacks, and mistakes as lessons learned and opportunities for growth.

Which mindset are you going to choose?

DON'T SAY YES TO EVERYTHING BY SACHA BLACK

This one is especially difficult because for a long time, you do need to say yes to everything. When you're a new writer you have no platform, no fans, and no readers. You don't have a reputation and you certainly don't have the sales. It's safe to say yes when no one knows who you are. Which means you have to work doubly hard to build all of those things. And that usually means saying yes—a lot.

But saying yes is exhausting, it's time consuming and if you're not careful, before long, you'll be doing speaking gigs, helping authors, Skype sessions, and critiques and—three months have passed and you haven't worked on any of the important jobs—like *your* books and *your* words.

It's one of the trickier things to balance. You need to do the awareness raising and platform building by partnering and collaborating and doing promotional gigs or whatever delectables come your way, but you also need to be creating new products to sell, otherwise all that engagement and fan base building is utterly pointless when you've still only got that one book on sale.

One book a career does not make.

In a 2019 study, Written Word Media showed that the average thriving author making six figures has 28 books on average—average is an important word, each author's journey is different and some make six figures on 2 books and others don't make it until they have 100 books. The lesson, though, is that if you keep saying yes, you'll keep compressing your writing time. That pushes the 28 books and an author career further and further away.

FOMO is a real kicker. For those not in the know, FOMO means "fear of missing out." That's one of the drivers behind saying yes. If you're a yes girl, then saying no is doubly excruciating, not only because you're missing out on a chance to platform build or sell books, etc., but also because you have to cope with anxiety-inducing FOMO.

What if someone else said yes and it's *the* opportunity that makes their career? What if something amazing comes out of the opportunity? What if the group of authors all forge an amazing friendship and I miss out?

Let me pull you into my inky arms. It's okay to miss out. If anything, I encourage it. Make missing out a choice. You can choose to spend your time on more important tasks, like writing those 28 books. Spend time on building the business and services that will bring you income.

Sure, you may miss out on some socials, or a cracking conference that may have gained you five minutes in the spotlight.

But people have short memories and I'm sure you know about the seven-touches principle of marketing. On average, it takes seven encounters with a product before a person will buy it.

Then there's that age ol' saying floating around the Internet that it takes reading four books before someone remembers your name. You're not missing out. That one thing you say no to, it's not make or break. For 999,999 people out of a million, there are no lightning bolts. You're going to be okay. In fact, you're doing yourself a favor by prioritizing the important work.

Let's not detract from the work you would be doing, though. Building a platform is essential. If you have a lot of books and no one knows about you, you're not going to sell any copies.

Likewise, if you have no books and a huge platform, you have nothing to sell. It's chicken and egg. Thriving authors know when to whip out their inner rebel and say no.

No one likes saying no. It's hard. Yes rolls off the tongue so easily. It's all silky and lubricated. No is hard in the mouth, it's a little sour, and has prickly edges. It's a difficult word to say and the consequences are harder to deal with. But that's what a thriving author does.

They prioritize the books and products first, always. Then comes the marketing and platform building.

Thriving authors know there's a time when you have to rebel against the yes vote and start saying no. That time is different for each author and some reach it early, some reach it later. For each time you face an opportunity, there is no right or wrong answer. And as much as I'd love to, I can't tell you when your time to start saying no will be. I'd like to say it's when you've written your third book and created a box set and done one audiobook. But I can't.

What I can say is, you'll know when you get there because your time is scarce and pressured. You'll know that spending time writing another book will earn you X dollars but participating in Y opportunity is a financial, growth, or productivity unknown.

Early in your career, saying yes is vital because you need the exposure in order to build your platform and sales. But once that work pays off, and your platform is at a level where you have an established audience and a solid income, your workload will have grown, too.

This presents an opportunity cost. Suddenly, your time is valuable and needed to create more books, products, and services that you can give to your now-hungry audience. While more exposure is valuable, it's not always more valuable than satisfying your current audience. Suddenly, you're running a business and you no longer have the time to say yes to everything because doing so does detriment to another part of your business.

When an opportunity presents itself to a thriving author, they'll always assess whether it's worth their time.

Is the opportunity big enough to sacrifice precious writing or creating time? What will the payoff be? What will the benefit be to your books and your career if you take on this opportunity? Versus how many words could you have written if you said no? Will saying yes mean you get to give back and help hundreds of fellow writers, or will it add too much stress and pressure on your plate?

Only you know the answer. Each opportunity will present a different set of options and challenges to be weighed against each other. Thriving authors might not like FOMO—but who does? They embrace the position they're in and carefully assess each choice and opportunity striking the best balance they can to continue propelling their careers forward.

DON'T SUPPRESS THEIR OBSESSION BY SACHA BLACK

I've met a lot of thriving authors and whether they'd like to admit it or not, there's one trait they all share. A controversial trait, as it happens: obsession. Stay with me, I know many of you will be screaming, "Obsession is bad," a terrible trait, it's... well... it's obsessive.

Yes, actually, that's sort of the point.

I can hear you screaming that obsession can't possibly be a trait that writers should have. But oh, dear sweet authors, it *is*.

It really, really is.

See, I believe that all the greats have obsession as a trait.

Look at history. Thomas Edison created 3,000 designs before he stumbled across the final light bulb. James Dyson made 5,126 prototypes before he finally iterated to bagless Hoover perfection. Gertrude Stein submitted poems for 22 years before she got one accepted. Jack Canfield and Mark Victor Hansen, authors of *Chicken Soup for the Soul,* were rejected 144 times before being accepted.

These are big numbers. That is a LOT of rejection and failure. There's no way you can argue that these guys were anything less than obsessed with their goals.

Now, before we dive into this essay, I feel like I should address the mental health aspect of obsession.

To be absolutely clear, I am not referring to "obsession" as a concept of unhealthy obsessions, nor am I referring to any instance of obsessions as defined by the DSM-5 (Diagnostic and Statistical Manual of Mental Disorders). What I'm referring to is healthy, obsessive passion. A tunnel vision of sorts, an unwavering determination and "grit" that leads so many creatives to success.

Of course, there is a very fine balance between keeping an obsession healthy and falling into something less healthy. And if you're in any doubt, you should always seek professional medical help.

But we're sticking with healthy obsession today, because I truly believe being obsessive in this way helps you to achieve your goals more quickly than lumbering through life doing a little bit of work here and there.

Obsession is a driving force. It means you can't leave the scab alone.

You take every opportunity you have to write words or learn about the industry or work on your marketing. You're the one at work who sits waiting for a meeting to start and scribbles part of a scene—everyone else? Well, they're busy talking inanely about the latest reality TV show.

Obsession drives you to consume information, to get better, to learn more, to practice more, to push through when others quit. I also think it means you're more likely to treat your writing like it's a profession, rather than viewing it as a hobby or pastime. There's nothing wrong with the latter, but this is about being a thriving author and you can't treat writing as a pastime if you want to have a career as an author.

Michael Phelps didn't become the most decorated Olympian by putting in a bit of effort here and there, or treating swimming as a hobby. No, Phelps smashed out training session after training session, getting in the pool twice a day—even when he didn't want to. He did his weights sessions religiously, even when his body protested. He ate set meals even when it was the 108th consecutive day that he'd eaten chicken and brown rice.

Phelps was obsessive.

Dyson was obsessive.

Edison, Stein, Canfield—all obsessive.

Thriving authors?

Yeah, they're obsessive, too.

Greatness requires obsession. I challenge anyone who says these greats weren't obsessed.

Obsession is also helpful to writers for another reason. See, we creatives often suffer with doubt, a vicious little parasite that likes to worm its way into our best creative cells and cannibalize any confidence we had.

But obsession is the antidote because even on your darkest, most unconfident days, obsession will keep driving you forward. As insidious as doubt is, obsession is more cunning. It multiplies harder and faster, and its claws are far sharper than doubts ever were.

You need your obsession, you need to embrace it, nurture it, and wear it under your suit like Superman.

Anyone can be a writer. All you have to do is write regularly. That, by definition, is a writer. But to be a thriving author, that takes something more—persistence and determination.

It takes obsession.

Obsession has become something of a naughty word. It's a word surrounded by shame and negativity. A trait we might have but "shouldn't" admit to.

I challenge that assumption and so do thriving authors. They rebel against societal expectations and embrace the true power of their obsessions.

A thriving author knows the value of their obsession and uses it to help them grow, learn and develop themselves, their craft, and their businesses. It's also a handy sword for those low days when the doubt-beast gets you.

Obsession drives you to go the extra mile.

When the average writer is tired, fed up or beaten down by a week of bad sales. A thriving author will dig deeper. They have a worm that's hungry, and there's only so long it will allow them to wallow. Eventually, a thriving author will research another advertising stream, they'll search for another author to collaborate with, they'll ask a friend to brainstorm marketing ideas or help them work through the plot issues.

It is always the extra mile that separates the average writer from a thriving author and that extra mile is gained in obsession.

Thriving authors don't allow the stigma and connotations surrounding the word obsession stop them from using its strength and power. They rebel against the notion that obsession is bad and instead choose to embrace it and use it for good.

How you use your obsession is up to you.

DON'T TRY TO BE LIKE THE CROWD BY SACHA BLACK

I don't care what you say, we all want to be liked. Even me. And I parade around convincing people my heart is black and my soul is made of coal... it is, I swear...

How dare you smirk at me. I didn't cry at *Toy Story 3*, my eyes were sweating.

Anyway, what I'm getting at is that humans are social beasts. We need contact and love and time to communicate with other evolved monkeys. As much as the introverts of the world love the rejuvenation of alone time, we still need contact with others.

Humans like to be liked—we like to be popular. It's genetically programmed into our DNA. Survival of the species requires mating and unfortunately, mating requires contact with other humans.

But there's a fine line between wanting to be liked and becoming part of the crowd. Being part of the crowd means you're taking the easy road, and the easy option. Being part of the crowd means letting your uniqueness dim and blend into the haze of everyone else's light. Why stand out when you can blend in?

If being a thriving author was easy, everyone would be on a white beach in Bali sipping cocktails with one hand and bashing out New York Times bestselling novels with the other.

But let's think about what being part of the crowd really means. When you're in the thick of blending in, you're distinctly average. The very purpose of being part of the crowd is to be like others—middle of the road. You can't be unique because then you stand out. You can't be better than others because then you stand out.

I don't know whether you've noticed, but thriving authors are anything but average. The average author earns a pittance; the average writer doesn't even finish a novel, let alone publish the thing. You can't be average, you can't be part of the crowd and still be a thriving author. It's like oil and water, the two don't mix.

Want to be liked? Sure, me, too. Who doesn't?

Want to be part of the crowd? Absolutely not.

Of course, not being part of the crowd has consequences. It can create tension between you and friends and family who might still be *in* the crowd. Those "in it" want their loved ones to be in it, too. Who wants to be on a different team to their family?

Those in the crowd won't like your defiance. They'll rail against it, try and convince you that it's a hopeless journey, that you'll never succeed. You're throwing your money away, doomed to failure.

But you have to remember, those in the crowd aren't thriving authors.

This isn't about rebelling for rebellion's sake. And it's not about being so difficult and contrary that you make yourself disliked. Far from it.

This is about not bending to peer pressure. Not thinking that the methods and tactics "everyone" else uses are right. It's about empowering yourself enough so you don't feel obliged to do... well, anything that doesn't sit right with your values and your journey.

Being an indie author is an opportunity to take your career by the reins and shape it the way you want. Being an indie author gives you the freedom from any boss making decisions for you, no interference from peer pressure, no gatekeepers determining whether you're allowed to publish or not, and no one to determine the right path for you.

It's total freedom and total choice. That amount of freedom is intimidating, which is what makes it so easy to see the crowd and run toward it. A crowd is a known entity, it's comfortable and safe.

Being a thriving author isn't safe. It's big and there's some risk, but it's also the most fulfilling, freeing life there is.

My wife uses an amazing analogy. She teaches kids who are struggling to stay in education or have chosen not to continue their formal studies and do apprenticeships instead.

She tells them at the start of the year, you can be a chicken or an eagle. But you can't be both. Then, she asks the students which one they want to be.

You have the same choice.

Chickens—and apologies to the chicken-lovers reading this—don't think for themselves, they follow the crowd, clucking and helpless; they all look the same and stick to the flock.

But eagles... they're different. They fly above the flock, they're leaders... actually, they're predators that eat the flock for breakfast[*]. Eagles are independent and think for themselves, hunting their goals without mercy. The herd watches the eagle, waiting for its next move.

*I'm not suggesting you start eating members of the writing crowd. That's going to be bad for business. Just go with the metaphor.

What I'm trying to say is that thriving authors are eagles. They could follow the crowd and be like and live like everyone else. But they don't. They rebel against it to create a different-shaped path, a unique one built on their values and what makes them happy.

A thriving author decides the route they want to take their career and ignores the rest. Thriving authors think for themselves and use their entrepreneurial streaks to help them stay independent.

But more than any of those things, thriving authors find the thing that's uniquely them, the aspects of their personality and the brand that set them *apart* from the crowd. Then they knuckle down on making it prosper so that they stand out, above, and away from the crowd.

So, let me ask you.

Are you a chicken or an eagle?

DON'T STICK TO THE RULES BY SACHA BLACK

I hate rules. I have a reputation for being a rebel. It's in my blood.

My great-grandmother was a rebel, so was my grandmother, and you can be assured that my father is. It's the reason I'm an indie. I couldn't bear the thought of a gatekeeper telling me what I could or couldn't do with my books and marketing.

Whenever someone places a rule on me, I have this primal fire ignite in my belly. A sort of inner scream clawing at my mind to find a way to break it. Doesn't matter how I break it—big break, small break—as long as I can subvert the rule placed on me, I'm all good.

Unfortunately, karma is a proverbial toe rag; it appears that my son has inherited my rebellious nature. Take this very morning as an example. He wanted to pour the milk in his bowl by himself, so reluctantly—in a bid to foster independence—I handed over the milk. He poured the milk in, and at the right point, I said, "Whoa, that's enough now."

He dutifully stopped pouring, then looked up, staring me square in the face and poured in another drop of milk. I must have pulled a pained expression because he continued to say, "Don't be grumpy, Mummy."

"I'm only grumpy because I told you not to pour any more in."

"Yeah," he said, grinning, "but it was only a tiny bit."

And here we have karma, my closest friend and my worst enemy.

Rules and rule breaking is a sticky topic.

There are some rules, like not murdering people, that are pretty solid. I'll be honest, I'm never going to break that one. Nor will I steal or commit any other acts of violence—except in my martial-arts fighting ring when it's fair game. I also won't perpetrate illegal crimes that would otherwise harm another person. I suspect the majority of you reading will agree that these are sensible rules to keep.

There are other rules such as sticking to a word count in flash fiction that also make sense. Those word-count rules are there to encourage your creativity. They restrict in order to foster outside-the-box thinking with words.

But other rules? Well, those were made for bending, twisting, and occasionally snapping.

See that derelict building with the no-trespassing sign? I probably climbed in to get some wicked dystopian photo inspiration for my next story. There was a time in my old day-job life when my boss told me I wasn't dressed corporately enough. Funny—I didn't realize the clothes that I wore directly affected how my fingers typed on the keyboard. I went to work in leggings and Converse trainers the next day, and the following day, and every day after that.

Some rules are silly. Others are made for breaking. And the truly terrible rules are designed to keep you stifled in a creative box. Those are the ones you need to set fire to as you burst free from their restraints in showers of glitter and rainbows.

Over the course of history, the greats have *had* to break the rules. Inventors have to break the confines of "current" design. Engineers have to think outside the box to create better, faster, more ingenious technologies.

Shakespeare practically rewrote the English language. According to Shakespeare.org.uk, he invented 1,700 new words that we're still using today. That's a serious amount of rule breaking.

But it's not just dead writers who break the rules. Mike McCormack broke all of the grammar rules with his 272-page novel, *Solar Bones*, published in 2016. The whole book is one sentence... ONE! Outrageous. That's not allowed. It's totally against the writing law.

But is it?

McCormack did it and he won a ton of awards for it. He broke the rules just like Shakespeare. Both men saw the "writing rules" and decided there was a better way around them. Was it controversial? Sure. Could it have gone wrong? Absolutely. But it didn't.

What rules you deem silly and ripe for breaking are unique to you and your moral inclinations. One person's Shakespeare is another's nightmare. But each and every thriving author will come across a rule that will test their moral fiber.

If you think about it, being an indie is a kind of rule break in itself. Every indie goes against expectation of "traditional" publishing and the gatekeepers and goes it alone. And at every step of the way, indies get to choose whether they break the rules or not—genre mash-up or write to market? On-brand cover design or slightly quirky and off-brand? On and on go the rules...

There are some writing rules that are sensible to keep. Tropes, for example, are based on reader expectations. Some tropes you may be able to bend and twist, but others—like a happily-ever-after in a romance book—you simply can't break without irritating your readers, which I don't advise doing.

But there are others like, "You must have a person on the front of your urban fantasy cover," that perhaps you could bend. Other rules such as, adverbs can't be used or you must always *show* emotion can also be bent.

Sneaking in some words at the office because you've finished all your work at the day job? I won't tell if you don't. Some rules come in waves and fads. Others, like you really shouldn't go into debt to fund your writing business, not so much. No-debt-to-fund-writing might not be a rule, but it should be. A thriving author knows the difference between the rules they should follow for the health of their business and sales and the rules they can break in order to stretch a genre, build their readership, create something spectacular, or fulfill their dreams.

Thriving authors don't break every rule, just the ones that restrict their creativity, their ability to write the best story they can, or their opportunities to experiment with marketing and promotion.

The beauty of a career as an author is the ability to make your life as you see it. Thriving authors get to make the rules and choose the ones they break.

Which rules will you break?

Don't Take on Expectations by Sacha Black

Expectations are powerful, but power has two sides, which means that expectations can be used for good or bad, depending on who, how, and why someone is placing them upon you.

They are so powerful that they can shape careers and lives, and veer potential off its creative path and on to something else, something "normal," expected—unwanted.

Following the law, for example, is a good expectation. It, mostly, protects people.

But other expectations, say, from your parents wanting you to go to an Ivy League school, or get a proper job, aren't so good.

The thing with expectations is that they usually come from a place of good intention.

Parents care deeply about us and our lives, they want us to do well, and to learn from the mistakes they made in their lives. But that's not how life works, at least most of the time. We have to carve our own paths, our children have to find their own way in life. It's your life. We only get one chance to make this life our own. None of us can or should live our lives for our parents or friends or loved ones. That's not how this works. Their choices are theirs, and ours are ours.

Expectations create social pressure to conform, to follow the crowd, to live the life someone else wants for you.

One of the most famous psychological experiments done by Milgram (1963) demonstrated how dangerous that expectations and obedience can be.

In the experiment, Milgram wired up a colleague to an electric-shock machine. The machine was clearly labeled from 0 volts to 400+ volts, which showed "danger." The participant then had to administer increasingly powerful electric shocks to the colleague every time they got something wrong. And each time a shock was administered, the colleague would shout in protest and pain.

Milgram would use phrases to place expectations on the participant such as, "please continue," and "you have no choice but to continue." Unbeknownst to the participant, the colleague was intentionally getting things wrong and was not, in fact, wired to the machine, but pretending to scream in pain.

Despite this, and despite the silence that came after the participant shocked the colleague at over 350v (indicating unconsciousness and death), 65% of participants continued to the end of the experiment.

What does this tell you? It tells you that expectations are immeasurably powerful. That most people will do as they are told, even when they know better and think they should be doing something else. Expectations breed obedience. And not all obedience is good. Yes, I'm suggesting that sometimes rebellion is not only needed, but essential.

The problem is, when you refuse to conform, it creates ripples, waves, and sometimes, tsunami-style repercussions.

Breaking expectations is so much harder than just not accepting them in the first place. Breaking them means going against the grain, defying loved ones, friends, or authority figures. It means standing out, going it alone, and facing consequences.

That's scary and pressured, and not everyone wants to be the one to break the mold. That's fine, you don't have to be. You also don't have to be a thriving author.

See, conforming to expectations that you don't agree with creates resentment. That resentment festers, it rots and sours and spreads. It makes people miserable and fed up, it ruins lives and mindsets, and your happiness.

It's not easy to reject expectation, but there comes a time in every thriving author's life when they have to do it.

It might be a parent telling them they expect them to fail because creative careers aren't financially viable. It might be a friend turning up their nose because you're choosing to self-publish and they expected you to try the trad route. Or it could be a spouse telling you they support you, but they don't expect you to leave your day job until you can afford to pay your share of the bills from your writing.

Whatever the expectation, thriving authors have to dig deep, grab hold of their unwavering faith, and fight their way through. A thriving author will examine the expectations that others try to put on them and only allow the ones that help them flourish.

No matter the consequence and fallout from not accepting others' expectations, thriving authors will first and foremost protect their own expectations ,regardless of whether they're expected to quit their job, to live the dream, to write full time, or to make X amount of income. These expectations are valuable because they drive an author forward and push them to achieve. They should be protected from the weight of others' expectations, even if it hurts their loved ones' feelings.

There are so many inspirational quotes and questions I could throw at you. But there's only one that really matters.

When you're lying on your deathbed in 50, 70, 90 years, do you want to look back and see a life lived for someone else?

Do you want to be shrouded in expectation and oozing with bitterness, or do you want to see a life full of vibrance and joy, no matter the outcome? Do you want regrets? Or do you want to look back free of, "I wish I'd done x, y, z?"

Remember those two little letters from the beginning of the book? Sometimes you have to say no. Even when it's scary and might upset others.

"No, you will not work a 9-5 job."

"No, you can't promise your spouse a stable paycheck."

"No, you don't want to submit traditionally."

Instead, thriving authors say yes to so many other wonderful things. Repeat after me:

"Yes, I do expect to quit my job."

"Yes, I do expect to make this my lifelong career."

"Yes, I do expect my writing business to pay my bills."

I can't tell you what expectations you should or shouldn't take on and neither can any other thriving author. What I can do is tell you that I'm a thriving author, I chose to rebel against others' expectations. I built my own, and you should, too.

Don't Refuse to Leap by Sacha Black

Luck.

There are two kinds of people in the world: Those who believe in it, and those who don't. I don't know about you, but I'm in the latter camp.

Dictionary.com defines luck as:

"the force that seems to operate for good or ill in a person's life, as in shaping circumstances, events, or opportunities:"

And there lies the issue; luck is a disembodied, intangible force, one that we as authors can't control. Luck is blind. It's based on faith of the inconceivable. It leaves life to chance and fate and to the whims of the universe.

I choose to reject this notion, and I believe that thriving authors do, too. There's nothing innately wrong with luck, but it's perilous and takes control of your destiny out of your hands. Ultimately, whether luck does or doesn't exist, and whether or not you believe in it isn't the point.

This is about mindset and choosing to pick up your career by the proverbial balls and charge forward with it. This is about choosing to believe you have the ability and the power to shape your destiny. And this is where we meet the leap.

You don't get to be a thriving author without taking at least one leap of faith. The likelihood is that you'll have to take many more after that, but the biggest leap is always saying "I quit" to the rat race and leaving the stability of your day job.

I'm not going to lie to you...

Each and every leap of faith is utterly terrifying.

It's every horror movie you've ever watched. It's every shot of adrenaline injected simultaneously straight into your carotid. A full-blown stomach-in-the-mouth-you're-going-to-puke feeling while standing on the precipice of a 300-foot cliff, your toes inched over the edge with nothing but thin air and sand particles floating beneath you. It's knowing that you have to jump despite the frothing waves crashing below, the salty wind chafing your cheeks, and your blurred vision. You have to jump, even though your insides are flip-flopping so violently that you're not sure whether to puke or faint or a combination of both—probably both.

What makes this leap scary is the blurred vision. A leap of faith is a jump into the unknown; when you tip off the edge, you can't see the landing point. The free fall is unguided, and you have to "make it up as you go." You jump with no idea whether you'll land on X or 100 feet to the left in a stinky sewage pit.

Every leap of faith feels this terrifying to some extent because inherent in every leap is a measure of risk.

Risk is scary. Our bodies have evolved to avoid it because evolutionarily, risk could mean death. Our autonomic nervous systems are quite literally wired to protect us from this kind of danger.

You know leaping is a free fall into the unknown and your brain is screaming, "Stop, stop, stop, the unknown is dangerous." It absolutely could be, too. You're flying blind, baby! Who knows if you'll sell enough books to make it? As if taking a leap wasn't hard enough, the act of leaping goes against every natural fiber in your body. Cheers, evolution.

Ultimately, it doesn't matter what the dream is, inside every single one is a healthy dose of risk. Risk is the yang to your dream's yin.

There's something important to consider—the consequence of not leaping is far worse than the roller-coaster free fall.

If you don't leap, it's the end. Why? Because when you reach a leap of faith, it's a crossroads. There are only two paths you can take: the leap toward your goal or a retreat back, away from your dream and into the normality of rat-race living and unfulfilled dreams. Leaps are black and white. Jump or don't. There's no in-between. And if you don't leap when the opportunity presents, there's no guarantee that you'll get another opportunity to leap toward your goal in the future.

I like to think of these leaps as personal tests. Like the hero of every story, can you leap over the obstacle and inch closer to your dream?

I still remember the abject horror I had facing my leap of faith. I'd just finished paying off all my debt when an offer of freelance work came out of the blue. I'd planned to leave my job a year later. This was unexpected, unplanned... out of control. The offer was perfect, though, it would bridge the gap between my current royalties and business income and what I needed to pay my bills. If I said no, I had no idea when or if I'd be able to leave my day job the following year. If I said yes, I had no idea if I could "do it," if I could ensure I earned enough royalties and business income.

I jumped, obviously. That's why I'm sitting here writing this. But I can assure you I wore my tightest underwear to make the leap!

While all thriving authors face a variety of different leaps of faith over the years, be it investing their life savings into Facebook ads, collaborating with a new author, or launching a service, there's one leap we all share: quitting the day job. I truly believe the first is the most terrifying. But you can't become a thriving author unless you quit the rat race and face the "to leap or not to leap?" question.

Leap, and you could grow and flourish. You could fulfill your goals and live the life you've always dreamed of, or you could fall flat on your face and have to skulk back to employment. It's an all or nothing situation. Either you make it, or you don't.

I can't promise you'll make it if you take the leap. But I can promise you that if you don't leap, you definitely won't.

There's real magic in saying "I quit" while still working your day job. Something intangible, ethereal, truly powerful. Maybe it's luck? Maybe in those moments, you make your own luck.

What I do know is that when a person throws caution to the wind, digs deep, and leaps into the unknown, good things happen.

I might not believe in luck, but I definitely believe in the universe. Not to get too woo-woo, but the universe helps, the universe *wants* you to succeed. When you leap, it gets the hell out of the way and gives you the room to fly.

DON'T IGNORE WHAT THEY THINK AND FAIL TO SPEAK UP BY SACHA BLACK

Speaking up is hard. It means going against the grain, doing the controversial thing, making a nuisance of yourself. It means rebelling against others. It opens you up to challenge and criticism, and the possibility of not being liked.

Being the only one with your hand up in class is awkward.

For a lot of people, those are seriously undesirable qualities to endure. No one wants to willingly submit themselves to criticism, potential conflict, or worse. We like to be liked, remember?

Saying what you think is hard. It's hard because most of us fear judgment. We fear losing valued friendships, and we fear the repercussions.

All understandable.

But worse, what if we do speak up and it turns out that we're wrong?

No one wants to submit themselves openly to a bully or be ousted out of groups because their creative thoughts don't match the group's ethos. But equally, there are times when a thriving author must speak out to protect themselves, their work, and their business.

But when? Well, let's say you get your brand-new cover design through a graphic artist. You're not happy. But you also don't want to be a pest, or you feel bad asking for the tenth tweak to the cover. The consequence of ignoring what you think and not speaking up is a half-baked cover. A cover that might not meet genre expectations and isn't going to give you the best first impression. A cover that will cost you sales.

What about a clause in a contract with a publisher? Fail to speak up and you could be needlessly giving away rights to your intellectual property. While it might not seem like a big deal now, if the lightning bolt strikes and your book goes to Hollywood, those are going to be pretty big tears you're weeping.

Or what about that editor who insisted you take out a subplot that you were certain fit the genre?

We have gut feelings for a reason. They protect us, tell us when danger is around, when to consider fight or flight. Just because you get those feelings behind a digital screen doesn't mean you should ignore them. Just because you're new, a first-time author, or perhaps a fledgling business owner, doesn't mean you should ignore your gut.

Yes, you might be new to writing, but this is your business. If you're a thriving author at heart, even if you're still one in the making, I'd bet you did your research and know exactly what your cover should look like, or the reason you purposefully added that subplot.

I learned this lesson the hard way.

The first cover I ever commissioned was from a designer who mostly worked with trad houses. An extremely talented designer, too. I still maintain that, despite what happened. But I was significantly overcharged, and it took over a year to get one cover finalized.

One. Single. Cover.

After endless shady communications and multiple occasions where weeks would go by before I heard from them, I finally decided enough was enough and spoke up. I whipped out the contract and a tightly worded email and received the files within 24 hours.

I'd ignored my gut and had been too afraid to speak up. I was worried about upsetting someone in the industry, afraid that this was just how the design process worked. If I hadn't spoken up, I'd have lost that cover and all the money I'd paid. Then I'd have had to spend my editing budget on a new cover.

I'm not telling you to start brawls and be a dick, but I am saying that sometimes you have to do what you know is right, even when it's hard to speak out. Even when you're afraid or worried that you're wrong.

There are worse things than to be wrong. And if you do happen to be wrong? There's a very cute five-letter word that works well: sorry.

This is your business. You are the only one who will protect it like a fearless mother.

No one else believes in your business like you do. You are the only person who can cultivate your career exactly the way you want it. No one else cares about your financial investments like you do. If you don't speak up and your business turns sour, there's only one business owner to blame.

Most of the time, authors, designers, editors, and industry professionals are lovely, genuine humans who will respect you more for being open and honest with them. Most of the time, speaking up will deepen your relationships. Sure, there are times when you have to speak up against something that's damaging your business, but hopefully, those occasions are rare.

But there's one person you may have to speak up against who won't want to listen: yourself.

Do you ever get those nagging itches that you're desperate to ignore, but you really shouldn't? Like reviewing your last three months and wondering why you've only produced X number of words when it ought to have been Y? Was it because you left social media notifications on, or because you allowed yourself to task-hop, or some other procrastinatory reasons?

It's a completely rhetorical question. But sometimes, there's a decision we don't want to make, or a habit that, deep down, we know needs addressing.

Thriving authors know they have to speak up. They know that the path to a full-time career in this world is fraught with difficulties and challenges and criticism. Thriving authors know that the *only* way to protect their work, their rights, and their business is to speak up, to not be afraid to stand up for what they believe in, to protect their rights and their work by calling out whatever their gut is worried about. Thriving authors know they are their businesses' first and last lines of defense—they are their own knights in shining armor, even when they, themselves, are the enemy.

DON'T THINK THERE'S ONLY ONE WAY TO AN AUTHOR CAREER BY SACHA BLACK

And here we come to the crux of this book and the egregious error made by many newer authors.

When you're starting out as a writer and you look at the bright stars of big indies, of the writers who are living the life you want to live, it's easy to think that's the model you should follow, and that there's only one way to create a career as an author.

Wrong.

So very, very wrong.

It's a simple mistake to make.

How many of us venture into huge Facebook groups, or attend conferences and see those "famous" indie authors on the main stage and think their way is the right way? I know when I went to my first conference, it felt like those authors were akin to all-powerful writing demigods. I mean, they'd achieved the high-ranking, high-paying, high-reputational status of "indie royalty." Their presence not only filled a stage, but billowed over it and spilled into the crowded theater. It made it easy to think their way was the right way. How could it not be?

Many indie authors-cum-teachers accidentally say things such as, "This is how you do it." They don't mean this is the *only* way to do it. Usually it's a throwaway comment. It's more efficient to say that this is how you solve the problem, rather than opening a can of philosophical worms about the many and varied routes to authordom.

These indies are sharing their successes and specific journeys to the heady heights they've reached. Of course, their way is right. It's right for them and their circumstances and their situation. But that doesn't take into account the newbie author staring at the Mount Everest of indie authors and the six figures they spend on marketing every year and wondering how on earth they'll achieve the same thing.

"This is how you do it" doesn't mean this is the only way you can do it. It means this is one way you can get there. But for the new author, they take the statement at face value and assume that you need a weighty pocket of change for advertising or for any other myth that permeates the community.

It's easy to stare at successful authors and the path they took to success and assume that is the way one must go. The only way.

It isn't.

It's not even close to the only way.

I've been lucky enough to meet a lot of authors. Authors like Michael Anderle, who's built an empire by publishing hard and fast and using Kindle Unlimited to grow his income.

But for every Michael Anderle I've met, I've met another author like Joanna Penn who publishes at a slower rate and wider, and makes six figures from her royalties and business.

Lest we not forget other authors who have grown their careers by building collaborations, like J. Thorn himself. Or what about thriving authors like Octavia Randolph, who's burrowed down into a tight niche like historical Scandinavian romantic action and now makes six figures a year!

There is no one path.

In fact, those who rebel against the expected path and find their own way are more likely to create their success.

I spoke to Joseph Alexander, musician, guitar teacher, and author about his journey. One that led him to his own rebellion and author career.

"My first book was rejected by a publisher because it came with three DVDs worth of musical examples. I literally got penalized for adding too much value which made the book too expensive to produce. So, instead of creating DVDs, I set up a WordPress site, hosted the audio myself, and added a link in my book, which I published on KDP. Everything was very low tech, but as my books started selling, I invested in my website, my mailing list, and building my audience. I kept writing, adding books, and building the site. When I ran out of things to write about, I partnered with other guitarists and split the profits. 120 books in four languages and 600,000+ sales later I'm still using this model and publishing some of the greatest musicians on the planet. It's amazing how an early rejection can focus your mind on building your own ecosystem once you begin to think outside the box."

What I love about Joseph's journey is that the tried-and-tested route didn't gel with his values. He *wanted* to provide more value. That was important to him and rather than rolling over and adhering to the "expected" route, he rebelled and created his own publishing path.

Our values are integral to creating the right path for us.

I, for example, after a long stint at risk of redundancy when I had a day job, no longer like being financially beholden to one organization. That's why I publish my books wide. It sits better with my values. Does that mean I never use Kindle Unlimited? No, not at all. I just carve a path that matches my values and makes me happy.

See, buried in all these chapters is a rebel mindset. Rebellion against expectation, against conformity, against being a yes man, against fixed mindsets, against staying quiet, against thinking there is only one way to build a successful author career.

At the heart of this book is a quiet revolution—your personal mutiny against what the world and everyone in it wants you to do. You need to drive your own uprising that will create a permanent change; it will empower you, inject you with thriving author rocket fuel that will grow your self-belief and shape the rest of your life, and your author career.

Joseph went on to say,

"It's important to remember that the people in charge of the traditional publishing industry aren't the arbiters of taste, quality. and 'art.' They're just trying to make a living by producing books that their audience will buy. In fact, when you think about it, a publisher was always just someone with enough money to access a printing press. They got to be gatekeepers by virtue of having cash (or a monastery full of monks and quills!). These days, things are different. We can bypass the monopoly of printing and distribution and talk to our audience directly using print on demand and eBooks. In a world of 8 billion people, your audience is out there. Invest in finding them, turn them into fans, and you'll always have a market for your books."

So, go rebel, my little wordsmiths, open your rebellious hearts and rebellious wings, and carve out the author career you've always dreamed of.

SELF-ACTUALIZATION

Is being a thriving author the highest goal in your life?

If you already are, is maintaining that status the highest goal?

What happens if you achieve that goal? Will you be fulfilled?

Most people who achieve lofty external goals will only feel fulfilled for a matter of hours, days, or possibly weeks. But very soon, the euphoria of the achievement wears off, and they're left with the same empty feeling. There is a sense that there must be something more to life.

Their goal had represented something more than it actually was. And after striving for that goal, and achieving it, they realize that they are still the same person. They were striving for transcendence, but all they got was a new job.

A *thriving author* isn't merely a term—it's an ethos. Much like the Zen archer, the thriving author can use their craft as a spiritual path, a vehicle for striving toward self-actualization.

Self-actualization is a term that was used by the psychologist Abraham Maslow. He described a hierarchy of needs that must be met for a human to have the motivation to become fully developed. The needs he identified are in a hierarchy because, to a large degree, the motivation to seek the higher needs depends on the fulfillment of the lower ones. Self-actualization—the fulfillment of one's personal potential—is at the peak of the pyramid.

From lowest to highest, the hierarchy of needs are:

Physiological—Food, water, shelter, and sleep.

Safety and security—Personal safety, emotional security, financial security, health, and well-being.

Social belonging—Friendship, family, and intimacy.

Esteem—Status, respect, self-esteem, competence, and self-confidence.

Self-actualization—The realization of one's full potential. The desire to accomplish everything that one can, to become the most that one can be.

Although the lower levels of need are extremely important, this section will focus primarily on the peak of the pyramid, self-actualization. We will make use of this helpful term to describe the internal path of the thriving author.

Transcendence and self-realization can be difficult to talk about directly. Such subtle and mysterious topics can sometimes only be explored through metaphor, which will be employed liberally.

Here is a quick summary of the areas explored in this book:

"Don't Avoid Adversity at All Costs" — Biological growth requires stress. That is most obvious when it comes to muscle and bone development. But the same is true of the mind and spirit. When this is understood, you can become a mental and spiritual weight lifter.

"Don't Ignore the Little Voice" — The voice of intuition is subtle and quiet. It is easily drowned out by the cacophony of everyday life. If not listened to, that quiet imperative will eventually tear its way into your life, resulting in a midlife or late-life crisis of priorities. But you can learn to integrate your intuitions.

"Don't Take Their Role as Writer Lightly" — Your readers aren't being merely entertained by your books. Whether they know it or not, your books are helping your readers to construct a picture of reality. Deep, universal themes can be transmitted through the most "low-brow" genre fiction. It is important for the author to understand the profundity of this.

"Don't Allow Themselves to Be Influenced by the Wrong Things or People" — Humans are suggestible—programmable, even. While this can initially seem disempowering, you will learn that true power lies in becoming self-programming.

"Don't Believe That They Will Live Forever" — Everyone knows that they will die one day, but few truly believe it. Belief is evidenced by action. The thriving author doesn't believe in putting today off until tomorrow, because tomorrow may never come.

"Don't Practice Things That They Don't Want to Improve" — Everything you do has consequences, one of them is that it will be a little bit easier to do same thing next time. With this knowledge, you can stop growing vicious snowballs and start building virtuous snowballs.

"Don't Succumb to Imposter Syndrome" — Imposter syndrome—the feeling of fraudulence while being seen by others as an authority—is felt by many successful creatives for one good reason: It's true. Sort of...

"Don't Starve the Dark Machine" — Your conscious mind is only the tip of the iceberg, the majority of your mind is dark, hidden. But it is a powerful machine whose output you depend on for insights. But it depends on you for input.

"Don't Ignore the Rest of the Pyramid" — Don't throw out the baby with the bathwater. The lower levels of the pyramid require daily maintenance. A failure at any level of the pyramid can sabotage your higher pursuits.

It is important to note that when we say "spiritual path," we aren't talking about religion, or even a substitute for religion. We use the word "spirit" loosely, and for good reason—that which it describes is difficult to put one's finger on.

Most of us have the sense that we have a potential for development, beyond body, emotion, or intellectual horsepower. Although we've come a long way, we know that there is a version of us that remains in the realm of potential. There is a version of us that is waiting to be found.

Unfortunately, becoming this "true self" doesn't seem to happen automatically. The wise people who have come before us indicate that this transformation requires discipline, intention, and sacrifice, i.e., real work. Perhaps not brute-force work, but work nonetheless.

This section only scratches the surface, but we hope that it will provide you with a few sparks. Hopefully, over time, you will kindle them into the fire that you need for your own inner journey.

DON'T AVOID ADVERSITY AT ALL COSTS BY JIMMY ESSIEN

"The impediment to action advances action. What stands in the way becomes the way." —Marcus Aurelius

When a bone in your body experiences stress, a hormonal cascade is triggered that sends resources to the affected area, thereby increasing bone mass.

When a bone experiences less stress than normal, the body determines that the highly-coveted resources stored in the bone are not needed and can be utilized elsewhere.

This results in osteoporosis or osteomalacia. It's the reason why astronauts can only remain in near-zero gravity for a limited amount of time. No stress, no growth.

Muscles will not grow in strength unless they are sufficiently damaged. Micro-tears in the fibers will trigger an inflammatory response and immune cells will repair the fibers, making them larger and stronger. When a muscle is no longer used, such as when in a cast from an injury, the muscle atrophies. No stress, no growth.

Calluses are often seen as a bad thing. When used figuratively, it is usually in the pejorative. But every manual-labor worker knows that calluses are their friends.

When you first begin working, your hands are soft and tender, not accustomed to the rough treatment. Over time, they get blistered, cut, and worn. But eventually, the skin gets thicker, providing much-needed distance between the nerves in the hand and the harsh external world. Without that padding, tools can't be wielded as expertly.

Whether you are digging a ditch, pulling a hoe, or swinging a sword, long and painful repetition will gain you the protection needed to deftly apply your full force.

There are countless examples of how our bodies require adversity and stress in order to grow.

Fasting is another example. Fasting increases Human Growth Hormone, known as the "fountain of youth hormone." Fasting also enables the body to break down stores of fat in and around the organs, leading to better general health.

The longer it avoids stress, the more fragile the body becomes. But it's not just the body—the mind also gets stronger when it is able overcome small difficulties, one after the other.

Writers, like everyone, need adversity to grow. There's no way around it.

But if adversity is so essential for growth, then why do we reflexively avoid it?

We don't avoid *all* adversity. For instance, we do get out of bed in the morning, even when doing so is sometimes difficult. We wash the dishes, even though we don't feel like it. Most of us keep up some modicum of physical exercise, even though we'd rather not have to.

Let's take the first example. There are a few common reasons that people overcome the unpleasantness of getting out of bed in the morning: We have responsibilities to attend to, that is, social pressure; we have an opposing unpleasant sensation, such as being hungry or needing to use the toilet; or finally, we are adhering to a discipline of getting out of bed at the same time every day for its own sake, that is, to maintain a standard.

Social pressure, a sufficiently strong opposing sensation, and maintenance of a standard of conscientiousness. One of these three is responsible for the vast majority of reasons that people voluntarily face adversity.

The problem with these common criteria is that they cast a fairly loose net. Opportunities for growth easily slip through.

We reflexively avoid adversity, and only deal with the problems that are unavoidable. But you can make more use of the adversity available to you. You can become the mental and emotional equivalent of a body builder by voluntarily taking on the problems that come your way.

The way to practice this is to begin doing things that you don't like doing. But start in small ways.

Find some small thing that you know you don't like, such as writing email newsletters. Treat each of those email campaign documents like you would a 30-pound weight. Your body doesn't really like lifting 30-pound weights, but if you're trying to build muscle, then you'll force yourself to lift that weight a few times every day, or a few times a week, or however many times per week that you decide.

You lift that weight—you work on the email newsletter. You don't do it because you like it, you do it because you *don't* like it. You're doing the thing that you don't like doing so that you become stronger. You're putting some stress on your preferences, but that stress will help build the strength of your mind, and maybe even the strength of your spirit. You may never come to enjoy writing the email newsletter, but as your strength grows, it will no longer be as difficult to manage as it used to be.

An email newsletter is just one example, but it will be different things for everybody. Some examples could be: Editing a manuscript one more time, journaling, networking with other authors or industry professionals, upgrading a website, practicing writing in unfamiliar genres, practicing reading in unfamiliar genres, etc.

The beautiful thing about treating your mind as a muscle that needs to be grown is that the practice will become habitual. You'll find yourself automatically viewing adversity as an opportunity for growth. This will express itself not only in author-related tasks, but you may find yourself viewing opportunities in your personal life as well.

We all know that life isn't fair. It throws adversity to people in different quantities. Having said that, nobody gets out unscathed.

But the secret in transforming difficulty into personal growth is in your attitude.

Going back to the 30-pound weight, if someone is handed this burden, the automatic tendency may be to hold it for only as long as it takes to put it down. But with a different attitude—an opportunistic attitude—being given that dumbbell can be an opportunity to do a few reps before putting it down.

As Marcus Aurelius said: "Just as nature takes every obstacle, every impediment, and works around it—turns it to its purposes, incorporates it into itself—so, too, a rational being can turn each setback into raw material and use it to achieve its goal."

Some adversity ought to be avoided. Things like addiction to heavy drugs, deaths of loved ones, and financial ruin are too dangerous, too terrible to seek out, and may never be recovered from.

These are not 30-pound dumbbells, these are pianos falling from the sky.

Luckily, they are relatively rare on a day-to-day level. But everyday adversity is plentiful, and practicing with the small problems will give you strength to survive the large ones.

Thriving authors don't avoid adversity at all costs.

Don't Ignore the Little Voice by Jimmy Essien

"Insight is not a light bulb that goes off inside our heads. It is a flickering candle that can easily be snuffed out." —Malcolm Gladwell

When you look up at the sky during the day, you don't see the stars. The stars are there, but the light of the sun is overpowering, preventing you from seeing them.

Our ordinary waking state is like the sun. The stars are the *little voices*.

Sometimes you wake up at 2 a.m. and you can't help but see the stars. They seem bright, urgent. But then you fall back to sleep, and when you wake hours later, they're no longer there. The full brightness of the sun obscures their subtle light.

You can gain the ability to see the stars during the day, but it takes practice.

The little voice can be seen as intuition—an imperative that surfaces from the depths of the unconscious mind. When it surfaces, it is often out of context, at odds with the rest of the daytime activities. For this reason, it is usually overlooked. It's too strange to take seriously. Too quiet to be relevant.

Perhaps your decision to become a writer was the result of a little voice that you could no longer ignore.

Many writers will tell of their own personal story, and how for years, even decades, the little voice was telling them that they needed to spend time writing. But they continually ignored the calling. Until one day—maybe they lost a job, got a divorce, or had a life-threatening injury or illness—they realized that the little voice was right, and they needed to pursue the calling.

Continuing our metaphor, a cataclysmic event in your life that makes you understand the importance of the little voice, can be seen as a solar eclipse. Something temporarily blocks out the sun, exposing the subtle light of the stars in the sky, the stars that were always there.

You don't have to wait for a rare solar eclipse that turns your life upside down.

The first step is to acknowledge that there are little voices beckoning for your attention. They tell you to zig when the rest of life is telling you to zag. They speak up when you're engaging in a daily habit that may be unbecoming. They might even tell you that the eastward direction in which you've been traveling for the last 20 years is altogether wrong, and to begin traveling west.

The next step is to make space in your life for it. Live *as if* you can see that star. Even though you can't sense or feel its power, have faith that it is still there, hidden within the noise.

In real life, there are some stars that can be seen during the day with a telescope or a powerful set of binoculars. The key to seeing them is in knowing exactly where to look. There are modern 'smart' telescopes with so-called "GoTo" features. The GoTo feature moves the telescope to the desired star using a GPS system and electric motors. When pointed directly at a bright star during the day, it can sometimes be seen.

Through practice, you can make your own internal GoTo system.

By creating a habit of continually listening in the direction of the little voice, that subconscious imperative will eventually become integrated into your conscious life.

Of course, the last step is to act on that intuition—if you dare. It isn't always wise to act on the slightest whim. But the little voices are not the same as everyday random impulses. You will know them because they are persistent. In those rare moments when the noise of life is diminished, they are there, every time.

It's all too easy to ignore the little voice, but we do so at our peril. Like a persistent tree root, the little voice, if left ignored, can slowly force its way through concrete walls. But that may not be the worst outcome. Much worse would be if the little voices never became loud enough to demand your attention, and it is only in the winter of your life that you notice how important they were.

In her book, *The Top Five Regrets of the Dying*, Bronnie Ware, a palliative care nurse who spent years caring for people in the last weeks of their life, described the patterns she observed among her patients.

Of note is that people didn't usually regret things that they *did* do, but rather, what they *didn't* do. The five most common regrets—expressed as wishes—were:

I wish I hadn't worked so hard.

I wish I'd had the courage to live a life true to myself, not the life others expected of me.

I wish I had let myself be happier.

I wish I'd had the courage to express my feelings.

I wish I'd stayed in touch with my friends.

What are those dim stars trying to tell you? Are you listening?

Don't ignore the little voice.

DON'T TAKE THEIR ROLE AS WRITERS LIGHTLY BY JIMMY ESSIEN

"Stories you read when you're the right age never quite leave you. You may forget who wrote them or what the story was called. Sometimes you'll forget precisely what happened, but if a story touches you it will stay with you, haunting the places in your mind that you rarely ever visit." —Neil Gaiman

We are all alone. No one can see your thoughts, feelings, and complex history. No one truly knows the sensations in your own body.

Those who know you well only have an approximate picture of your inner world. They will never understand you perfectly.

And the same goes for others; you will never truly see through another's eyes.

We are alone, but we are alone together.

Being alone is not the same thing as being lonely.

Gaining the capacity to embrace aloneness is the path to true maturity.

You find yourself in an empty building. It's a mysterious tower. Without being told why you're there, and without being given an instruction manual, you are understandably afraid. But you have a choice: You can cower in the basement and wait for time to take its course, or you can stretch yourself out, light the fireplace, decorate every room, and claim the castle as your own.

In a world full of single-occupant castles, communication becomes very important. Lonely, you stand on the balcony waiting for a carrier pigeon to arrive with messages from life beyond your confines.

It is difficult to see the other castles far away in the distance, but they are there. What is life like for the occupants? Why is everyone stuck in these magnificent prisons?

You learn some things about the outer world on our own. From the balcony, you notice the birds flying in patterns, you feel the seasons change predictably, and you see the gradual growth of the surrounding forest. But to learn deeper truths about yourself and humanity, you need to communicate with others.

A carrier pigeon arrives with a note. The paper is soggy. The ink didn't adhere. Nothing was communicated.

Another message arrives. The paper is dry and brittle. It disintegrates when you unfold it. Still, nothing was communicated.

Then a third paper is delivered. The quality of the paper is pristine and durable. Words are written legibly with good ink.

The author of the note says that they, too, find themselves alone in a castle. They, too, had to find the will to leave their basement and begin exploring the other rooms. But as you read on, you realize that they learned things about their domain that you have yet to. They give instructions about how to fix various appliances. They give advice about how to arrange the office so as to make the best use of the light coming through the window. And most intriguing, they've found secret rooms...

You apply what they've written, unlocking some secrets within your castle. With the help of this new information, you even make chance discoveries of your own.

Feeling gratitude for the help you received via messages written on sturdy paper, you learn how to construct your own paper. Now you can send your own messages into the world, telling of your discoveries. Helping others in this way becomes meaningful. Meaning becomes an end in itself.

Story is the substrate on which reality is communicated.

As a crafter of story, your experience of life will be communicated through your work. And that's no small thing. The difference between "alone" and "lonely" can be a fine one.

Sometimes all it takes is a whisper from the right person at the right time to make a small change in one's life that dramatically alters the trajectory.

This isn't relegated to self-help books, nor to ten-pound Russian classics. A sci-fi alien action-adventure novel can have all of the same themes as *Crime and Punishment*. And the more expertly the story is crafted, the easier those timeless themes will enter the reader under the radar. The transmission of theme is *deep communication*. That is, a form of communication that speaks to the part of us that longs to understand our place in the world.

Deep communication is an antidote to loneliness.

When loneliness is overcome, aloneness can be embraced.

When aloneness is mastered, reality can be communicated to others in need.

When reality is communicated, meaning is created. In this way, deep communication becomes an end in itself.

This is the cycle that powers humanity's progress. If you have the skill of storytelling, then you have the power to move us forward, and the motivation to do so. That's no small thing.

Civilization has come a long way in the last 5,000 years. Many of the concepts that we hold dear today—and that are often taken for granted—were injected into culture and successfully propagated via story. Without those skilled storytellers, such fundamentals as human rights, freedom of expression, and the importance of following one's conscience may not exist.

There is still a lot of room for progress, and there are an unimaginable number of people standing on balconies, waiting for a message.

Thriving authors don't take their role as writer lightly.

DON'T ALLOW THEMSELVES TO BE INFLUENCED BY THE WRONG THINGS OR PEOPLE BY JIMMY ESSIEN

"You are the average of the five people you spend the most time with." —Jim Rohn

We are the products of our influences. No? Does this undermine free will?

This is not a chapter about free will versus determinism (in either case, it makes sense to behave as if we have free will). But that doesn't mean we are invulnerable to influences. In fact, it is easily demonstrable that we are—as the first line stated—the products of our influences.

In his book, *Predictably Irrational*, Dan Ariely described an experiment in suggestibility. Undergraduate students from New York University were asked to do some word puzzles. The puzzles consisted of rearranging seemingly random words to form sentences.

What the students didn't know was that half of them were given words that primed them to think about the elderly, such as "Bingo," "Florida," and "Ancient." When the mock experiment was over, the researchers then timed how long it took them to walk down the hall as they left the building. Those with the words associated with the elderly walked more slowly down the hall than the control group.

We see here the power of subtle influence.

While we don't seem to have much choice as to whether we will be influenced by our surroundings, we can—to a large degree—choose our surroundings.

People trying to break an addiction to a narcotic or alcohol know that one of the first actions that needs to be taken is to remove themselves from access to the substance, which usually involves removing themselves from those people with whom they would take those substances. It's one of the most basic, and somewhat obvious, things that can be done to help a person break a bad habit.

But what about establishing a good habit? We don't often think of that as the opposite of breaking a bad habit or addiction. But why not? If you remove yourself from certain people in order to break a bad habit, shouldn't you surround yourself with certain others to create a good habit?

It might be that we don't think of good personal qualities and characteristics as habitual in nature. This is a different way of thinking about psychological characteristics. But it can be very useful to think of psychological characteristics as habits, because *we feel like we have more control over habits than we do control over who we are intrinsically.*

Personal characteristics can begin with habits of mind.

One way to change yourself is to seek out an individual who embodies the characteristics that you wish to have. Spend time with that person—in person, if possible, but at least remotely. Try to work on a project with them, or help them accomplish one of their own goals.

Through unconscious observation of their micro-mannerisms, you will see how they go about solving problems and tackling issues. Eventually, you will begin to automatically imitate them.

It might begin with finding yourself imitating their verbal quirks or tone of voice, and maybe even facial expressions. That level of imitation is useless, and a bit embarrassing. But with time, you will imitate their responses to various problems and opportunities. Their work ethic will rub off on you. You will come to view the world a little bit more as they view it.

Those are the habits that you want to instantiate in yourself, because those automatic responses determine your success or failure in an enterprise.

These changes in you may be subtle, but as we see in the New York University experiment, subtle influences can shape measurable behavior.

Viewing yourself as a programmable being is disconcerting at first. It can even become depressing for a while. But if you persist in viewing yourself in this way, and act accordingly, it will cease to be depressing, and will become empowering.

You are a programmable machine, *but you are also the programmer*. You'll see how for most of your life, you were the former but not the latter. Life was the programmer. Your parents and friends and coworkers were the programmers. You were at their mercy. But now that you understand your open-source nature, you can protect yourself from those who would knowingly or unknowingly upload malware into you.

You will also see how sensitive you are. Even if you are not consciously paying attention, your unconscious mind is taking everything in. Such a sensitive being should be handled intentionally.

Put up defenses in some areas, and lower the drawbridge to other areas. Seek out your influences.

Embracing your suggestibility—your propensity to be hypnotized—can be fun, rewarding, and ultimately, the beginning of self-mastery.

Don't allow yourself to be influenced by the wrong things or people.

DON'T BELIEVE THAT THEY WILL LIVE FOREVER BY JIMMY ESSIEN

"You act like mortals in all that you fear, and like immortals in all that you desire." —Marcus Aurelius

Everybody knows that they will not live forever. But there's a difference between intellectual knowledge and the palpable knowledge of the present moment.

Everybody knows that standing on the ledge of a tall building is dangerous. But if you do it yourself, you will feel the danger—and the instinctive need to take a step backward—that transcends the single-dimensional "knowing."

Everybody knows that if you were to go on a three-day fast, you would experience hunger at times. But it isn't until you are deep into that fast that the urgency of the hunger will grip you.

Everybody knows that one day they will die. Brushes with death can give the type of urgency that one experiences like the examples above. But most of us don't have such an intense acquaintance with death to make us feel the reality of our own mortality for an extended period of time.

Our finite time in this life is one of the most important aspects of it. Time is our most precious resource, yet we're always looking for ways to spend it, waste it, and kill it.

A common form of resistance to creation is the impulse to put off something until tomorrow, as if tomorrow we will be in a better state of mind, or will have more creative resources. The problem is that tomorrow isn't any different than today. What we put off today until tomorrow gets put off tomorrow until the day after, and so on.

One of the chief differences between a thriving author and a struggling writer is the belief in tomorrow. Thriving authors don't believe in tomorrow. They know that tomorrow is snake oil being sold to them by Resistance.

The thriving author knows that tomorrow is an unwritten story, one whose climax will be determined by today's choice.

The thriving author knows that reliance on tomorrow is akin to a refusal of the call. Their own hero's journey won't proceed until they accept the call to adventure.

The thriving author knows that the arc of their own hero's journey is the length of a lifetime, but it is also the length of a project, and the length of a day. There are daily journeys, with all of the same progressive steps. Like scenes in a novel, their daily choices determine tomorrow's outcomes and options. The call to adventure occurs every day.

An ever-present, intimate awareness of one's own inevitable death is a capacity that we all possess. But that capacity won't be filled automatically. It requires conscious work—for most of us, that is.

There are some who receive a medical diagnosis that dispels them of the comfort of ignorance. Every caring and reasonable person should see such a diagnosis as unfortunate, but many of those who survive a medical scare say that it was the best thing that ever happened to them, because now, they value every single day.

You don't need to wait for a terminal illness to begin treating every day as your last.

There are many ways that this can be done, but here is one exercise: Each day, choose a single person that you are interacting with—a spouse, grocery store clerk, or co-worker—and while looking at them, silently tell yourself that they were once babies, like you. They grew up and now have hopes, dreams, and sorrows, like you. And they will one day pass away, just like you. This need only take ten seconds.

Marcus Aurelius suggested another practice. He said, "Stop whatever you're doing for a moment and ask yourself: Am I afraid of death because I won't be able to do this anymore?"

A little bit of conscious focus on death every day will slowly build the muscle needed to look directly at it and gain inspiration from it. But it's painful at first.

Increasing your capacity to focus on your own mortality is a bit like learning to take an ice bath. As soon as you get in, almost every fiber of your being tells you to get out. There is only a small part in your mind—a part that now seems overwhelmingly outnumbered—that knows that this is not going to kill you. It knows that there are benefits to the exercise. It wants to go through with the ice bath.

The key to remaining in the water is to relax, and to stop fighting the discomfort. After repeated attempts, most people reach a stage where—through relaxation and breathing—they are able to accept the pain. No longer resisting the sensation, it ceases to be uncomfortable, and instead, becomes empowering and exhilarating.

Pain is only a sensation, and when you remove the negative emotion attached to it, suffering vanishes.

The awareness of your own mortality is scary at first. But with persistence, relaxation, and sincerity, there will come a moment when you accept the pain, and in so doing, find that it is no longer uncomfortable. You will then possess the perspective that you need in order to do the things you feel called to do, and become the person you were meant to become.

As Epictetus wrote: "I have now made a habit of being prepared in all affairs of life for the worst. As death, when we come to consider it closely, is the true goal of our existence. I have formed during the last few years such close relationships with this best and truest friend of mankind that his image is not only no longer terrifying to me but is indeed very soothing and consoling, and I thank my God for graciously granting me the opportunity of learning that death is the key which unlocks the door to our true happiness."

DON'T PRACTICE THINGS THAT THEY DON'T WANT TO IMPROVE BY JIMMY ESSIEN

"The only difference between a groove and a grave is the depth."
—Jane Heap

We are creatures of habit. More so than we realize. Inertia can be your worst enemy, but it can also be your greatest ally. This is why practice is so important.

But what is practice? We casually think of practice as the *deliberate carrying-out of an activity that we want to get better at.* Unfortunately, practice doesn't care whether we are aware of it or not.

It helps to try to think about practice differently: *Practice occurs when you carry out an activity.*

Too broad?

Look at what happens when you borrow an unfamiliar car or buy a new one. It's awkward. You flail around for the windshield wipers. Your hands don't know what to do. You don't know where the blind spots are. The seat and steering wheel are in the wrong position.

But you keep driving, day after day. Before long, your hands know what to do. You mindlessly adjust the wipers, stereo, and mirrors as needed. It's as if you've driven this car your whole life.

Were you deliberately practicing driving the car? You probably weren't thinking of it like that, but it happened. You kept going through the motions until your body was good at it. Some people call this "muscle memory."

Take a different example. You've been waking up to your alarm at 5 a.m. every morning for the last two weeks. You've been surprised at how it got easier and easier to stay awake and get up when the alarm went off. But one morning when you are especially tired, you give in and hit the snooze button. "Just this once," you say. Then the next morning when the alarm goes off, the residue of yesterday's snooze-hitting is still fresh in your memory, and how sweet it tastes. Yesterday turned out fine, you tell yourself, so what's the harm in doing it one more time? So you hit snooze. What will happen on the third day? We are all familiar with how things like this can become vicious snowballs.

The same happens with diets. You can be on the straight and narrow for weeks. Then, in a moment of weakness, you indulge in your favorite pastry. "Just this once." How much easier will it be tomorrow to do the same? And the day after?

There is also something like muscle memory in the mind. Mental muscle memory is more difficult to see. You won't see it unless you try to change the way your mind works. An object in motion will remain in motion unless acted upon by an external force.

Many writers struggle to break free from their inner-editor while writing. It's an important thing to do. The mind gets analysis-paralysis and the fingers grind to a halt. The way to overcome this is to force yourself to keep writing, knowing that you will edit later. Easier said than done. But you take it one step at a time. When you find yourself not typing because you're unsure of how that last sentence was phrased, you let it go and proceed to the next sentence. Success!

But it doesn't stop there, because the next sentence isn't quite right either. Stop, let it go, and proceed. Another success!

Do this ten thousand times and it will become second nature—as if you've been driving this car your whole life.

Much can be learned from these small successes, these *virtuous* snowballs. The mind is extraordinarily receptive to practice, deliberate or not. This isn't to be feared. This is a superpower.

They say that fear is the mind-killer. But, through practice, fear can also be the mind-reminder.

Fear has a way of training us and guiding our paths, like runoff water flowing through grooves in the sand at the beach. With every day that passes, the grooves get deeper, and the water is more bound to the path. When we notice the deep groove we are in, it can be discouraging. But virtuous snowballs have small beginnings.

There are many ways to apply the power of practice to erode the walls of your groove of fear.

For example, observe yourself when you are in front of the grocery store clerk. Many of us habitually close ourselves off when in front of a stranger, and we get better at it every day. We avoid eye contact, and shift our bodies so that we are not directly facing the other person.

If this is you, try standing up straight, face the clerk head-on, and make eye contact. For some people, there is aversion to practicing this. It's as if we are afraid, even if we don't *feel* afraid. But if you can compel yourself to practice this, it will be a small win.

Another thing you can do is to think of a conversation you've been avoiding having with a spouse, friend, or business associate. Not a big issue, just a small issue that you have some petty aversion to dealing with. Deliberately initiate the conversation. Tell yourself, "I'm not doing this because I'm *not* afraid. I'm doing this because I *am* afraid."

The key to creating virtuous snowballs is to start small. Facing one's fears can become habitual, believe it or not. And noticing an aversion in yourself can become a reminder to practice.

That doesn't mean it will be easy, but you *can* get free from the groove that fear places you in.

But make no mistake, if the snowballs in your life are not virtuous, then they are vicious. Things move up or down. Nothing in life is static. Make sure you are practicing the right things. Thriving authors don't practice things that they don't want to improve.

DON'T SUCCUMB TO IMPOSTER SYNDROME BY JIMMY ESSIEN

"You might not understand your experience, but you can know your experience." —Annie Lou Staveley

Imposter syndrome is the feeling of self-doubt that is experienced when one gets recognition for one's accomplishments.

Why this feeling of doubt? Wouldn't recognition from others be the validation needed to know that you are not an imposter? And why do people at the top of their profession, who undoubtedly deserve the recognition they receive, also experience imposter syndrome?

Consider this: Your constant conscious identity began when you were three to five years old. People told you that you existed before that, and you have no reason to doubt them. As you got older, you saw pregnant mothers, and you saw babies, so you naturally assumed that this was what happened to you, and that you were simply too young to remember being a baby yourself. You were also told about the history of your mother and father and of your grandparents, and you began to understand human lineage.

You still don't remember anything before a very young age—and you were never given an instruction manual for this life—but you may have been given an explanation for your existence by your parents or your culture. Perhaps it was a religious story, or maybe a scientific one.

Regardless of what the explanation was, what became more important with every passing year was the avoidance of pain.

Life can be very painful, physically and emotionally, and much bandwidth is taken up by learning how to not experience unnecessary pain. Similarly, you learned how to increase your chances of experiencing a sense of well-being. The older you got, the more you were preoccupied with avoiding pain and seeking well-being. The utterly strange fact that for all of eternity you didn't exist, and then one day you did exist, gets buried beneath this preoccupation.

The older you got, the more complex life became. But you were learning the rules of the game that you were in: Get an education so that you can get a better education so that you can get a good-paying job so that you can have a sense of well-being in the future. Avoid pain, seek well-being, and invest one's energies into future well-being. This is an all-engrossing enterprise that can consume one's entire attention.

In your quest to avoid pain and seek well-being, you found yourself attracted to certain pastimes. You practiced more than others did, and you gained skill in these areas. Practice makes perfect, they say, and soon, you were attracting attention from others. While you were not the best in the world, people saw you as an authority on the subject, at least in comparison to the rest of your circle.

You know some things, but that knowledge is like a matchbox floating on a cosmically vast ocean of ignorance. If you feel like an imposter, then your feeling is partially correct. You are an imposter.

What your feeling is wrong about is that other people are not imposters.

In a way, we are all imposters. None of us know the punch line, none of us remembers choosing to be who we are. We are all, to some extent, flailing. If your imposter syndrome is telling you that you are the only one experiencing this, then it is not telling you the truth. In this way, you are probably not an imposter.

There is a difference between being an imposter and having an incomplete understanding of life.

In a world full of flailing beings who are trying to avoid pain and seek well-being—and if there is any bandwidth left, to seek understanding—there is a huge need for those with expertise or insight that they picked up along the way. We need your *honest* take on life, so that we might benefit from it. We need your understanding, incomplete though it may be, so that we might have a better chance at acquiring understanding and well-being ourselves.

The antidote for imposter syndrome is sincerity.

Is your writing fundamentally based on your own experience? Or are you simply regurgitating what you've read in other books? Are the human interactions in your books something that you've seen with your own eyes? Not that you can't write fiction, but is the underlying characterization of the conflict between your characters something that you have observed in the humans around you? Is your expertise on a subject derived from your experience from walking that path? Or can it be reasonably extrapolated from your own experience? If so, then we need to hear it. We need to read about it.

The reason we need your take on life—or a small aspect thereof—is not because we think you have all of the answers. We need it because if it's honest, then it is unique. No one has seen exactly what you have seen. No one stands precisely where you stand.

In *The Hobbit*, Bilbo is in a position to notice a missing scale on Smaug the dragon's chest. Bilbo is in no position to take advantage of this vulnerability because he is no warrior. But he gets the message out to Bard, a true warrior, who is able to shoot an arrow through the gap in the armor.

If you communicate what you see from your own unique perspective, it may enable others to slay their own dragons.

You might not understand the nature of human conflict that you have observed, but you can *know* what you saw. You might not understand why you feel a certain way in certain situations, but you can *know* that you felt it. You may not have the answers to your most-pressing questions, but you can *know* that those questions are important to you.

And if your writing is founded on what you know, what you have experienced, then you have every right to convey that in written form. What's more, if you feel called to write, then you may have an obligation to put it to paper.

Remember that Resistance—the internal force that will always try to sabotage your creativity—will use imposter syndrome for its goals.

Don't be fooled by it.

Thriving authors don't succumb to imposter syndrome.

DON'T STARVE THE DARK MACHINE BY JIMMY ESSIEN

"You are the books you read, the films you watch, the music you listen to, the people you meet, the dreams you have, the conversations you engage in. You are what you take from these. You are the sound of the ocean, the breath of fresh air, the brightest light and the darkest corner. You are a collective of every experience you have had in your life. You are every single day. So drown yourself in a sea of knowledge and existence. Let the words run through your veins and let the colors fill your mind." —Jac Vanek

Your writing is the product of a dark machine. The processing that takes place within the dark machine is mysterious. Its conclusions are presented in the form of pictures, thoughts, feelings, and stories. The dark machine feeds on experience and knowledge—it doesn't generate something from nothing.

The dark machine is like a harvesting combine used in agriculture. The combine will harvest (automatically gather the crop), thresh (loosen the grain from the chaff or stalk), and winnow (separate the grain from loose husks and dust). In other words, things go in rough and whole, and come out more refined.

A combine can't process what it doesn't harvest. The dark machine can't digest what it doesn't consume.

The unconscious mind has been likened to the massive majority of an iceberg, submerged underwater and out of view. Whereas, the conscious mind is like the tiny tip of visible ice.

One could argue that we are not the thinkers of our thoughts, or generators of our emotions. Rather, we are the receivers of thoughts and feelings. They spring forth from the event horizon of our subconscious minds.

If you are struggling with a challenging problem that requires a lot of thought, people will say to "sleep on it." While sleeping, the subconscious mind does its magic. It's like a super-computer, crunching data, eliminating redundancies, and clearing caches. When you wake up the next morning, the solution to the problem may be offered up to you with clarity and simplicity.

"How could I have not seen this before?"

Knowing that many of your thoughts, beliefs, and feelings are the product of unconscious processing can feel limiting or deterministic. It can even make you feel like a slave to an unknown agenda. But with some reframing, it can be empowering and even liberating.

You are the *owner* of a powerful machine. It will refine what you put into it. It will extrapolate events of the past and offer up a warning if you are in danger. It will present powerful metaphorical images when words won't do.

It wants a master. It wants to communicate with you. It wants you to listen.

You can harness the power of the dark machine by doing two things: Feed it intentionally, and listen carefully.

What does it mean to feed intentionally?

If you aren't learning new skills, visiting new places, meeting new people, reading unfamiliar books, or taking on new responsibilities, then you are driving your harvesting combine over barren land. Nothing new will be produced.

Viewing new experiences as unrefined food for your mind can change your relationship with life. For example, you may not feel the desire to go to coffee with, and get to know, a new person. But what if something about their personality is the key piece of data needed for your dark machine to unlock something previously not understood about human psychology?

There's only one way to find out.

A Wikipedia article might contain all of the information you need to write a scene set in a city where you've never been. But what if taking a day trip there so engorges the dark machine full of sounds, sights, and smells that it is able to present a richer and more integrated depiction for your book?

It's time to buy a bus ticket.

In this way, things once viewed as chores can become engaging hunts.

Another form of feeding is to ask it questions. We rarely think to ask ourselves a question, because we assume that the conscious tip of the iceberg makes up the totality of "I." But when you acknowledge that "you" are largely a mystery to your conscious mind, the natural thing to do is to begin communicating with yourself.

If there is something that you wish to understand—about your inner world or the outer world—write it down on a small piece of paper. Pull it out of your pocket throughout the day and read it. Then, before you fall asleep at night, read it one last time. You may be surprised to find an answer rising up to the surface upon waking the next morning.

There has been a lot of research confirming that while we sleep, the brain reorganizes information to facilitate problem-solving. In his novel, *Sweet Thursday*, John Steinbeck wrote: "It is a common experience that a problem difficult at night is resolved in the morning after the committee of sleep has worked on it."

That committee works for you.

What does it mean to listen carefully?

Out of the darkness will come images, stories, metaphors, poetry, and ideas. You need to carve time out of your day to accept the gifts bestowed.

There are many ways to do this, but in general, it requires sensory silence. It is difficult to assimilate your new insights if all of your downtime is spent staring at a smartphone. Taking time out of the day to simply do nothing can feel awkward—even indulgent—at first. But it is essential if you want to partake in what has been collected and processed.

By analogy, when you walk into a forest, the wildlife nearby goes still and silent, waiting for you to leave. However, if you sit down and stay still for twenty minutes, you'll notice a rustle here, and a chirp there, until finally the forest comes back alive around you.

It's important to remember that the dark machine also communicates via emotional feelings and bodily sensations. Most of us are not in the habit of giving these phenomena their due attention. When you form the habit of paying more attention to the sensations of your body, you will see interesting patterns.

Why does my body feel colder when I talk about certain subjects?

Why do I get nasal congestion *before* eating certain foods?

Some physical and emotional phenomena are like breadcrumbs, which, if followed, will lead to surprising discoveries. And those things need to be discovered.

In the darkness lives a powerful friend that wishes for your self-actualization. But it can only meet you halfway.

Don't starve the dark machine.

DON'T IGNORE THE REST OF THE PYRAMID BY JIMMY ESSIEN

"What a man can be, he must be." — Abraham Maslow

Don't throw out the baby with the bathwater.

Being all-consumed by the pursuit of excellence and accomplishment through your craft can blind you to the foundation on which you stand.

The lower levels of need must be satisfied before a person will be sufficiently motivated to strive for the higher levels.

Physiological needs, safety, love and belonging, and esteem. If any of these is compromised, the highest aim of self-actualization may fade into what feels like an unattainable luxury. Ill health, abuse, divorce, public shame, financial trouble—each of these can derail your motivation to become what you were meant to become. For this reason, the thriving author is careful to maintain those states of being.

Although Maslow himself never used the pyramid as a model for his theory—that came after, as others built upon his work—the principle, if simplistic, is still useful. Remove too many blocks from the lower levels and the apex falls.

It is important to remember that *self-actualization is still possible when the lower needs are not being fully satisfied*. But what will be threatened in that scenario is the *motivation* for self-actualization.

We are beings with limited resources. We only have so much energy, attention, and time. Feel-good platitudes will only get you so far. The thriving author is a realist.

The thriving author knows that if the body is sick, their work won't be optimal. Junk food will only get them by for so long before the machine will wind down to a grinding, inefficient, slow burn.

Humans are wired for physical activity, and writing is the exact opposite. Therefore, the thriving author goes out of their way to give the body the exercise it requires.

Sleep is not an option. While they can get most mundane tasks accomplished day after day on inadequate sleep, the deep work needed for self-actualization requires an extra hour or two of sleep.

The thriving author knows that they need to feel safe and secure. A constant, background anxiety about finances can use up a large portion of their much-needed bandwidth. The line between financial calm and financial crisis can be two-dollars wide: Having a dollar left over after paying all of one's expenses, versus being a dollar short.

Therefore, the thriving author maintains a cushion—if only modest—which allows them to focus wholly on their work when they need to. They also know that abuse in the household or living in a dangerous neighborhood will undermine attempts to focus deeply and put resources toward their own evolution as a person.

The thriving author knows that they need loving relationships. The road to realization leads through, and is powered by, the heart. But without intimacy, the heart closes. Loving relationships teach us about ourselves. The avoidance of intimacy can become a dangerous habit. Isolation is self-perpetuating, and can turn into a deep hole that is difficult to crawl out of.

The thriving author knows that esteem is not always egotistical. We are tribal creatures; it's how we became such a successful species. Our ancestors were those who could cooperate and remain in good standing with the tribe.

Today, that tribe doesn't have to be the entire country, nor an entire city. It can be a small group of family, friends, or colleagues. But no matter the scale, we need to feel that we are being accepted to some degree—that we aren't being shunned and pushed out of the camp. Historically, humans that were exiled from the community didn't live for very long on their own. Part of us remembers this fact. Excessive self-esteem can lead to egomania, which will eventually sabotage the thriving author's journey. But a healthy self-esteem is essential to having the energy to do one's work.

The thriving author doesn't maintain these aspects of themselves in order to live a more comfortable life. Comfort is subordinate to the goal. They maintain these aspects of themselves because they know that they need every advantage that they can get.

Motivation to pursue higher ideals doesn't come out of thin air, it rests upon a healthy foundation.

The thriving author is constantly reminding themselves that nobody is going to do the work for them. All of life isn't trying to help them to realize their full potential—much of life is working against them. Every inch of ground gained is hard-won. And every new success brings its own peril in the forms of egotism, distraction, or complacency.

A warrior's spirit is needed to walk the road to realization.

Fortitude is needed to constantly reinitiate the work, moment after moment, day after day.

Faith is needed to believe that there is a self to be discovered, mysterious though it may be.

We wish you good luck on your journey.

If you do follow your bliss you put yourself on a kind of track that has been there all the while, waiting for you, and the life that you ought to be living is the one you are living. Follow your bliss and don't be afraid, and doors will open where you didn't know they were going to be.

—Joseph Campbell

ABOUT THE AUTHORS

Sacha Black

Sacha Black is an author, rebel podcaster and speaker. She writes sapphic books for teens and other books about the art of writing. When she's not writing, she can be found laughing inappropriately loud, sniffing musty old books, fangirling film and TV soundtracks, or thinking up new ways to break the rules. She lives in Cambridgeshire, England, with her wife and genius, giant of a son.

sachablack.co.uk

Zach Bohannon

Zach Bohannon is a horror, science fiction, and fantasy author. His critically acclaimed post-apocalyptic zombie series, Empty Bodies, is a former Amazon #1 bestseller. He loves hockey, heavy metal, video games, reading, and he doesn't trust a beer he can see through. He's a retired drummer, and has had a beard since 2003—long before it was cool.

www.zachbohannon.com

James R Essien

James R Essien is an author of both fiction and non-fiction. He is also a home builder, woodworker, Qigong practitioner, and recovering songwriter. He lives in the Columbia River Gorge in the Pacific Northwest.

jressien.com

Janet Kitto

Janet Kitto writes both fiction and non-fiction, diving into family relationships as well as the author life. Janet and her husband sold their home and most of their belongings to travel with their truck and a 20-foot RV trailer in 2018 and 2019. From her new home base in Nova Scotia, Janet explores the local beaches and trails on her dual-sport motorcycle.

https://janetkitto.com

J. Thorn

J. Thorn has published two million words and has sold more than 185,000 books worldwide. He is an official member of the Science Fiction and Fantasy Writers of America, the Horror Writers Association, and the Great Lakes Association of Horror Writers.

Thorn earned a B.A. in American History from the University of Pittsburgh and a M.A. from Duquesne University. He is a husband, father, full-time writer, part-time professor at John Carroll University, founder of The Author Life Community, podcaster, FM radio DJ, musician, and owner of the Three Story Method Editing Agency.

theauthorlife.com

Daniel Willcocks

Daniel Willcocks is an international bestselling author and award-winning podcaster of dark fiction. He is an author coach, founder and CEO of Activated Authors; one quarter of digital story studio, Hawk & Cleaver; co-founder of iTunes-busting fiction podcast, 'The Other Stories';' CEO of horror imprint,

Devil's Rock Publishing; and the host of the 'Activated Authors' podcast.

Dan is furiously passionate about all things creativity and productivity. He has written 60+ books since 2015 for himself and on behalf of ghostwriting clients. His mission in life is to activate creatives and authors to ensure they keep their creative flames and passions burning in a sustainable, positive, and healthy way.

danielwillcocks.com

Lightning Source UK Ltd.
Milton Keynes UK
UKHW010651090223
416681UK00007B/1996